CUBAN ZARZUELA

SUSAN THOMAS

Cuban Zarzuela

PERFORMING RACE AND
GENDER ON HAVANA'S
LYRIC STAGE

UNIVERSITY OF ILLINOIS PRESS

URBANA AND CHICAGO

Library of Congress Cataloging-in-Publication Data
Thomas, Susan
Cuban zarzuela : performing race and gender on Havana's
lyric stage / Susan Thomas.
p.   cm.
Includes bibliographical references and index.
ISBN-13 978-0-252-03331-5 (cloth : alk. paper)
1. Zarzuela—Cuba—Havana. 2. Sex role in music.
3. Music and race.
I. Title.
ML1714.T46   2009
782.1'2097291—dc22   2007046796

Contents

Credits

Acknowledgments

This book is the result of both institutional and personal support. The initial research for this project was funded by the Women's and Gender Studies Program at Brandeis University. Its further transformations were made possible by the generous support of the Willson Center for Humanities and Arts at the University of Georgia.

The writing of this book has taken me down many roads, and I did not travel them alone. I am deeply indebted to Robin Moore, whose large library of recordings initially inspired this project and without whom research would have been a much more arduous task. Robin graciously showed me around Havana, introducing me to many scholars, musicians, and archivists, and even carting me around town on the back of his *bicicleta china*. The community into which Robin introduced me became a vital resource for me throughout this project. Through those introductions I acquired many more personal debts.

The list is long. My lengthy stays in Havana would not have been possible, nor as productive, without the support, mentoring, and friendship of my hosts Leonardo Acosta and Michi González. I am deeply grateful for Radamés Giro's profound generosity with both his information and his time. Rogelio Martínez Furé and Tomás Fernández Robaina both gave of their time and provided valuable insight on sociocultural issues. Juan Benkomo, drum maker and pedagogue, introduced me to many people at the National Opera and Pro-Arte Lírico, helped me to locate scores, and to understand the nuances of libretto texts. Reinaldo Fustier, professor of voice and tenor with the Centro Pro-Arte Lírico de La Habana, became a valuable resource for information on performance practice, as did his son, pianist Antón Fustier. My understanding of singers' lives during the 1930s and 1940s was profoundly shaped by Pedro Arias, one of the founders of the Pro-Arte Lírico. Arias's mother, Raquel Domínguez, appeared in several of Lecuona's productions. He was kind to share with me his excellent collection of photographs from the period, as well as several librettos and musical scores. Pedro's greatest gift, however, was to introduce me in the summer of 1998 to the late Pedrito Fernández. The late comic tenor was Lecuona's personal secretary, and although he was elderly and frail at the time of our interview (he died only a few months later), his memory was unparalleled.

I would like to thank the singers of the Pro-Arte Lírico for allowing me to observe them in rehearsal and for taking the time to discuss their views on the zarzuela with me. I am grateful to Nelson Moore, cofounder of the Pro-Arte Lírico, for making it possible for me to observe rehearsals and especially to the late maestro Manuel Duchesne Cuzán, director of the National Opera, for making himself available for interviews.

Musicologist José Ruiz Elcoro not only shared his work and ideas with me, but also shared his extensive collection of wax cylinder and Victrola recordings from the Cuban popular theater. Musicologist Enrique Rio Prado graciously gave of his time to discuss his work. Ramón Fajardo's support, guidance, and friendship has been invaluable. I am especially grateful to him for sharing a number of historic recordings and photographs with me—and for his fine cooking.

The bulk of my archival research was carried out at the Museo Nacional de la Música Cubana, and it would have been impossible without the support and interest of director Jesús Gómez Cairo. Special thanks are due to Rolando Delgado Miranda for his assistance, Alicia Medina Martín and Sonia Guillén Álvarez for their help locating scores and librettos, Leonor Borges Linton and Ada Lidia Céspedes Pacheco for their advice and for rescuing me from the uncomfortable metal chairs in the courtyard, Pepe Piñeiro for his historical expertise and aid with recordings, and Raul Martínez for taking an interest in my project and making himself available for discussion.

Thanks also need to be expressed to the late composer and conductor Félix Guerrero, who took the time to discuss his long collaboration with Ernesto Lecuona with me, and to his wife, soprano Lucy Provedo, for her artistic insight and her always gracious welcome. I would also like to thank composer Roberto Sánchez Ferrer, pedagogue and founder of the Coro Nacional Cuca Rivero, as well as Olga Bosque Prats, Esther Borja, the late Jorge Antonio González, and Rosita Fornés.

I am very grateful to the community of scholars who, in different capacities and at different times, helped to make this book happen, especially Miranda Pollard for her excellent editorial guidance; Allen Keiler, Jessie Ann Owens, and Gabriela Cruz for their mentorship; John Turci-Escobar, Alejandro Planchart, and Roberto Echevarría for their much-needed advice; and Greg Brown, for his help in formatting the musical examples. After many discussions about the racial and gendered performances that took place on the zarzuela stage, artist Alexis Esquivel created the painting that appears on this book's cover. I am honored by his interest and touched by his generosity.

None of this would have been possible without the support of my family and especially the patience and understanding of my husband, Freeland, who lost me to Cuba for months at a time and married me anyway.

CUBAN ZARZUELA

Introduction

Our campaign in favor of Cuban theater, of *criollo*[1]
theater, poses this problem: Should local customs be
maintained, being treated in the *sainete*, in *revistas* and
zarzuelas within an environment of low morality and
patent bad taste?
The answer, evidently, is negative.
Criollo theater cannot acquire a position among that of
other American countries so long as it does not dispose
of certain conventions that it has maintained through a
grave error of vision and of the appreciation of the authors
themselves.

—*El Mundo*, September 16, 1928[2]

Nationalism, culture, and morality. For cultural critics like
the author of the *El Mundo* editorial cited above, nothing less was at
stake in establishing a local form of music theater, a form that came
to be known as the Cuban zarzuela. The source of some of the Western Hemisphere's best-loved melodies, the zarzuela is one of the most
oft-mentioned and least discussed genres in Cuban music history. The
zarzuela's peculiar blend of elite culture and popular entertainment, its
exploitation of folklorisms and racial stereotypes, its social moralizing
and its penchant for tragedy, as well as its explosively short life span,
have attracted only cursory attention from historians of both Cuban and
American musics. Yet it is precisely the zarzuela's incongruous set of
characteristics that positions it as a linchpin in understanding Cuba's
cultural and musical slide into modernity. Bringing together Old World
theatrical and rhetorical traditions with New World themes, the primary
composers of Cuban zarzuela, Ernesto Lecuona (1895–1963), Gonzalo
Roig (1890–1970), and Rodrigo Prats (1909–80), created a national mu-

1

sic that bridged perceived gaps between art music and entertainment, much like their North American counterparts George Gershwin, Aaron Copeland, and Leonard Bernstein. The zarzuela not only exemplifies how the culture industry in Cuba participated in ongoing debates regarding nationalism, gender roles, class warfare, and racial politics, it also provides perspective in understanding how the competing experiences of colonialism and postcolonialism, imperialism, and nationalism affected cultural production throughout the Americas.

Created by composers, librettists, and impresarios to fill a growing demand for family entertainment, the zarzuela evidenced the emerging economic and cultural power of Cuba's white female bourgeoisie to influence the entertainment industry. It was this audience and their desire to see theatrically portrayed the racial and gender vision of their class, as well as to have their cultural supremacy musically celebrated, that fueled the zarzuela's success. Yet far from being a triumphant rhapsody to this new bourgeois female class, the musical and dramatic rhetoric of the zarzuela voiced the limitations of female advancement and buttressed the patriarchal status quo. Indeed, no issue appears to have occupied the minds of librettists, composers, impresarios, and the paying public as much as the question of sexual difference. The plots that were set to music in the 1920s and 1930s reflect considerable ambivalence concerning the role of women in a rapidly changing Cuban society. The musical scores of zarzuelas represented a remapping of Cuba's cultural crossroads, merging the conventions of Spanish zarzuela with the sounds of Italian bel canto and operetta, and Cuban popular comedic traditions and blackface performance practices, as well as with song styles emerging from North America's Tin Pan Alley. Cuban zarzuela was also a primary vector for the Afrocubanist movement, helping to popularize genres such as the *son, rumba,* and *tango-congo,* and it provided Cuban music with some of the best-loved standards in its repertoire. These conventions were more than mere signposts of popular taste, however; they were part of a musical discourse that indicated how the treacherous terrain of class, racial, and sexual conflict should be traversed.

The zarzuela developed during a period of explicit intellectual concern regarding the necessity of creating a Cuban art music, particularly a national opera. Although Cuban composers and impresarios participated in a nationalist discourse that aimed to locate Cuba internationally and to redefine it against the ever-present presence of the United States, the zarzuela's main focus was a domestic one. Zarzuela responded to the corruption of the Machado regime (1925–33), racial tension, student unrest, and an increasingly dilapidated economy, all factors illustrating the enormous social and political changes in late 1920s Cuba. A fascination with black music and dance styles exemplified the perverse contradictions of the Afrocubanist movement that influenced all areas of Cuban arts in the 1920s, and musical genres once vilified as belonging to the black underclass were popularized through all sectors of Cuban society. The zarzuela played an important role in this popularization, its "respectability" granting access to middle- and upper-class women who might not otherwise have heard such music.

A young nation that had inscribed its incipient identity on the bodies of women during the wars of independence, Cuban society was nonetheless unprepared for its women to behave in revolutionary ways after independence was won.[3] Young single women from the countryside migrated to Havana in the first decades of the twentieth century, seeking work in the city's shops, factories, and domestic services. The newly visible presence of single, independent, and mobile young women was considered by many to be a threat to the public order. Simultaneously, middle- and upper-class women echoed the suffrage movements fought and won in Britain and the United States, becoming increasingly radical in their political claims. Havana's well-to-do women were also determined to make their mark on the emerging national culture, publishing journals, heading concert societies, and organizing artistic and musical events.

The Cuban female bourgeoisie represented an organized, motivated, and underserved audience base. Impresarios rushed to fill that gap, renovating theaters, revising plots and musical scores, and effectively engaging in a theatrical respectability campaign that would attract elite women and their families. Composers, librettists, and impresarios also had enormous female talent at their disposal; middle- and working-class women had flocked to music schools and conservatories in the 1920s, resulting in unprecedented numbers of trained singers and musicians who viewed professional performance as a respectable career. Yet paradoxically, while women provided the zarzuela's most talented performers as well as the majority of its spectator base, men dominated the zarzuela's business, authorial, and musical output. The works they created placed female protagonists in moralizing plots in which they either emerged virtuous and unscathed or were led to a tragic end by their wayward behavior. The zarzuela thus became a musical and dramatic pedagogical tool, instructing Havana's increasingly liberated women on the roles available to them.

The zarzuela is not unique in its expression of gendered and racialized identities via a coded musical rhetoric. Interest within the opera-studies community has led to a blossoming of scholarship on the subject. Wendy

Heller has shown that in the seventeenth century, composers and audiences drew a connection between women characters' socially ascribed virtue and melodic and harmonic simplicity (or silence), and between sexual or mental deviance and extreme expressions of orality. Carolyn Abbate's work has called into question not only the rhetorical power of a performer's sung speech, but the ability of the *performance itself* to supersede, if temporarily, the power relations laid out in the plot. Heather Hadlock and Mary Ann Smart have offered new perspectives on studying the operatic representations of gender, sexuality, and madness. Mary Hunter and Wye J. Allenbrook have examined the intersection between the musical and dramatic portrayals of class and gender in Mozart opera and the social identities of the operas' audiences. Susan McClary's work on *Carmen* and Catherine Clément's writings on *Otello* examine the musical and dramatic representation of race and racial hierarchy.[4] Similar strategies of representation are at work in the Cuban zarzuela, where the interrelationship of gender, race, and musical genre is not only a central preoccupation of the zarzuela, but an obsession.

Examining Cuban zarzuela as a specifically racialized genre continues the work being done by musicologists, ethnomusicologists, and cultural critics on the intersections between musical culture and racial meaning, as illustrated by recent volumes such as Ronald Radano and Philip Bohlman's edited anthology *Music and the Racial Imagination* and Jonathon Bellman's *The Exotic in Western Music*.[5] The Cuban zarzuela offers a uniquely New World perspective to the growing body of literature that explores the relationship between operatic discourse and colonial and postcolonial contexts. While much of the scholarly focus has been on Europe's relationship with either Africa or an imagined Orient, the zarzuela offers us a glimpse into postcolonial Cuba's conflicted identity politics regarding gender, race, imperialism, nationalism, and class. Expanding on Jill Lane's excellent study of racialized performance and the use of blackface theater in Cuba,[6] this text examines how blackface and other racializing practices were adapted in the twentieth century to meet the specific circumstances and needs of the zarzuela, its consumers, and its critics. I argue that for contemporary Cuban audiences, the *music itself* came to be freighted with racialized and gendered interpretations that maintained their efficacy and resonance even when divested from explicit visual caricature. Rhythmic patterns, musical form, even harmonic motion were part of a sophisticated system of musical hermeneutics that acculturated listeners and performers would have easily interpreted.

As the zarzuela is an American art form that utilized overt racial caricature and blackface performance practices, it has an obvious and compelling parallel in the simultaneously occurring practice of minstrelsy in North America. The work of Eric Lott, William J. Mahar, Robert Toll, Alan Green, and Paul Gilroy demonstrates that the manipulation and exploitation of black bodies on the minstrel stage was part of a larger cultural project whose aim was not so much to define blackness and its role in white society as to define whiteness itself. By identifying the space occupied by the dark-skinned Other, white space and white privilege were also identified and protected, making the appropriation of black bodies, mannerisms, and music in North American minstrelsy what George Lipsitz has called a "possessive investment in whiteness."[7] While it resulted from very different cultural and theatrical traditions than North American minstrelsy, blackface theater in Cuba can be seen as having played a similar role. An appreciation of the zarzuela's manipulation of racial stereotypes not only contributes to our knowledge of Cuban musical culture, but also leads to a fuller understanding of the complex web of power, prejudice, and privilege that has accompanied the history of African slavery and its aftermath in the Americas.

Archival sources present unique obstacles to documenting the zarzuela and its role in Cuban history. The musical scores to many zarzuelas are not readily available, or have been lost entirely. Not a single zarzuela score was ever published, which has made their reproduction problematic and complicates research efforts, as well.[8] Composers maintained direct control over the orchestral parts and the conducting score, and rented out individually hand-copied parts to the theaters producing the work. Such control was jealously guarded, and one reason for the absence of publications appears to be that composers feared that copies would be made without their permission.[9]

Concern over copyright did not extend to a preoccupation with the authenticity or integrity of an "official version" of the musical or dramatic text. Orchestrations were often changed to accommodate the personnel of individual theaters,[10] and it was not uncommon for a composer to appoint someone else to orchestrate his work. Lecuona is the most famous example of this practice; the majority of his compositions were arranged by Félix Guerrero, while others were orchestrated by Gonzalo Roig.[11] Roig and Prats, both bassists and conductors, orchestrated their own works, although re-orchestrations for subsequent productions were not uncommon.

Some aspects of performance practice were not written down at all. Percussion parts, for example, were often not fully notated. While the parts for Western percussion instruments, such as timpani or snare, were usually written out, the parts for drums and hand percussion drawn from

Cuban popular music often were not. In many cases, the composer merely notated the kind of dance rhythm that a piece is based on and provided specifications for what kinds of percussion should be playing and where they should enter.[12] The flexible nature of the musical score makes any kind of urtext document impossible and, I would argue, irrelevant. This was show business, and theatrical fluidity and flexibility was crucial for success in the economically tumultuous environment within which zarzuela composers functioned.

It is likely that more music exists than is currently documented, but a combination of poor organization, lack of communication, and economic considerations have kept it from being accounted for.[13] While excellent general histories of Cuban lyric theater have been written by Cuban scholars, most notably Edwin Teurbe Tolón, Rine Leal, and Jorge Antonio González, lyric theater has not been privileged by later generations of Cuban music scholars, who have tended to invest their efforts primarily in folklore, reference texts, and biographies of famous popular music performers.[14] The lack of scholarly attention has placed lyric theater collections at the bottom of the priority list in many archives, where inattention has led to the deterioration of scores and documents and, in some cases, their theft.[15]

A higher percentage of librettos survive. The librettos themselves are a fascinating resource. One of the most important sources of librettos is the private collection of the late comic tenor Pedrito Fernández.[16] Fernández was Lecuona's personal secretary, as well as a member of his company, and his collection includes many scores, along with mimeographed librettos onto which he has penciled in the names of original cast members.[17]

Perhaps even more than the musical scores, the librettos have gone through constant revisions. Works were made shorter or longer, dialects were changed or altered, and entire scenes may appear in one version but not in another. In some librettos, there are texts for musical numbers that the composer appears to have ignored or rejected. In cases where the music for a zarzuela has been lost, the libretto can be a valuable resource. The libretto can provide clues about the missing music, by stating the rhythmic genre of individual musical numbers, such as *marcha* or *tango-congo;* a piece's poetic form; or the way the soloist interacts with the chorus.

In the musical and literary analyses in this book, I confine myself to a select group of compositions that, in the judgment of contemporary critics, historians, and the authors themselves, were central to the genre.

Because of the fluid nature of zarzuela orchestration and the difficulty in obtaining orchestral arrangements of entire works, I have relied primarily on piano-vocal scores, which are much more readily available. Individual orchestral parts have proven invaluable in confirming performance dates and also in understanding elements of performance practice, such as the cutting or insertion of musical numbers, as well as the behavior of non-notated parts, as other players often notated the entrances of such parts in their own scores. Orchestral parts also serve as a source for contemporary humor and critique. Many players defaced their parts with biting commentary regarding the quality of the performance, the lack of clarity on the part of the conductor, and occasionally their salaries.

In order to understand how the libretti and musical scores of the zarzuela communicated meaning to contemporary audiences, understanding of the political, historical, and cultural context of the zarzuela is critical. Chapter 1 illustrates how the historic circumstances of the early Cuban Republic contributed to the zarzuela's rise, and it places the zarzuela within the trajectory of Cuban theater. This chapter also addresses the confusion surrounding the zarzuela's nomenclature that pervades the existing literature.

Chapter 2 examines the gendered production, reception, and political economy of the zarzuela. A genre created by men to fill a growing need for women's entertainment, the zarzuela can be considered anti-femininst but pro-*feminine*, its plots focusing on female protagonists and its musical scores showcasing the female voice. The zarzuela owed its popularity to a peculiar set of social, political, and economic conditions, all of which hinged on the role and behavior of women in Cuban society. Written, directed, and financed by men, zarzuela performances reflected the increasing feminization of professional music making in Cuba, and working-class singers and actresses gave voice to the perceived needs and desires of women and to larger concerns regarding gender in a rapidly changing Cuban culture.

Chapters 3 through 6 scrutinize the musical and dramatic characterization of the zarzuela's stock character types. The first of these representational studies, Chapter 3 explores the social and historical conditions that produced the stereotype of the *mulata*, or mixed-race woman. This chapter examines her role as a figure of ambivalence standing as both an icon of national identity and also as a symbol for the threat of cultural and racial destruction. Focusing on the title characters of *María la O*, *Cecilia Valdés*, and *Amalia Batista*, the chapter explores how they express their "*mulata*-ness," that is, how they are identified in terms of race, Otherness, and female behavior. The site for these protagonists' self-identification, and the focus of this study, is a new zarzuelistic convention: the *mulata*'s entrance aria, known as the *salida*.

Chapter 4 underscores the importance of ideologies of sex and gender in the performance of Afrocuban male roles by white actors appearing in blackface. The majority of zarzuelas produced between 1927 and the early 1940s include black male characters, and an examination of these works shows that composers and librettists followed two strategies for representing black masculinity on the zarzuela stage, both of which stemmed from theatrical and literary traditions that date back to the era of slavery. Focusing first on the *negrito* and then on the *negro trágico*, I discuss the historic roots of both strategies and examine the ways that these already well-worn types were adapted by composers and librettists. The zarzuela's manipulation of the black male image evidences the influence of a racialized gender politics on theatrical production, and this chapter places special emphasis on how the *negro trágico*—and his music—served the white female imagination.

White women, the zarzuela's target audience, were also represented on the zarzuela stage. Chapter 5 examines the dramatic formulas that composers and librettists used in their portrayal. Musical genres that were already strongly coded with race and gender (such as the *salida*) were adapted to be sung by white women. Of critical importance to this chapter (and to the political economy of lyric theater production) are zarzuelistic connections between class and virtue, for it is through these connections that the social vision of the zarzuela's audience and creators can best be observed.

The *mulata*, the black man, and the white ingenue/fallen woman all represent, in one way or another, the fantasies of patriarchy. These characters' inability to supersede their social restrictions is the foundation of the zarzuela's tragic ethos, an ethos that is expressed not only by characters' struggle to improve their situations or to realize their desires, but also by their restriction to particular musical genres. The character of the young white male represents the other side of the equation of power. Yet in its analysis of the two most popular representations of white men, Chapter 6 shows that such characters inhabit an expressive world equally constrained by social constructions of identity, and that the musical expression of the elite *galán* and the rural *criollo* is heavily fettered by concerns of gender and class.

After the zarzuela's heyday, it increasingly became a revival genre, with a handful of the most popular works being performed over and over again as "classics," while the rest of the genre faded from view. The Epilogue to this volume addresses the zarzuela's postrevolutionary history and examines successes and strategies of various revival movements in Cuba and the United States.

Inherent to this study are the suppositions that the zarzuela's musical hermeneutics outlived the genre that produced them and that as the zarzuela fell victim to economic decline and waning popularity, the musical and dramatic elements that sustained it were appropriated by other genres and, as such, remained part of Cuban musical discourse. A comprehension of the zarzuela's musical and dramatic rhetoric is thus useful not only in interpreting Cuban cultural and musical history of the early twentieth century, but also provokes intriguing questions regarding musical meaning in later performance practices.

1 Cuban Lyric Theater in Context

Our theatrical personalities are exclusively "ours,"
we find them sometimes in everyday Havana life, but
they would be exotic and incomprehensible in other
circumstances, in other places. Their conventionality
lacks any possible universality. They would say nothing
to a Spaniard in Spain, or to a Frenchman in France,
or to any of our Latin Americans in their respective
countries, if they were not familiar with Havana, if they
had not lived here enough time to be in contact with
"our" *mulata* from the tenement house, happy and
featherbrained, our comic and fun-loving *negrito,* our
policemen . . . and the naturalized Spaniard that feels and
lives "in Cuban" and has assimilated our bad and rowdy
habits.

—*El Mundo,* August 7, 1928[1]

The local characteristics that marked Cuban lyric theater grew
out of an ongoing dialogue between the island and the metropole. On
the one hand, Cuban performance and composition of operas, zarzuelas,
and vaudeville-style reviews was a local reaction to shifting cultural
hegemonies: an adaptation of the styles of the moment emanating from
Madrid, Paris, Rome, or New York. At the same time, however, while
Cuban artists and audiences self-consciously reproduced metropolitan
cultural products, they also developed their own local forms. In spite
of the *El Mundo* writer's protestations that one must live "in Cuban"
to understand island entertainment, new Cuban products increasingly
returned to colonial (and postcolonial) centers, creating a transnational
dialogue in which Cuban cultural exports had a growing influence.[2]

The development of the Cuban zarzuela and other forms of lyric theater should be seen as part of this ongoing dialogue. This chapter begins
by exposing the cultural counterpoint taking place between Cuban and
Spanish theaters in the nineteenth century and relates how the zarzuela's
social status, its musical and dramatic rhetoric, and its importance as
a marker of national identity developed in reaction to the political and
economic conditions peculiar to Spanish colonialism and the Cuban plan-
tocracy. The 1898 U.S. intervention in the Cuban War for Independence,
the subsequent four-year North American occupation of the island, and
the continuing economic, political, and cultural intervention of both the
U.S. government and U.S. corporations had lasting effects on all forms
of Cuban entertainment. The second part of this chapter examines how
rising nationalist sentiment, turbulent economic and political conditions,
and an increasing awareness of North American culture contributed to
the development of the Cuban zarzuela and its subgenres. The chapter
closes with a detailed description of the zarzuela and its nomenclature.

Historic Antecedents

The term *zarzuela* was initially used to describe the sung theater with
spoken dialogue that was first performed in Spanish courts in the mid-
seventeenth century.[3] Taking its name from one of the hunting lodges
of King Philip IV, the genre mixed blank verse and prose with a variety
of musical styles in vogue at the time. It was not unusual for zarzuela
scores to include solo numbers in the form of *coplas, tonadas,* or *ro-
mances,* orchestral interludes and dances, choruses, and arrangements
of popular songs.[4] The genre fell out of favor during the reign of Felipe V
and María Luisa Gabriela de Saboya,[5] for the Bourbon monarchs favored
the sounds of Italian opera, importing the foreign genre with such force
that some historians have called it an "invasion."[6]

It was not until the early nineteenth century, when a series of laws
banned foreign-language operas and non-Spanish singers, and Spanish
cultural nationalists became obsessed with developing a national form
of opera, that the zarzuela was reinvigorated.[7] The zarzuela's revival was
aided by the opening of the Real Conservatorio de María Cristina in Madrid in 1832.[8] The conservatory's expansive curriculum in composition,
vocal and instrumental instruction, and acting provided the foundation
for the development of a renewed zarzuela, which blended musical gestures from Italian and French opera with elements of the *tonadilla escénica,* Spanish popular theater.[9]

The following decade saw zarzuela composition increase dramatically. Composers and librettists experimented with the combination of sung music and spoken dialogue to create new genres, including the *zarzuela parodia*, which poked fun at the bel canto style of Donizetti and Bellini, and the *zarzuela andaluza*, which was the earliest form of the zarzuela to exploit local types, making use of both regional dialects and Andalucian musical style.[10] This nineteenth-century exploration of local "exotics" shows an early influence of the literary *costumbrismo* movement on music, and it evidences a move toward musical nationalism in the zarzuela.[11] The inhabitants of Madrid's poorer barrios also became the subject matter for many zarzuelas. These "exotics close at hand" reflected the general fascination that swept much of western Europe in the nineteenth century for the exotification of the poor.[12]

Curiously, 1832, the year that saw the opening of the Conservatorio Real in Madrid, was an equally important year for cultural institutions in Cuba, for it marked the completion of Havana's Teatro Tacón. The theater became the center of theatrical production in Cuba, producing spoken and lyric theater by local artists, as well as hosting touring performances from Spain, Italy, and elsewhere in the Americas.[13] In 1853, the Teatro Tacón was the site for the first Cuban performance of a Spanish zarzuela, Rafael Hernández's *El duende*.[14] By the end of the year, there were two zarzuela companies in Havana, that of Catalán impresario José Robreño in the Teatro Tacón and another that took up residence in the Teatro Villanueva.[15] Local composers quickly embraced the new genre; the 1853 season included several zarzuelas by Cuban composers. While written in the Spanish style, these early examples illustrate that Cuban composers and librettists were already searching for ways to infuse the zarzuela form with local color. Two works from the 1853 season, *Trespalillos o El carnaval de la Habana* and *El industrial de nuevo cuño*, both portray elements of local color and details of Cuban daily life, bringing the Spanish vogue of *costumbrismo* to the Cuban stage.[16]

The exploitation of local types was also the basis for Cuban popular comedy, or *teatro vernáculo*. Using stock characters based on local, racial, and ethnic stereotypes, the *teatro vernáculo* was performed primarily by white actors, often with the aid of blackface.[17] This type of Cuban comedy had its origins in the early nineteenth century in the work of comic actor Francisco Covarrubias (1775–1850), whom theater historians widely regard as the progenitor of Cuban popular theater and of nationalism in the arts.[18] Covarrubias and his troupe introduced local characters onto the stage for the first time, including the *negrito* (comic black man), *gallego* (Spaniard), *mulata* (mixed-race woman), and *guajiro* (poor white farmer).[19]

The Cuban practice of caricature was inherited from the Spanish, whose history of representing local types goes back to the thirteenth century.[20] Theatrical representations of regional stereotypes and exotic Others were commonplace in the works of Spanish Golden Age playwrights such as Lope de Vega.[21] The practice continued in New World colonies, including Cuba, through the the *villancico*, where ethnically suggestive musical numbers such as the *negro* or *negrilla* featured hemiola shifts between 3/4 and 6/8 meter and a call-and-response structure with alternating solo and choral entrances.[22] Later, the cultural exchange resulting from the Bourbon monarchy brought a taste for the stock characterizations of the Italian commedia dell'arte and their French derivatives.[23] However, whereas the comic opera traditions of Europe adapted the stock characters of Italian popular comedy to speak for rising social and class tensions, Cuban entertainers used popular local idiom—and a fair amount of blackface paint—to make those characters speak for the racial tension resulting from Cuba's headlong rush into slavery.[24]

At the end of the 1860s, composers and librettists began to see a new potential in lyric theater. This movement, too, would begin in the metropole. The decade of the 1860s was politically turbulent in Spain. The Glorious Revolution (1863–1868) ended with the dethroning of Queen Isabel II and constant infighting among moderates, unionists, and progressive factions of the new government. The economy grew increasingly precarious. Spain's political and economic crisis was matched by a cultural crisis in which the zarzuela suffered, as well.[25] The genre's unflattering equation with the status quo, along with the increased economic risk faced by impresarios, caused a sharp decrease in zarzuela production that the closure of Madrid's Teatro de la Zarzuela in 1866 only worsened.[26]

Out of this instability, a new form, the *género bufo*, developed. The *bufo*'s arrival was announced by the performance in 1868 of a new work, *El joven Telémaco*, performed in Madrid by Francisco Arderius's new troupe, the Compañía de los Bufos Madrileños. Adopting the style of Jacques Offenbach and the Bouffes Parisiens, the Bufos Madrileños made use of musical parody, contemporary satire, and the exploitation of stock characters built from local stereotypes.[27] Arderius's production was a huge success. The piece was the first in a huge wave of production in the *bufo* style that both stimulated Spanish lyric theater and provoked heated criticism.[28]

Just months after the premiere of *El joven Telémaco*, the Bufos Madrileños traveled to Havana, where they presented the work.[29] The fast-paced wit, scalding political satire, burlesque, and caricature of popular types used by the Spanish *bufos* were instantly popular in Havana and quickly imitated by a troupe of Cuban actors. Calling themselves the Bufos de La Habana, they adopted the style of the Spanish troupe and used it to address contemporary Cuban issues, namely the growing discontent with Spanish governance.[30] The genre's stock characters were recast in local molds; the *negrito, gallego,* and *guajiro* already found in Cuban popular theater were quickly absorbed into the new *bufo* style.[31] Havana was completely under the thrall of *"bufomanía,"* and within eight months, seven different *bufo* troupes sprang up in the capital.[32] The homegrown *bufos'* presence in Havana created an artistic revolution that marched alongside nationalist political sentiment. *Bufo* theater challenged the hegemony of "foreign" genres such as Italian opera and Spanish zarzuela and created a new type of music theater in which "local" music predominated. For the first time, working-class music with Afrocuban roots, such as *guaracha* and *danza,* was publicly appropriated and identified with being Cuban.[33]

Bufo theater's popular sensibility and its penchant for political satire and nationalist politics continued into the twentieth century, when the targets for performers' humor were more likely to be the United States, rather than Spain, or local Cuban politicians. The zarzuela, which had acquired a reputation for pro-Spanish and conservative politics during the prolonged independence struggles of the nineteenth century, continued to be associated with a conservative agenda, and imports of Spanish zarzuelas and Cuban-produced imitations were primarily relegated to Havana's Teatro Albisú and Teatro Irijoa.[34]

Twentieth-Century Popular Theater: The Teatro Alhambra

The stock characters introduced in the *teatro vernáculo* and later refined by the *teatro bufo* maintained their importance in the twentieth century. The trio formed by the *negrito, gallego,* and *mulata* was particularly important in the repertoire performed in theaters such as the Shanghai, the Molino Rojo, and the Alhambra, where racial burlesque and political humor were blended with more than a touch of vulgarity.[35]

Of these theaters, the Alhambra stands out as a critical antecedent to the development of Cuban zarzuela. The theater first opened in 1890 and underwent several transformations in the years leading up to independence. In 1900, under the direction of Regino López, the theater began turning out its own brand of *teatro vernáculo* in an unprecedented theatrical run that lasted thirty-five years.[36] The theater, which performed picaresque comedy for all-male audiences, further popularized and codified the representation of local character types, establishing musical and dramatic conventions that later found their way into the zarzuela. Furthermore, the Alhambra's role as a male public space that served as a venue for contemporary politics, off-color humor, and burlesque became a point of contrast against which the zarzuela could be developed.

Eduardo Robreño writes that the "miracle of the Alhambra" was not due to any miracle at all but rather to the quality of the productions.[37] The list of names of those responsible for the Alhambra's creative output is impressive. Manuel Mauri, brother of opera composer José Mauri, was the house composer until 1911. His successor, Jorge Anckermann, composed over four hundred musical scores for the theater. Other composers who wrote music for the Alhambra include José Marín Varona, Eliseo Grenet, Jaime Prats, and Gonzalo Roig. The Alhambra's librettists include some of the most important literary names of the early Republic: Federico Villoch, Agustín Rodríguez, Gustavo Sánchez Galarraga, and the Robreño brothers. The theater's productions were also praised for their innovations in stage technology; under Pepito Gómiz and later under Nono Noriega, the Alhambra made advancements not only in scenography and special effects, but also in the development of new ways of effecting scene changes.[38]

Yet quality alone cannot explain the Alhambra's success and unprecedented endurance. Perhaps of equal importance was the theater management's ability to mythologize the Alhambra environment. The theater's fame was as a "male-only" establishment, ostensibly because of the risqué nature of many of the productions and the supposedly rough house that the theater would attract.[39] Audience members came from the working classes as well as the social and political elite, and the theatrical space became an important political forum.[40] Alhambra productions lampooned political events and critiqued social conditions.[41] The theater received its share of moralistic criticism,[42] and although its productions did often employ the use of racy double entendre, scantily clad women, and vulgar language, their content rarely descended to the level of pornography found in other theaters with all-male clientele, such as the Teatro Shanghai or the Teatro Molino Rojo.[43]

Despite its "male" reputation, the Alhambra's most successful works were frequently transferred to other Havana theaters, such as the Payret, Nacional,[44] or Martí, where they could be enjoyed by mixed audiences. The amount of revision that was deemed necessary in adapting Alhambra works to be shown for mixed audiences on Havana's most prestigious stages is open to debate.[45] It is clear, however, that the mixed-gender audiences of the Payret, Nacional, and Martí theaters eagerly awaited the next performance by López's troupe and upper-class, "establishment" newspapers such as *Diario de la Marina* hailed upcoming presentations outside of the Alhambra without a hint of embarrassment.

The repertoire performed in the Alhambra remains little studied. The scholarly work that has been done by writers such as Rine Leal and Eduardo Robreño, and the popular treatment in Enrique Piñero Barnet's 1989 film *La bella del Alhambra*,[46] has been valuable in helping to reconstruct the theater's past but has also resulted in an imbalance. Scholars have tended to favor the librettos over the music, at times considering the music to be inconsequential. Even Rine Leal, Cuba's most celebrated theater historian, excused himself from discussing the music of the *teatro vernáculo* by stating, "I don't talk about what I don't know."[47]

The lack of engagement with the musical scores for the theater has prompted the myth that Alhambra productions were primarily spoken, with only incidental music, and that Alhambra employed untrained singers whose vocal abilities were not terribly important. Both Anckermann's musical scores and recordings made by members of Regino López's company refute this view.[48]

Anckermann's works are full-fledged musical scores. They typically incorporate eight to twelve musical numbers, the majority of which are integral to the overall plot of the work. Light operatic numbers are interspersed with popular genres in vogue at the time, such as the *rumba* or the *tango-congo*, and stylized versions of song forms from folk music, such as the *décima* and *canción*. Foreign genres such as the fox-trot and tango are well-represented. *América en la guerra*, a surprisingly pro–United States piece that documents North American involvement in World War I, even includes an instrumental rendition of the U.S. national anthem after an American officer falls wounded on the stage.[49]

The myth that the repertoire performed in the Alhambra was primarily spoken theater may have arisen from the fact that some of the theater's most celebrated performers could not sing.[50] Recordings made by personnel from the Alhambra between 1910 and 1920 should dispel the notion that "legitimate" singers did not perform in the theater. These recordings typically have a spoken comic sketch on one side and a musical number on the other. The music is frequently vocally demanding, and the voices of singers Margarita Cueto and Ramón Espigul, who perform on many of the recordings, are fluid and reflect a classically trained aesthetic.

Understanding the Alhambra's repertoire as sung theater illuminates the connection between *teatro vernáculo* and the zarzuela and reveals that the two genres shared much more than mere repetition of character types and plot formulas. Rather, they shared an intertextual bond and thus could comment on each other in substance as well as content. The presence of *mulatas* named Cecilia and María la O on the Alhambra stage is provocative when one considers their later incarnations as zarzuela protagonists,[51] as is the use of light operatic music associated with the zarzuela in contemporary popular theater.

Opera in Cuba

It should not be seen as a contradiction that an operatic sound was employed in the Alhambra and other "popular" theaters. Opera *was* popular, at least among the theatergoing public. Cuba's love affair with opera began with house performances in the early days of colonialism and flourished in the nineteenth century, when traveling European troupes made Cuba a first stop on their overseas tours.[52] During the twentieth century, Cuban audiences continued to demand international troupes; operas by Verdi, Donizetti, and Bizet were especially popular.[53]

The Cuban love for opera did not extend only to the consumption of a repertoire of Italian and French "hits." Cuban composers, in their search for a national music, led various attempts to create a national opera. *Patria*, by Hubert de Blanck, was completed in 1899.[54] The work documents the painful struggle for Cuban independence, recounting the starvation and misery of Cuban civilians, the fraternity among Cuban independence fighters, or *mambises*, and the bravery and strength of Cuban women in the face of incredible hardship. The opera does more than merely treat a historical Cuban plot; it also engages local musical material. In the score, de Blanck uses a variety of Cuban musical genres, most notably the *habanera* and the *décima*, both of which take on strong nationalistic symbolism. *Patria* also provides early evidence that particular musical genres and styles were associated with the racial, gender, and class attributes of characters.[55]

One of the most important currents in the movement to develop a national opera was led by Eduardo Sánchez de Fuentes. The portrait historians paint of him is not always a positive one.[56] Openly racist, the composer and essayist was one of the harshest critics of the growing Afrocuban influence on Cuban music and culture.[57] Sánchez de Fuentes was the leading proponent of *indigenismo*,[58] a movement that traced the percussion instruments and rhythmic complexity of Cuban musical genres not to Afrocubans, but to Cuba's long-disappeared indigenous population of Taino and Arawak peoples. The composer led the charge to create a uniquely Cuban national music through the "rediscovery" of indigenous music.[59] His first opera, *Yumuri* (1898), is based on events that took place during Columbus's second voyage to the island. The work is only the second opera composed in Cuba to be based on a Cuban theme and is considered by some to be the first truly Cuban opera.[60] Sánchez de Fuentes's nationalist agenda, however, does not extend to his musical language; the music of *Yumuri* is entirely European in sound and has been described by some critics as being Wagnerian.[61] After a venture into *verismo* with the operas *Il naufrago* (1901) and *Dolorosa* (1910), Sánchez de Fuentes returned to his interest in writing "indigenous" opera with *Doreya* (1918). The composer claimed to incorporate authentic elements of Taino music into the opera, although it is doubtful whether many witnessing the work actually believed this to be true. L. Fernándo Ros wrote in his column in *La Noche*, "the dance numbers offer a strange rhythm that's said to be authentic, coming from rhythms used by the Tainos in their *areitos* and [the dances are] the best part of the work."[62] While the music contains its fair share of open fifths and "exotic" rhythms, the score owes much more to contemporary Italian opera than to the composer's re-creation of lost indigenous dances.

Cuban opera also dealt with the question of racial identity. José Mauri's opera *La esclava* (1928),[63] for example, tells the story of Matilde, the daughter of a wealthy Spanish landowner. Upon the death of her father it is discovered that she is the granddaughter of a slave and that her birth was illegitimate, making her a slave, as well. Betrayed by her former fiancé, who first seduces her and then watches dispassionately as she is being sold at auction, Matilde eventually is saved by her admirer Miguel, who buys her her freedom and gives her what would have been her rightful inheritance. The intervention comes too late, however, for the young woman cannot overcome the horror of what has been done to her, and she dies of grief. *La esclava* may be the first musical portrayal of the tragic *mulata*, a character type that would become a mainstay of twentieth-century Cuban zarzuela, although in the zarzuela it is not usually the *mulata* who dies.

Afrocubanismo

One of the most pervasive cultural movements that characterized Cuban intellectuals' search for national identity was an increasing valorization and popularization of elements of Afrocuban culture, a movement known as *afrocubanismo*. In *Nationalizing Blackness: Afrocubanismo and Artistic Revolution in Havana, 1920–1940*, Robin Moore documents the ways in which, after a virtual separation between white Cuban and black Cuban culture, the 1920s were witness to an explosion of interest in and exploitation of Afrocuban cultural forms that affected all areas of cultural production. Scholars Fernando Ortíz and Israel Castellanos gave Afrocuban cultural products a newfound institutional legitimacy (albeit an ambivalent one) by devoting extensive attention to cataloguing and recording black "folkloric" practices.[64] Poets Nicolas Guillén, Emilio Ballagas, and others explored the linguistic vitality of the sounds and rhythms of black speech, as did novelist Alejo Carpentier. Images drawn from Afrocuban ritual and religious experience influenced the work of visual artists, most notably Wifredo Lam and Eduardo Abela, and composers of concert music Amadeo Roldán and Alejandro García Caturla attempted to define a new national art music by blending European compositional techniques with Afrocuban sonorities and rhythmic patterns.[65]

Nowhere was the trend of *afrocubanismo* more apparent, however, than in popular music. Dance genres associated with black urban street life, such as the *son* and *rumba*, were appropriated and popularized by white audiences, although often in considerably "refined" versions.[66] While dances like the *son* retained their associations with the underclasses for many of the elite,[67] the emergence of a wide variety of salon-style popular songs and piano music by composers such as Ernesto Lecuona, Eliseo Grenet, Ernestina Lecuona, Ignacio Villa, Moisés Simons, and others made it possible for "contained" Afrocuban musical elements to be performed and heard by whites in their own homes.

The lyric stage was another medium that allowed for careful containment of the presentation of Afrocuban culture, which made it an ideal vehicle for the spread of *afrocubanismo*. Moore considers the zarzuela as one of the three pillars of *afrocubanista* composition, along with salon music and music for dance bands.[68] The zarzuela's inheritance of racialized character types from the *teatro vernáculo* made it a likely vehicle for this style of composition and its preference for nineteenth-century plots provided a corps of "slave" choristers and dancers for whom elaborate folkloric production numbers could be written and staged.

Ensemble and production numbers based on Afrocuban themes are found in the majority of zarzuelas produced in the period 1927–40. *El cafetal* (1929) and *Cecilia Valdés* (1932) both contain large slave choruses. *María la O* (1930) is filled with *afrocubanista* musical numbers, including a huge production number showing a *comparsa*, or street parade, for the Kings' Day celebration, a chorus of *curros*,[69] and a number written for the protagonist and a group of *chancleteras*, women wearing wooden sandals that could be used, effectively, like tap shoes. *Afrocubanista* compositions could also be much smaller in scale, such as Felo and Chea's duet from Lecuona's *Julián el gallo* (1934) and Dolores de Santa Cruz's popular *tango-congo* from *Cecilia Valdés* (1932), "Po po po."[70]

The presentation of the *mulata* character, by far the most prominent protagonist on the zarzuela stage, was also heavily influenced by the popularity of *afrocubanismo*. It is through the *mulata* that truly hybridized musical compositions are expressed, blending stylistic elements of European classical music with refined rhythms and a "popular" vocal style drawn from Afrocuban dance genres.[71]

A Word on Nomenclature

It is a curious irony that the term that defines the genre being studied here is itself the source of considerable controversy and confusion. *Zarzuela* is often used by Cubans in the abstract to refer to the lyric theater, based on Cuban themes, that was produced in the second quarter of the twentieth century.[72] These works, sparked by the success of *La Niña Rita* in 1927,[73] alternate musical numbers with spoken dialogue in the tradition of Spanish zarzuela. Yet *zarzuela*, as used in the abstract, does not distinguish among the specific subgenres of music theater produced in this period. Its general usage does not identify dramatic structure or musical or thematic characteristics. Rather, *zarzuela*, or the more open *la zarzuelística*, is often used as an umbrella term to describe a variety of genres, including the *revista*, *opereta*, and *sainete*, and also, confusingly, the zarzuela.

However, in spite of the ease with which the term *zarzuela* is applied to describe this period of musical theater at large, its usage becomes much more controversial when it is applied as a descriptive label to specific works. Nomenclature is a recurrent problem in discussing the music theater produced in Cuba from the late nineteenth century until the 1950s. Spanish, French, and American theatrical styles—and their vocabulary—combined with local forms, and the terminology used to describe the resulting genres is not used with any consistency. Generic labels found on title pages of works produced between 1920 and 1940 show a stunning variety of classificatory options, including *sainete*, *revista*, *opereta*, *comedia lírica*, and more fanciful denominations such as *boceto lírico*, *juguete cómico*, and *revista fantástica*. These labels generally serve more as dramatic description rather than providing any kind of specific taxonomy of genre. For example, *La blanca negra* (*The Black*

White Woman), performed in the Molino Rojo between 1912 and 1917 with music by a young Gonzalo Roig, is labeled as a *juguete cómico-racista* (a "comic-racist plaything"), a label that provides very little insight into the work's musical or dramatic form but, rather, prepares the audience for racial burlesque. Generic titles were usually provided by librettists rather than composers, and in cases where they are used beyond mere description to actually define genre, their usage tends to be literary, referring to plot formulas rather than suggesting musical and formal content.

One of the greatest difficulties in understanding the practice of genre classification is that the nomenclature solidified after the fact; it is the product of analytical critique rather than artistic forethought.[74] As the process of canonization began in the 1940s and 1950s, an evolutionary genre hierarchy began to develop, with the short sketches of Cuban popular theater at the bottom and opera at the top. Lecuona, Roig, and Prats all played a part in this movement, with Lecuona dreaming of writing and producing his first opera and Roig and Prats making respective additions to *Cecilia Valdés* and *Amalia Batista* with the lofty goal of the works' eventual conversion to opera always in mind.[75]

It was within zarzuelistic *culture* to use nomenclature both as classification and description. Cuban sources, particularly firsthand accounts, often mix the two approaches, occasionally appearing to be quite contradictory. Understanding is further complicated by the fact that theater historians, rather than musicologists, have done the majority of work on the music theater of this period,[76] and they have developed a taxonomic nomenclature that refers almost entirely to the librettos. Musicologists have tried to use the same terminology to also encompass the music, leading to different, and often confusing, results.[77]

Since librettists and composers did not employ their terminology with anything approaching an exact science, the productivity of trying to force works into a belated generic taxonomy is questionable. This book employs this nomenclature as classification in the loosest of senses; my use of the nomenclature is based on an interpretation of the primary sources; the work of several Cuban scholars, most notably Rine Leal and José Ruiz Elcoro; and personal observation. I am less interested in the generic classification of individual works than I am in the zarzuela convention as a whole; thus my use of nomenclature is descriptive rather than discriminating and I analyze and discuss works within these pages that are technically *sainetes* or *revistas* but that are considered part of the larger zarzuela convention.

Sainete

As relatively short (forty-five minutes to an hour and a half) one-act works, *sainetes* are part of the *género chico* tradition that evolved in Spain during the decade following the 1866 "Glorious Revolution."[78] On both sides of the Atlantic these works employed simple, linear plots and were colored with local customs and musical styles. In Cuba, the *sainete* became a favorite medium for the classic triangle of the *negrito, mulata,* and *gallego,* developed in the *teatro vernáculo.* The trio's sharp-witted comedy made the *sainete* a perfect vehicle for political humor and satire, and it was a form widely used in Cuban theaters that specialized in political and burlesque comedy, such as Havana's Teatro Alhambra.

   Sainetes tend to be shorter than works given the denomination *zarzuela.* Responding to economic necessity, *sainete* casts are generally small, with few singing characters. While the humor may be quite sophisticated, the plots themselves tend to be rather simplistic; it is rare for more than one subplot to be happening at a time.

   However, there are some works that seem truly zarzuela-like. They are longer, have more complex plots and more developed musical scores— and yet they are labeled *sainetes.* In these cases, the decision to label them *sainetes* rather than *zarzuelas* appears to have been based on content rather than structure, length, or the quality of the musical score. Works that highlight lower-class characters and share themes with Cuban popular comedy, such as life in urban tenements (*solares*), casual interracial relationships, or prostitution, tend to be called *sainetes,* whereas works that showcase middle- and upper-class characters and milieus are more likely to receive the label *zarzuela.*[79]

Revista

Another one-act genre with a duration of an hour or less, the Cuban *revista* was heavily influenced by the North American review, which was brought to Cuba with the U.S. occupation beginning in 1898.[80] However, the form and basic dramatic function of the genre, derived from the French *revue,* was brought to Cuba from Spain, where the *revista* was hugely popular in the latter decades of the nineteenth century.[81] In the *revista,* musical and dance numbers are strung together by a loose plot, which serves more to promote spectacle than to tell a story. Such pieces are always of a light, comic nature. Musical numbers are relatively short, often in the style of popular song, and there is no thematic cohesion from one piece to the next. They are usually scored for solo voice or for ensemble (duets are rare), and the solo personnel tends to change from one number to the next with a clear preference for female, rather than male, vocalists. Dance numbers are interspersed with vocal pieces, and the cast often includes a pair of solo dancers as well as a small dance troupe, usually made up of women.

The *revista*, along with the *sainete*, was well suited for political satire. Rodrigo Prats recounts that a 1933 performance of his *revista* titled *Quítate tú para ponerme yo* contained a string of musical numbers that satirized Cuba's presidents up until Ramón Grau, who became the *de facto* president after President Gerardo Machado was overthrown in 1933.[82] Such performances were not always well received.

> The day of the opening nothing happened, but in the next performance there were tremendous problems. It seems that someone brought the news to the authorities of what happened in the work and that night the theater was full, which was strange because the piece wasn't [meant] for a big public. We didn't notice the rabble that came in! From there until I began to play the known popular piece and an actor imitated Grau on stage, it began to rain, from the audience, tomatoes, potatoes, rocks, and a group of policemen dressed as civilians began to shoot. It was necessary to close the curtain, or they would have killed the actors. At the same time I began to direct the Himno [national anthem] but not even this calmed those lunatics. In the end I was left alone with my trumpet, because the whole orchestra had taken off [put their feet to dust].[83]

Zarzuela

Cuban zarzuelas are usually lengthy one-acts with several scenes and are only occasionally split into multiple acts. They feature linear plots of a romantic nature that almost invariably resolve in a tragic ending. This is a major contrast to the majority of Spanish zarzuelas, which close with happy endings, typically a wedding or multiple weddings. Zarzuela plots are based on Cuban themes, and their musical scores feature rhythms and song forms from Cuban popular music, such as the *tango-congo*, *guaracha*, and salon *rumba*, alongside more classically inspired, aria-like *romanzas*, *lamentos*, *duos*, and ensembles.[84] The use of more elaborate musical numbers and orchestral introductions sets the zarzuela apart from the *sainete* and *revista*, as does the use of recurring musical themes to create musical and dramatic unity.

Opereta and *Opereta Cubana*

European-style operetta was quite popular in Cuba, and works by composers such as Lehar and Offenbach were performed regularly. Lehar's *The
Merry Widow*, in fact, was such a permanent fixture that it can almost
be considered part of the Cuban repertory.[85] The Cuban *opereta* follows
the multi-act format of the European operetta, and, like the zarzuela, it
features a musical score separated by spoken dialogue. The difference
lies in the subject matter. Works designated as *operetas* are usually based
on European (non-Spanish) plots or are staged in exotic faraway lands.[86]
Operetas also occasionally take place in precolonial Cuba, among the
island's lost Taino and Arawawk population.

Adding to the confusion, there are also works that are referred to by
librettists as *operetas cubanas*, which in their length, musical score, and
treatment of Cuban themes appear to be quite similar to Cuban zarzuelas.[87] *Operetas cubanas* are consistently multi-act works, while works
labeled *zarzuelas* may be one-acts with many scenes. The most significant
difference, however, is that they invariably focus on white, and generally
upper-class, plots.[88] The *opereta cubana* lacks a strong presence of characters from Cuban popular theater and does not include stylized Afrocuban
production numbers, as do many zarzuelas. This division of nomenclature,
using *zarzuela* to denote works with more popular themes and *opereta
cubana* for those that dealt with upper-class issues, is similar to the division found in the United States between operetta and musical comedy.[89]

Both the "exotic" *opereta* and the *opereta cubana* were performed as
elaborate productions. Lasting up to two and a half hours, *operetas* employed large casts, full orchestration, extensive sets and backdrops, and
lavish costumes. These features set them apart from the lower-budget
sainetes, as does their reliance on a greater number of trained voices in
the cast.

As most broadly defined, the zarzuela can be seen as the result of, and
the engagement in, multiple cultural and historical dialogues. The genre
was a major outlet for the growing popularity of Afrocuban styles. At the
same time, however, it responded to audiences' expectations based on
their familiarity with opera and popular theater. The zarzuela was also a
participant in another cultural discourse, one that concerned the role of
women and the construction of gender identities. Just how the zarzuela
fit into early twentieth-century proscriptions regarding gender in Cuba
is the subject of the following chapter.

2 Eminently Feminine: The Politics of Gender and Genre

The zarzuela's rise in Cuba occurred at an unlikely moment, for it flourished during a period of both economic and political turmoil. An independent republic for barely three decades, Cuba had fallen victim to government corruption and increasing U.S. economic exploitation. The gap between rich and poor remained wide and grew even wider during the years of the *vaca gorda,* when rising sugar prices took the Cuban elite on a wild and euphoric, if short-lived, ride. By 1920, sugar prices had fallen, the Cuban economy was in disarray, and shortages of food and other resources were becoming commonplace.[1]

In 1925, General Gerardo Machado was elected president of Cuba. Although he was elected by popular vote, Machado's presidency soon proved itself far from democratic. In 1927, Machado called a special constitutional assembly that changed the rules for term limits and guaranteed him power until 1935.[2] The president ruled with an iron grip. The period of Machado's presidency, known as the *machadato,* was a reign of terror, with the *porra,* the dreaded secret police, murdering the president's critics and occasionally innocent bystanders.[3]

Machado was finally overthrown in August of 1933 in what has been called the "frustrated revolution,"[4] for the uprising and removal of Machado did not end the terror on the streets, economic unrest, or political corruption. By January of 1936, the island was under its sixth government and had already experienced two military coups, both masterminded by military leader Fulgencio Batista.[5] Batista himself would become president in 1940, in an administration racked by increasing social unrest. Batista was voted out of office in the presidential elections of 1944, and although there was a peaceful transfer of power, the polemics of his regime were translated into violence on the streets as armed gangs representing opposing political factions resorted to terrorist tactics.[6] Eight years later, Batista regained government control following a military coup; he maintained his despotic grip until the 1959 revolution.

Curiously, it was precisely in this time of political turmoil and economic collapse (1927–44) that the zarzuela rose to prominence. Zarzuelas, with their emphasis on historic plots, Cuban themes, and local music, participated in a growing quest to define national identity, at a time when that identity was undergoing tumultuous change. All constructions of nationalism, Anne McClintock reminds us, are "constituted from the very beginning as gendered discourse."[7] The zarzuela was no exception.

Andrea García, writing about the Cuban zarzuela in 1987, called the theatrical genre "eminently feminine."[8] This sexual label was self-evident to the reviewer. Yet it directly echoes an anonymous writer in the 1930s who called the zarzuela "the most feminine of genres."[9] Neither critic specifies what aspect of the zarzuela qualified it as feminine, or indeed what the meaning of *femininity* might be in such a context.

Certainly, the most notable quality of the zarzuelas produced in the decade following 1927 is the prominence of female protagonists. The titles of some of the genre's best-known works—*María la O, Cecilia Valdés, Amalia Batista, Rosa la China, María Belén Chacón, Lola Cruz*—show that women, or at least women characters, are at the heart of this genre. The zarzuela's connection to women is much stronger than a mere predilection of plot, however. This chapter examines how women, directly and indirectly, influenced the zarzuela's production, reception, and performance. The zarzuela's promoters created a genre that would appeal to a previously underserved market: Havana's middle- and upper-class women. Librettists and composers worked to maintain much of the flavor of *teatro vernáculo* while reworking the humor to make it suitable for family audiences. Zarzuela plots centered around female protagonists, and their musical scores showcased the female voice. Furthermore, the theaters that promoted the zarzuela provided an important public space for women, a space that opened a new feminist politics, countering the all-male spaces of theaters like the Alhambra.

The Women's Movement and
Female-Led Institutions

In Cuba in the 1920s, the behavior of women was a growing concern in the public arena, as, in the midst of an already volatile economic and political situation, women began to organize for their rights. The Cuban women's movement was increasingly active during the first three decades of the Republic and was directly affected by, and interactive with, current political events. The movement was led by upper- and middle-class women, many of whom were married to and entertained highly influential men. These women were portrayed by civic leaders, politicians, and the media as the keepers of Cuban morality, an image they promoted themselves as they sought to define and protect Cuban motherhood, family values, and, ultimately, nationalism itself. K. Lynn Stoner points out that the privileged status of these women led them to pursue goals that were more reformist than revolutionary.[10] Nevertheless, their positions were far from heterogeneous, and the mere existence of such groups was implicitly subversive.

In 1923, the Federación Nacional de Asociaciones Femininas held its first National Women's Congress. Social concerns such as the rights of illegitimate children and prostitutes were the most controversial subjects addressed at the Congress, along with criticism of the nation's divorce and adultery laws. Division over these social issues led to a split between conservative feminists, who focused their energies and resources on suffrage, and radical feminists, who campaigned more heavily on social issues. The split widened at the second National Women's Congress, held in 1925. Recently elected President Machado spoke at the opening ceremonies. Machado's nominal support for suffrage earned him the backing of politically conservative feminists and caused many, men and women alike, to temporarily reject the suffrage campaign as complicit in the Machado regime.[11] Machado, however, never had any intention of giving women the vote, and as his tyranny grew, women's organizations became one of the most effective forces against him.[12]

Women's efforts to achieve political recognition were only one of many ways in which they were making their influence felt on Cuban society. While they might not have been able to vote, Cuban women from the upper classes were increasingly organizing the fabric of public life.[13] Cuban women had traditionally put their influence—and their money—behind many philanthropic causes. They supported charities for poor women, financed foundling hospitals, and organized to fight the scourges of society, such as prostitution, alcoholism, and gambling.[14]

Charities and public works were not the only outlets for Cuba's well-to-do women, however. Women also founded and ran some of Cuba's most powerful cultural institutions. The Pro-Arte Musical, founded in 1918 by María Teresa García Montes de Giberga, was the first organization dedicated to the promotion of art music and became home to Havana's first orchestra and symphonic concert hall. The society also published a magazine, *Revista Pro-Arte Musical,* which included concert reviews, interviews with well-known performers, and articles on music history and style. The magazine mirrored the Pro-Arte Musical's function of providing high-class cultural *entertainment.* However, beyond proclaiming the cultural superiority of European concert music over the popular rhythms emerging from both Cuban composers and North American dance bands, *Revista Pro-Arte Musical* was not a forum for aesthetic debates over the future of musical composition.

A more serious venue for musical debate was found in the pages of *Musicalia,* founded in 1928 by María Muñoz de Quevedo, a respected composer, professor, and supporter of new music. Muñoz de Quevedo's musical and professional activities already placed her well into the public domain before her decision to start the magazine. Yet it is clear that Muñoz de Quevedo recognized the extent to which music magazines and the concertgoing public fell into contemporary conceptions of the feminine sphere and, in spite of their many differences of opinion on musical (and one suspects political) matters, she respected García Montes's mastery in catering to the whims of this public. Upon the death of García Montes in 1930, *Musicalia* published a eulogy of the Pro-Arte Musical founder written by Muñoz de Quevedo herself.[15] In the eulogy, the author recounts that when she decided in 1928 to publish *Musicalia,* she first paid a visit to the offices of Pro-Arte Musical, to seek the advice—and the blessing—of García Montes. At the time, the Pro-Arte Musical offices were located in García Montes's home, thus placing the seat of one of Havana's most powerful cultural institutions in the private, domestic sphere of one of the city's most influential women.

Women were part of the most important cultural institutions of Republican Cuba. Feminist writer Mariblanca Sabas Alomá was one of the founding members of the Minoristas, a progressive, left-leaning, intellectual group of writers, artists, and musicians, and she was one of its only two female members.[16] Both women appear to have been active participants, in spite of their poor reception by some of the men.[17] Yet, while fellow members of the Minoristas might not have taken the presence of women in the intellectual group seriously, it is clear that women did have power in similar cultural organizations, and that power was respected by their male colleagues. José Manuel Carbonell, for example, writes that when the Sociedad "Teatro Cubano," an organization that flourished under the auspices of the Sección de Bellas Artes del Ateneo de la Habana, wanted to open its board to members of Havana's intellectual community, he and fellow committee member Gustavo Sánchez Galarraga[18] first obtained the permission of Laura G. de Zayas Bazán, of the Ateneo.[19]

That women were such avid consumers and promoters of theater should not come as a surprise. Despite twentieth-century anomalies like the Teatro Alhambra, theater in Cuba had always been a strangely female province. The earliest theatrical performances on the island were held in private homes as the wives of colonial officials sought to provide an air of sophistication to the rough and raucous culture of the colonial port.[20] Havana's first theater, the Teatro Coliseo, was billed as an urban renewal project and, to gain the support of the local bishop, the theater's promoters, the Marqúes de la Torre and Governor Don Felipe Fondesviele, proposed that the Coliseo's proceeds should go to a local orphanage.[21] The Coliseo's opening in 1775[22] can be seen as beginning a collaborative relationship between artistic production and charitable organizations—many of which were headed by women—that would outlast colonialism.

Cuban women had a real need for public spaces such as the Coliseo. In *Fighting Slavery in the Caribbean: The Life and Times of a British Family in Nineteenth-Century Havana,* Luis Martínez-Fernández pieces together accounts from diaries and travelogues to conclude that elite white women in Havana were more restricted in their movement and behavior "than [their counterparts] in any other Western society."[23] Women from the upper classes lived cloistered lives, their mobility strictly controlled. It was considered unseemly for a woman to walk in the street, and she could never do this alone. Houses had barred windows at street level, through which women could converse with passersby. The lives of these urban elite women were largely spent in the cool recesses of the dark, high-ceilinged houses of Havana's wealthy neighborhoods, leading some visitors to Havana to decry these women's "imprisonment."[24]

As an interior yet public space, the theater provided one of the few secure civic spaces in which elite Cuban women could mingle. In the upper boxes of the Teatro Tacón, for example, unaccompanied women could see and be seen, experiencing a moment of physical liberation normally denied to them.[25] But the theaters did not just offer an opportunity to display attractive hairstyles and daring décolletage. By the middle of the nineteenth century, the theater also became a public arena for women to display their political affiliations. During the thirty-year period of independence struggle, it was not uncommon for women to arrive at the theater wearing the colors of the banned Cuban flag.[26]

During the early years of the Republic, theaters such as the Payret, the Martí, and later the Auditorium[27] continued to provide the women of Havana's upper classes with a public space in which they could meet and socialize. The importance of theater in elite women's lives is evidenced by the fact that the *Diario de la Marina* printed the theater and society pages side by side. In "Habaneras," the daily society column, readers could catch up on the local gossip, learn of upcoming events (including theater openings), and read interviews with visiting musicians and artists.

Newspapers such as the *Diario de la Marina* reveal that not only was there a strong connection between female readers and the entertainment economy, but that theater was itself tied up in an emerging female identity in Republican Cuba. Appearing on the theater page, along with announcements for openings, touring Italian opera companies, instrumental recitals, visiting symphony orchestras, and showings of new American films, are occasional announcements for meetings. It was not unusual for Havana's theaters, especially the Gran Teatro Nacional and the Payret, to be used by politicians for fund-raisers and political gatherings; few other such large spaces were available. However, these are not the meetings advertised in the theater section. Rather, listed under the heading "Teatros," and appearing alongside the listings for concerts and theater premieres, are announcements for the activities of the Alianza Feminista Cubana, the Club Feminino de La Habana, and notices for the attendees of the Women's Congress of 1927. These listings reveal connections among a female public, an interest in women's issues, and theatrical production.

Until 1927, the political humor that permeated so much of Cuban popular theater, as well as the male exclusivity of burlesque theaters such as the Alhambra and the Molino Rojo, further distanced middle- and upper-class women from theatrical entertainment. Unable to vote, women lacked a direct connection with the electoral politics that were the focus of so much of Cuban popular theater. As the suffrage campaign grew in the 1920s, the "male-only" dictate of the Teatro Alhambra did more than protect women from the off-color humor and occasional nudity of the *teatro vernáculo*; it barred them from political space. The Alhambra was as much a forum for political debate as for entertainment. There, politicians, officials, judges, lawyers, clerks, businessmen, and workers met to cheer or jeer, to censure by catcalls or rotten fruit. The theater's male-only policy explicitly represented and enforced women's separation from the political process.

Feminist concerns and the drive for suffrage were treated on the stage, although not necessarily in a flattering manner. The Amazonian society found by the two travelers in *La tierra de Venus*[28] poked fun at the idea of political governance by women, showing feminism as something alien and, ultimately, antimale. *La liga de las señoras* (*The League of Women*) (1927), which also premiered in the opening season of the Regina Theater, and Gonzalo Roig's *El voto femenino* (*The Feminine Vote*) (1932) were more direct references to the women's movement, and although neither libretto nor complete scores can be found for either of these works, existing musical fragments, as well as media accounts, suggest that both works treated the subject more as lighthearted farce than harsh critique.

The women's movement was also undercut in ostensibly nonpolitical works, such as Gonzalo Roig and Agustín Rodríguez's *La Habana de noche* (1936), which portrayed women as childish, frivolous, and unable to lead. In the work there is a sprightly mazurka over which a women's chorus sing of the challenging activities in their days. "At ten o'clock we drink our hot chocolate and we go to bed after we pray. And then at six we get up in a hurry and go to Mass without having breakfast."[29] Other works that similarly portray women in contemporary society show them as being obsessed not with societal goals but with fashion.[30] Similarly, the rising ranks of working women were also a source of ridicule. Shopgirls and female clerks were often viewed on the stage as morally suspect, their lives in the public sector conflicting with traditional societal values.[31]

Theater "for Families" and the Opening of the Regina

On a professional level, Havana's theater scene remained very much apart from the institutionalism promoted by the city's wealthy women and instead was run by male impresarios, directors, composers, playwrights, and designers. While the infrastructure that supported the city's concert scene might have been based in private parlors and salons, the *business* of running Havana's theaters was conducted in cafés, in government offices, and in the theaters themselves.

By the 1920s, the economic potential of female theatergoers began to influence the production of Cuban theater. The unstable economy of the *machadato*, combined with government censorship and the threat of violence, made political comedy increasingly unprofitable. Traditional

Cuban comedy also had to compete with movie houses, which drew away audiences with inexpensive admissions and continuous showings. Profits reached all-time lows, and actors had to survive on barely subsistence wages.[32] Given the economic instability of the theater, it seems only natural that impresarios and theater organizers would have looked for a way to diversify and expand their audience base. This diversification was found in the presentation of popular theater for "family" audiences, in other words, audiences that included wives, sisters, and daughters.

The inauguration of the Regina Theater on September 29, 1927, was a direct response to the economic potential of family entertainment and, more subtly, women's need for a new public space. It is perhaps symbolic that the Regina Theater, whose opening began what many consider to be the "golden age" in Cuban lyric theater, occupied the same building that had housed the Teatro Molino Rojo, which specialized in picaresque comedy for male audiences. The building's restoration was more than a mere makeover. Rather, it was something akin to a respectability campaign. The Molino Rojo's tendency toward pornography had earned the theater a sordid reputation. Making the new theater fashionable, or even respectable, would take a gargantuan effort on the part of its organizers.[33] In a 1936 tribute to Lecuona, an unknown author acknowledges the importance that the rehabilitation of the Molino Rojo had in the creation of a new genre: "Ernesto Lecuona is the creator of lyric theater in Cuba, and to create it he realized the miracle of converting the repugnant 'Molino Rojo' into a theater that families comfortably attended. It's just to say that an adept enterprise, formed in part by Don Luis Estrada, took the place of that low-class theater, where impudence and lewdness had reigned, with a hall that was nice and attractive."[34]

The remodeling of the Molino Rojo thus represented both an architectural and a moral conversion, and the refurbished building was lauded in the press with the joy of the return of a prodigal son. The theater's inauguration was a grand affair. The theater section as well as the society column in the *Diario de la Marina* began hinting about the event weeks in advance. The theater promised to be the epitome of luxury. "The attractive building lacks not one single detail of comfort or of good taste," crowed the paper.[35] A building that had once kept out only good taste was now open to Havana's most select elite; invitations for the building's baptism were doled out "by rigorous invitation," going to authorities, the press, and "the most exclusive families of our elegant world."[36] The same select public appears to have been present at the theater's opening, as the *Diario de la Marina* trilled the day following the premiere, "all of the *highlife*, all the *elite*, the complete *bon ton* . . . made itself comfortable in the brand-new boxes of the brilliant coliseum."[37] News of the inauguration filled the society column for days. The day following the event, the column "Habaneras" enthusiastically reported the names of women who had been seen at the event, among them the wives and daughters of politicians, military leaders, and important businessmen.[38]

There is remarkable agreement among both music and theater historians that the opening of the Regina Theater marked the birth of the Cuban zarzuela. Such agreement is striking, particularly since neither of the two works that were presented to the public on that day, *La Niña Rita o La Habana en 1830*, with music by Eliseo Grenet and Ernesto Lecuona, or *La tierra de Venus*, with music by Lecuona, is actually a zarzuela.[39] *La Niña Rita* is a *sainete*, a shorter, one-act work from the tradition of the *género chico*.[40] *La tierra de Venus* is a *revista*, a string of colorful production numbers held loosely together by a fragile plot. The theater's opening, which will be discussed later in greater detail, was an immense success, and the Regina would become the most important location for works by Lecuona and Sánchez Galarraga until the spring of 1929. While both *La Niña Rita* and *La tierra de Venus* are indebted to the Spanish and Cuban musical theater performed in Havana at the time, there are also real differences apparent in these two works that help to account for their popularity and their influence in the creation of a new genre.

At first glance, the plot of *La Niña Rita* is an insipid love story indistinguishable from any number of Spanish zarzuelas.[41] The *sainete* was notable, however, for its inclusion of local themes and especially for its historical plot. The press responded positively to the debut, stating, "*La Habana en 1830* is a delicious *sainete*. The retrospective local setting is treated with finesse and admirable grace."[42] *La Niña Rita* can be considered responsible for starting the vogue of nineteenth-century plots that would fill the zarzuela stage in the decade to come.[43] The *sainete* was influential for its blending of an upper-class love story with scenes of lower-class life, its inclusion of stylized black speech in the libretto, and its use of Cuban musical genres that previously would only have been found on the *vernáculo* stage.

While Cuban scholars cite *La Niña Rita*'s influence on the development of the zarzuela, *La tierra de Venus* is mentioned only in passing. The work's failure to maintain its popularity through revivals has created a misleading historical record, and writers often brush *La tierra de Venus* aside as the "filler" that accompanied *La Niña Rita* in the Regina's opening. One suspects that the piece would hardly be mentioned at all but for the fact that two of Lecuona's most enduring songs, "Siboney" and "Canto Indio," premiered in the work. Longer and containing far more music than *La Niña Rita*, *La tierra de Venus* was a huge success. It contained multiple showcases for stars Rita Montaner, Dora O'Siel, María Ruíz, and Caridad Suárez. The elaborate praise it received in the press was even more enthusiastic than that garnered by *La Niña Rita*.

> *La tierra de Venus* was interesting from the first scene. It's a *revista* full of light and color, a picturesque parade of animated scenes that keep the public constantly curious. The work was splendidly staged. The scene changes were smooth, under the expert direction of Esteban Palos, who, moreover, together with Strabeu, with Paquita López, and with María Verdiales, showed us that he is [also] a notable dancer. In the role of the governess in *La tierra de Venus*, Soledad Pérez was a great success. She wore a turban, a creation of the elegant Maison de Ketty, that strongly drew the attention of the ladies. E. Lecuona and E. Grenet deserve recognition, the first for his work as artistic director and the second for directing the orchestra.[44]

It is not only *La tierra de Venus*'s popularity, however, that suggests it should be viewed as equally important in the creation of the Cuban zarzuela as *La Niña Rita*. The *revista*'s formula of linking elaborate musical and production numbers that bear little relationship to the overall plot becomes a crucial element of the zarzuela and is particularly evident in works by Ernesto Lecuona and Rodrigo Prats. *Revista* strategies are used most frequently in zarzuelas that showcase representations of Afro-Cuban music and dance.[45]

As the title suggests, *La tierra de Venus* is striking in its foregrounding of women, who sing all of the work's musical numbers. There is a preponderance of lyrical ballads intended to be sung by the *revista*'s four soprano leads, and, while this might not seem like skillful dramatic programming, the subsequent publication and distribution of these works as sheet music points to the composer's considerable market savvy. For those less interested in lovely vocal moments, a leggy dance corps dressed up (or down) as a variety of exotic women—harem girls, nubile Arawaks, submissive geishas—offered a visual display for members of the audience who might have otherwise preferred to attend the burlesque performances of the Alhambra. In *La tierra de Venus*, Ernesto Lecuona and librettist Gustavo Sánchez Galarraga discovered a feminine formula that would power the future of lyric theater for the next decade.

The *revista* was the genre for which the Regina was best known, and Lecuona composed more *revistas* for the theater than any other genre. They include *Carrera del amor* (1927), *Es mucha Habana* (1927), *Chauffeur al Regina* (1927), *La liga de las señoras* (1927), *Cuadros nacionales*

(1927), and *Alma de raza* (1929). With the exception of *Alma de raza,* all of these *revistas* were performed in the opening season of the Regina Theater. All of them, including *La tierra de Venus,* employ light social satire, a quality that is not found in the love dramas typical of later zarzuelas.[46]

The Regina's importance was not merely as a precedent to the zarzuela boom. On March 1, 1929, the theater presented the first work considered to be a true Cuban zarzuela: *El cafetal,* with music by Lecuona and libretto by Sánchez Galarraga. *El cafetal* can be distinguished from previous works because it contains a longer, more elaborate plot than earlier *sainetes* and because it includes more complicated musical numbers, particularly duets and ensembles.[47] *El cafetal* is also important because it is one of the first works of the emerging genre to mix serious dramatic characters with characters drawn from Cuban popular theater. There is no happy ending to *El cafetal;* the work ends in tragedy, a recurring trait in future zarzuelas.[48]

The Importance of Theatrical Space

It is no coincidence that the names of particular theaters have occupied such a prominent position in the telling of this history. Theaters themselves were important players in the zarzuela's development. The genre emerged almost entirely on a handful of Havana's stages: the Regina, Payret, and Martí theaters and occasionally the Auditorium. Public space was a valuable commodity during the tumultuous period of the Republic; Havana had few buildings suitable to hold large gatherings, and theaters were often pressed into service to house political meetings.[49] Space was hard to come by and even more difficult to maintain, and the need to find a permanent, stable home for the production of zarzuelas was a problem that Lecuona, Roig, and Prats all had to grapple with.

Shortly after its presentation of *El cafetal,* Lecuona's company lost its lease in the Regina Theater and was forced to seek out a new home for the emerging genre. Late in 1929, under the direction of Gustavo Sánchez Galarraga and Ernesto Lecuona, the company relocated to Havana's Teatro Payret, where they would remain for several months.[50] *María la O,* perhaps Lecuona's best-known work, was produced during this period.[51] Given the political and economic instability of the time, finding a permanent home for lyric theater was extremely difficult, leading Lecuona to quip in frustration, "In Cuba there can't exist in any stable form a real company of Cuban theater with the prestige that it deserves as long as the government does not offer it protection."[52] In spite of Lecuona's considerable influence within the entertainment establishment,[53] efforts to obtain a permanent home in the Teatro Payret failed and Lecuona was never again able to locate a stable home for his company.

In 1931, Gonzalo Roig partnered with Alhambra librettist Agustín Rodríguez and impresario Manuel Suárez in the formation of a zarzuela company in Havana's Teatro Martí.[54] The troupe would perform in the Martí until political and economic pressures forced the theater's closure in 1936.[55] The theater's significance for the zarzuela is hard to overstate. Rodrigo Prats recounted,

> The importance of . . . the Martí is its five consecutive years (1931–36), the number of works premiered, and the felicitous development of the lyric genre. They were performances, almost all of them, with a full house, with showings in the afternoon and at night, with a cast that never got sick or even hoarse. It's also necessary to point out that this season was maintained thanks to the work of the composers and librettists who collaborated on this arduous enterprise, in spite of suffering under the current political crisis.[56]

Some of the zarzuela's best-known works premiered in the Martí. Among them were Roig's *Cecilia Valdés* (1932), *El clarín* (1932), *La hija del sol* (1933), *Carmiña* (1934), *La Habana de noche* (1936) and *Cimarrón* (1936), and Rodrigo Prats's *Soledad*, (1931), *La Habana que vuelve* (1932), *Leonela* (1932), *María Belén Chacón* (1934), and *Amalia Batista* (1936). Even rival Lecuona participated in the Martí's success; his zarzuela *Rosa la China* (1932) opened just a few months after the premiere of Roig's *Cecilia Valdés*, attracting sellout crowds and helping to assure the Teatro Martí's place as the center of lyric theater production in the mid-1930s.

Havana Sings: Concerts, Conservatories, and the Marketing of the Female Voice

One of the factors that made the zarzuela such a success was the organizers' sage showcasing of female talent. This was a quality that marked the zarzuela from the opening of the Regina Theater in 1927. The cast of *La Niña Rita* and *La tierra de Venus* highlighted four soprano soloists, a gender imbalance that was treated favorably by the press. "When it opened, the Regina was put in the hands of Lecuona, who, so that everything would be new, also put together the four sopranos that would be seen in his works. They were Rita Montaner, everyone knows how far she has gone; Caridad Suárez, who also rapidly rose in her reputation and admiration; María Ruiz; and Dora O'Siel."[57]

Lecuona was an important agent in the recognition and promotion of local female talent. He was aided in his efforts by the fact that in the 1920s and 1930s there were a tremendous number of trained female singers. These women were the product of a burgeoning music education business, a business largely run by women. In 1927, Havana was home to more than forty music conservatories.[58] The majority of these conservatories were small schools that focused on piano, voice, and dance and whose students and faculty were primarily women. Musical skills were considered a sign of refinement, and in the difficult economic times of the *machadato,* teaching music was a socially acceptable way for young women to earn money. Professional performance careers were still not viewed as an acceptable choice for bourgeois women and were even more discouraged after a woman had children. Baritone Pedro Arias, one of the founders of the Pro-Arte Lírico, recounts that his mother, Raquel Domínguez, a professional soprano who appeared in the premiers of several of Lecuona's works, was forced to retire from the theater after the birth of her daughter.[59] Rita Montaner faced similar pressure from her husband after the births of her children; she later divorced him.[60]

Young singers found an invaluable venue in the Sunday concerts of "Typical Cuban Music," organized by Lecuona, Sánchez de Fuentes, and Anckermann.[61] The concerts were intended to combat the increasing influence of foreign music by reintroducing audiences to Cuban music. They became important meeting places for those interested in the promotion of Cuban music (or at least the promotion of the music written by those who ran the concert series). They also became the proving grounds for an entire generation of Cuban singers, particularly female singers. Esther Borja, Sarita Escarpenter, Candita Quintana, Hortensia Coalla, Rita Montaner—the women who would become the focus of the stage works written by Lecuona—all had their starts at these concerts. The Sunday concerts gave Lecuona a hand-picked talent pool, a place where he could train singers until he felt they were ready for the stage.

In spite of the prejudice against women pursuing professional performance careers, increasing numbers of trained singers poured from Havana's conservatories. While upper-class women tended to perform in private recitals or even an occasional benefit concert in the Auditorium Theater, young women from the middle classes edged toward performance.[62] For these women, the Sunday-morning concerts were a valuable venue. The concerts targeted family audiences. Held late enough so that families could arrive just after attending Mass, the Sunday-morning time slot gave the concerts an aura of respectability and a certain cultural elitism—only the people who truly loved music would be willing to get up on Sunday mornings to come.[63] Rather than being praised for their dramatic or comic abilities, Lecuona's singers were presented as delicate and refined beauties, even described in the press as "confections."

Lecuona's preference for female talent had economic benefits beyond the box office. The music popularized by female singers was published and sold as sheet music. Women would buy the music to perform it at home, enjoying the tunes as much as the fantasy of sounding as enchanting as Esther Borja, singing "Damisela encantadora."[64] Marketers of other products, too, recognized the draw that zarzuela heroines and the women who performed them had for female audiences. Products such as soap, stockings, dresses, and malt drinks were sold with reference to zarzuela heroines or their performers. An ad for La Llave soap, for example, reads, "María la O, Rosa la China, y Lola Cruz. If they were women of today, they would wash with 'La Llave' soap."[65]

The lyric theater that began with the 1927 season in the Regina was associated with the female on many levels. The creation of the zarzuela responded to a need for female entertainment and showed that women continued to view the theater as a public, and sometimes political, forum. The plots of zarzuelas also catered to a female audience by showcasing female protagonists, and the music popularized on the stage was marketed to women for home use. The disproportionate number of trained female singers exiting from Havana's many conservatories helped to satisfy a preference for female protagonists. The ways in which those singers behaved musically and dramatically and the messages that could be gleaned from their performances is the subject of the following chapters.

3 The Mulata Makes an Entrance: The Salidas of María la O, Cecilia Valdés, and Amalia Batista

Of all the stock characters from Cuban popular theater that were appropriated by the zarzuela, the *mulata*, or mixed-race woman, is perhaps the most visible and well-worn. Musically appropriated by zarzuela composers and librettists, the *mulata* is creatively reinvented, despite being a character type that already had a long history in Cuban arts and letters.[1] From her earliest appearances in popular theater, the *mulata* is portrayed as a beautiful young woman whose exotic genetic makeup is the source of both her character and the intrigues, comic and tragic, that shape her life.

María la O, Cecilia Valdés, and Amalia Batista, the title characters of zarzuelas by Ernesto Lecuona, Gonzalo Roig, and Rodrigo Prats, are arguably the most famous protagonists in the zarzuela repertoire. The three characters are *mulatas*, and their theatrical representation and their dramatic predicaments are drawn directly from artistic conventions established in the nineteenth century. The zarzuelas themselves were composed within a span of six years, with *María la O* premiering in 1930, *Cecilia Valdés* in 1932, and *Amalia Batista* in 1936. The works, among the most popular in the zarzuela repertoire, share more than a passing similarity; all are tragedies based on a love affair between a beautiful *mulata* and a high-society white man. *María la O* and *Cecilia Valdés* actually draw their subject matter from the same literary source: Cirilo Villaverde's nineteenth-century novel *Cecilia Valdés.*

In spite of their similarities, each zarzuela takes a different approach in the representation of the *mulata* character type, a type that, by the 1920s, was the subject of an intricately woven mythology. This chapter begins with a look at the social and historical conditions that produced the stereotype of the *mulata* and examines the *mulata*'s role as a figure of ambivalence, standing as both an emblem of national identity and as a symbol of cultural and racial destruction. Later, I explore how the title characters of *María la O, Cecilia Valdés,* and *Amalia Batista* express their "*mulata*-ness," that is, how they are identified in terms of gender, race, Otherness, and behavior. The site for these protagonists' self-identification, and the focus of this study, is a new zarzuelistic convention: the *mulata*'s dramatic entrance aria, known as the *salida.*

The three famous *salidas* examined here are all subject to the conventions of genre and character type, and composers and librettists manipulated these conventions to achieve a staged poignancy that resonates with deeply ingrained prejudices of class and racial hierarchy. The zarzuela's treatment of the *mulata* protagonist illustrates the instability, or what Homi Bhabha has called the "ambivalence," of stereotype, for while zarzuela *mulatas* do repeat theatrical clichés, they do not necessarily affirm their assigned identity.[2] Instead they often use the tropes of their type self-consciously, sometimes fulfilling them, sometimes dismantling them. The audience's pleasure thus reverberates with a heady blend of familiar social norms and risqué new identities; their fluency in the stereotypical tropes of *mulata* performance allowed familiar comedic formulas to be recast with an ironic, bitter, and ultimately disorderly tinge.

The *Mulata* Type in Cuban Arts

The tragic protagonists of *María la O, Cecilia Valdés,* and *Amalia Batista* represent a relatively new vision of a character type that had a long history in Cuba. By the time *María la O* premiered in 1930, prescriptive portrayals of a sexually aggressive, clever, and comic *mulata* were de rigueur in popular theater. Yet while the zarzuela's creators now fashioned *mulata* protagonists who were tragic rather than comic, deeply romantic rather than merely flirtatious, and naive instead of streetwise, the theatrical tropes of the comic *mulata* type—reprinted, replayed, and repeated throughout Cuban popular culture—were an inescapable component of her character.

The literary and theatrical ancestors of the zarzuelistic *mulata* can be traced back to Golden Age Spanish theater, where playwrights such as Lope de Vega used racially exotic characters to enliven their works through song and dance.[3] The *mulata* character became a fixture in Cuban popular theater in the mid-nineteenth century, at the same time that the island began its turbulent journey toward independence from Spain. The stage *mulata* and other racial and ethnic caricatures, such as the *negrito*, were formalized and developed alongside increasing white unease about the ever-growing population of slaves brought to work on Cuba's sugar plantations. The relationships among racial caricature, the social and political circumstances created by Cuba's full-fledged entry into the slave trade, and the development of Cuban national identity has been well established.[4] Reynaldo González and Vera Kutsinski, in particular, have greatly added to our understanding of the historical processes that shaped the stereotyping of the *mulata* in the nineteenth century.[5] Both writers show that the *mulata* served both as a symbol of sexual desire and as an icon for the danger of racial contamination through miscegenation. In colonial Cuba, the *mulata*'s mere physical presence was a visual signifier of an illicit sexual union between a white man and a black woman.[6] In the dominant racialist imagination, black female sexuality was viewed as voracious and uncontrollable, overwhelming the supposedly helpless white masters and overseers who fell victim to its charms.[7] Yet in popular culture, the *mulata*'s mixed-race features came to be viewed as possessing an exotic loveliness, while her beauty ironically recalled the troubled condition of her conception. The danger posed by the *mulata*, her beauty, and her sexuality became a recurring theme in nineteenth-century Cuban arts, letters, and popular culture, where the *mulata* was routinely regarded as a threat, not only to the individual white men she encountered, but to the very future of white supremacy in Cuba.[8]

Paradoxically, while the *mulata* was viewed as a destructive sexual agent, she also became a potent symbol (albeit a conflicted one) of Cuban nationalism.[9] As Cuban nationalists sought to affirm Cuban identity by differentiating the Caribbean island from peninsular culture, the *mulata*'s specifically *criollo*[10] difference—her Otherness—marked by a phenotype that only the island itself could produce, made her an earthy symbol of nationhood. In poetry and prose she is described with such images as a tobacco blossom or a sugar cane flower,[11] objects that were not only seen as uniquely Cuban, but that were also the driving force of the island's economy. The metaphorical equation of the *mulata* with Cuba's economic resources brought the ownership of those resources into

The Mulata Makes an Entrance 43

sharp focus at a time of increasing tensions between Cuban and Spanish interests. Islar/peninsular tension is also at play in the representation of what is perhaps the most famous fictional *mulata* of all time: the title character in Cirilo Villaverde's 1882 novel *Cecilia Valdés*. The author uses the protagonist's overwhelming beauty and tragic fate to ground an attack on Spanish colonialism and the slave system.[12]

On nineteenth-century stages, comic and sultry representations of mixed-race women personified aspirations for an independent Cuba free from Spanish control, and the *mulata* herself did not just voice these aspirations—she sang them. The *mulata* type was inseparably associated with the genre she sang: the *guaracha*. Perhaps the most prominent musical form used on the popular stage, the nineteenth-century *guaracha* was an upbeat topical song whose lyrics often involved sexual humor and bawdy *double entendre*. The genre typically showcased a female singer dressed in the long ruffled train, or *bata de cola*, of the *mulata del rumbo*,[13] alternating stanzas with one or more male singers. Moving at a sprightly tempo, *guarachas* generally alternated between simple and compound meters, and both the vocal and instrumental lines were highly syncopated. It was actually through the mouth of the *mulata* character type that music with Afrocuban influences was first popularized on the stage; the *guaracha* is one of the first instances where professional musical entertainment for the Cuban middle and upper classes was accompanied by instrumental ensembles employing overtly Afrocuban rhythms.[14]

Guaracha texts read like recipes, with the protagonist providing a list of ingredients to describe what she is made of—often with literal references to foodstuffs. This listing of traits—physical attributes, sexual prowess, and dancing ability—is central to nineteenth-century representation of the *mulata*, and its influence continued to be felt well into the twentieth century. The most enduring of these textual tropes is the presentation of the protagonist as a *mulata del rumbo*, a provocatively dressed woman who walks the streets alone, attracting constant attention from men. A typical *guaracha* text from the nineteenth century, aptly named "La Mulata," employs images that reappear again and again in song texts, detailing the *mulata*'s sexualized interaction with the white men who pursue her. The woman's frank comparison of her sexuality to both sugar and fire is common in many *guaracha* lyrics, as are her flamboyant vanity and regal pride. The *estribillo* (chorus), sung by male ensemble members, burlesques men's inability to resist the *mulata*'s physicality.

Yo soy la Reina de las mujeres
En esta tierra de promisión;
Yo soy de azúcar, yo soy de fuego,
Yo soy la llave del corazón.

Estribillo
No sé lo que tengo aquí
ni lo que me da;
¡Ay! ¡Ay! ¡Ay! ¡Ay!
No tiene cura mi enfermedad.

Si algún blanquito me dice:
"Mulata santa te quiero yo,"
Doy media vuelta y me queda preso
en las varillas del malecó.

Yo soy la causa de que los hombres
a las blanquitas no den amor,
porque se mueren por mis pedazos,
y los derrito con mi calor.

Yo soy de azúcar, yo soy de fuego,
Si corresponden á mi pasión;
Pero si quieren de mí burlarse,
furiosa rujo como un león.[15]

I am the queen of women
in this promised land;
I'm made of sugar,
I'm made of fire,
I am the key to the heart.

Chorus
I don't know what I have here,
Nor what it gives me;
Ay! Ay! Ay! Ay!
My sickness has no cure.

If some little white guy says to me:
"Saintly *mulata*, I love you,"
I half turn around and capture him
In the bathhouses of the *malecón*.[16]

I'm the reason that men
Don't give love to white women,
Because they die for bits of me
And I melt them with my heat.

I'm made of sugar, I'm made of fire,
If they return my passion;
But if they want to laugh at me,
I roar furiously like a lion.

Like its protagonist, the *guaracha* became a resonant political symbol. Beginning with the outbreak of the Ten Years' War in 1868 and throughout the three decades of struggle for independence from Spain, the *mulata* became the central figure of Cuban lyric plots, and Rine Leal asserts that the use of the *guaracha*, her favored mode of musical expression, became a catalyst for discussing the very *mestizaje*, or racial mixture, of the Cuban nation. As audiences recognized her as a national allegory, they would also recognize her theme song, the *guaracha*, as a reference to her, and by extension, Cuba itself.

By the early twentieth century, the stage *mulata*'s association with overt sexuality, nationalist sentiment, and physical humor reached Cuban audiences via the *teatro vernáculo*, where she continued to be associated with a musical genre also called the *guaracha*. However, these early twentieth-century *guarachas* were generally solo songs and no longer included ensemble commentators. The formal structure changed, moving away from the verse/*estribillo* format of earlier *guarachas* in favor of two-part or through-composed forms. Twentieth-century *guarachas* shared with their predecessors the use of picaresque subject matter, metric shift, and patterns of syncopation, and they continued to develop the same poetic tropes found in nineteenth-century *guaracha* texts, focusing on the *mulata*'s sexuality, her role as an object of voyeurism, and her conversion to a symbol of nationalism.[17]

Yet while the stereotype of the sexy, saucy, and politically savvy *mulata* replicated itself on the popular stage, a new vision of the *mulata* began to appear in the lyric theater in the late 1920s, a vision more tragic than comic, more romantic than picaresque. There were precedents for this change; portrayals of the *mulata* as a tragic figure were well established in the literary and artistic realms.[18] An early theatrical interest in this representation can be found in Federico Villoch's highly nationalistic *La mulata María* (1896), where the *mulata* protagonist represents romantic seriousness, although the overall tone of the work is still quite lighthearted. Yet it is José Mauri's 1921 opera *La esclava* that presents the first truly tragic *mulata* to appear on the Cuban lyric stage. The opera, discussed in Chapter 1, tells the story of Matilde, a virtuous and apparently white young woman who learns, after the death of her wealthy guardian, that she is actually of mixed-race parentage and that her mother was a slave. The tragic heroine of Mauri's opera is a "*mulata blanconaza*" (a "whitened" *mulata*, or a *mulata* who can "pass" for white), in Cuban racialist nomenclature. The presence of the *mulata blanconaza* was a frequent strategy employed in Cuban theater and literature, facilitating white spectators' and readers' identification with—and voyeuristic pleasure in—the tragic protagonist. In *La esclava*, the discovery of Matilde's ancestry directly leads to her death. Sexually abused by her former suitor, abandoned by her friends, and facing a life of servitude, the young woman dies of sorrow.

The *Mulata* in the Cuban Zarzuela

Blending the literary and operatic vogue for racial tragedy with lighter musical and dramatic elements from popular theater, the tragic *mulata* type quickly emerged as the protagonist of the most prominent works of the zarzuela repertoire. In 1930, Lecuona's *María la O* was the first zarzuela to successfully exploit this type, and the work set a precedent for how racialized romantic tragedies should be handled on the stage. Among the most important conventions that Lecuona established was the use of the *salida*, or entrance aria, sung by the *mulata* protagonist. The *salida*, whose formal characteristics are described below, became the primary genre through which the *mulata* would identify herself. So closely associated was the zarzuela *mulata* with the *salida* genre that the form itself became a musical sign for desire, social danger, low moral character, and sexualized behavior. The convention became so popular that non-*mulata* characters in future zarzuelas often had to adapt to the *salida*'s peculiarities, as we will see later.

Similar in function and structure to the operatic cavatina, *salidas* typically begin with an onstage chorus announcing the *mulata*'s entrance.[19] Because *salidas* almost invariably occur at large public events onstage, events such as dances and parties, the choral introduction provides an excellent opportunity for the composer to create local color by showcasing local rhythms and popular dance genres. An example of this can be found in the introduction to the *salida* of María la O. Here, after a lively fanfare-like orchestral introduction, the chorus announces María la O's entrance while alternating between 6/8 and 3/4 time (Example 3.1).

Unfolding as it does, the *salida* is not only critical as an element of cultural and musical discourse; it also serves as the dramatic foundation for the zarzuela itself. Typically, after a grand choral entrance, the soloist will begin a slow, melodic introduction, in which the chorus may or may not interject. The slow introduction offers a tantalizing first glimpse into the *mulata*'s personality: how she carries herself, how she treats others, and the manner in which she chooses to present herself socially and musically. The *salida*'s introductory section is followed by a faster dance section, or series of dance sections, in which one or several of the earlier *guaracha*-based musical and poetic elements may be present. The

Ex. 3.1

meter may alternate between duple and triple divisions, and the melodic line may employ commonly used rhythmic patterns taken from dance music, such as the *cinquillo*.[20] Some *mulatas* will actually sing a *guaracha* embedded within their *salida*, a practice that appears in both *María la O* and *Cecilia Valdés*. However, the most consistent of these popular, *guaracha*-identified traits occurs in the text, which introduces the singer according to the poetic tropes of the *mulata del rumbo*. With self-reflexive voyeurism, the protagonist describes how she walks in the streets alone, how the men follow her, and what a good "natural" dancer she is. Other dance sections that follow the *guaracha* portion might include *danzas*, *tango-congos*, or *danzones*. Many *salidas* have a slower last section, often over a slow *tango-congo*, *son*, or *bolero* rhythm, in which the soloist introduces the tensions and inadequacies that will eventually destroy her, foreshadowing for the audience the zarzuela's incipient tragedy.

Staged as a public performance, then, the *salida* does the dramatic and cultural work of the original *guaracha*. Sharing a material connection as well as a rhetorical one, the *salida* is, like the *guaracha*, a type of musical allegory. It is the *mulata*'s calling card, the site where her "*mulata* nature" is expressed and explored. The *salida* presents the *mulata* according to the prescription of her type; she repeats well-worn gestures and clichés. Simultaneously, however, the *salida* is also the space where the *mulata*'s inherent instability is exposed, for the *mulata*'s performance of her identity, or—to borrow from Benítez-Rojo—her *"cierta manera"* ("certain way") of repeating her own clichés, reveals her not as an ordinary creature, but as an intrinsically disruptive and disorderly force.[21] Thus, the *salida* is the space where an unwary discursive truce is negotiated, between the *mulata* as cultural icon and the *mulata* as social individual. Examining the *salidas* from three of the most popular zarzuelas from the repertoire, *María la O*, *Cecilia Valdés*, and *Amalia Batista*, allows us to best understand this tension between the mulata as a cultural (stereo)type and the mulata as an anxiety-creating form of social disorder that shapes each zarzuela's tragic events.

María la O

When Lecuona began work on *María la O*, he had every intention of converting Cirilo Villaverde's 1888 novel *Cecilia Valdés* into a musical work for the stage. By popular account, he had already begun when word arrived that Villaverde's heirs had refused to give him the rights to the novel.[22] Lecuona met with his librettist, Teatro Alhambra veteran Gustavo Sánchez Galarraga, and, with a new libretto and some name changes, they were able to salvage much of Lecuona's work.

The resulting libretto is only loosely tied to Villaverde's novel. Published in New York while Villaverde was in exile during Cuba's struggle for independence, the novel *Cecilia Valdés* is an uncompromising attack on slavery and Spanish colonial rule. In the novel, the political message is framed by a tragic love story in which Cecilia, a very light-skinned *mulata*, falls in love with the rich, white Leonardo, who, unbeknownst to either of them, is really Cecilia's half-brother. Cecilia has a daughter by Leonardo, but he abandons her nonetheless in order to marry the socially acceptable Isabel. Cecilia's jilted admirer, the free black José Pimienta, stabs Leonardo to death to avenge his true love. The interwoven racialized drama of romance, rejection, and murder serves Villaverde well as a tableau of slavery's malignant effects, at the same time as it ideologically upholds the very same social and economic structures so critical to racial hierarchy.

In his revised libretto, Sánchez Galarraga changed the names of the main characters and reoriented the plot's dramatic denouement. Cecilia, Leonardo, José Pimienta, and Isabel become María la O, Fernando, José Inocente, and Niña Tula, respectively. The incest plot, which assumes such critical importance in Villaverde's novel, is dropped from the story altogether, and Sánchez Galarraga also makes several changes in location and occupation of characters.

The similarities between the two tales are readily apparent, however. In the zarzuela, the *mulata* María la O has a love affair with a wealthy young white man named Fernando who leaves her to marry the socially acceptable Tula. María la O's jilted admirer, the free black José Inocente, attempts to kill Fernando to avenge his true love. However, in a major deviation from the original plot, María la O arrives first, stabbing Fernando herself. María la O thus becomes the romantic victim who is able to take revenge herself, a more powerful protagonist than the novelistic Cecilia.

Yet despite this narrative switch, *María la O* is not inherently more radical than Villaverde's novel. Written with a strong abolitionist sentiment, much of Villaverde's novel takes place among Havana's population of mulattos and free blacks, focusing on educated members of the lower middle class who run small businesses and are artisans, poets, and musicians. Villaverde went to great lengths to make his nonwhite characters accessible to white readers, drawing attention to the familiar aspects of their environments and describing their daily lives in often excruciating detail. Villaverde's obsessive description of Cecilia's racial ambiguity had rendered her a sympathetic object for the readers' consumption; she is exotic yet familiar, mysterious yet ultimately containable. In contrast, the distinctly racialized characters in *María la O* were not meant to be identified with, but to serve as exotic spectacle. Sánchez Galarraga and Lecuona increased their characters' Otherness by removing them from the middle-class milieu painstakingly documented by Villaverde. Much of the zarzuela's action is provocatively located in one of Havana's most infamous Afrocuban *barrios*, the Manglar.[23]

By far the strongest character among the famous trio of zarzuela protagonists, María la O is not the passive beauty of Villaverde's novel. Indeed, she has few points of commonality with upper-class white audiences. María la O is poor; she moves more easily through Havana's underworld than though the well-mannered salons of elite society, and her presence becomes a source of chaos that will result in violence. The dangerous aspect of María la O's sexuality is made dramatically transparent from the beginning of the work. Spoken dialogue reveals that she wears a knife strapped around her ankle, and she hints that she does not carry it just for defense. "If I had any doubt of your word," says María la O to Fernando, her white lover, "you can be sure, I either would have died, or I would have killed you! Killed! . . . Like the *maja* in Spain, I also carry a knife under the train of my dress!"[24] The castrating power hidden under María la O's skirts directly connects her character with other popular representations of the *mulata* as a devouring sexual deviant, and her inherent threat is expressed not only within the classic symbolism of the *vagina dentata*, the sharp weapon hidden under her open skirts, but also through the ultimate gender transgression—her possession of the knife/phallus.

María la O's reference to the *maja* in her sexual threat also creates an intertextual dialogue on other levels. *Maja* and *majo* refer to popular representations of members of Spain's poor and working class, particularly those found in the Madrid *barrios* of Lavapiés and the Barquillo. The *maja* and *majo* became stock characters in nineteenth-century Spanish zarzuelas and could be recognized onstage by their flamboyant dress and tendencies toward amoral and violent behavior.[25] The *maja* appears to have provided the closest model on which the *mulata* type was fashioned, perhaps even providing the *mulata del rumbo* with her Andalusian-inspired ruffled gown.[26] Regardless of the Cuban racial distinctiveness of the *mulata*, the direct reference to the Spanish character draws a connection between María la O's threatening moral character—her aggressive sexual appetite and violent potential—and her social class. The decision to couch María la O's degeneracy in terms of social inferiority points to the class-demarcated nature of Cuban society. In María la O's case, though, the social and sexual threat is overlaid and remade racially. Thus the *mulata*, musically announced in the *salida* that facilitates her theatrical entrance, becomes a vital and complicit element upholding the fluid hierarchies of Cuban racial ideology.

Just as María la O's class status is confirmed early in the libretto, so, too, is her subordinate racial identity. Gone is the racial subtlety of *Cecilia Valdés* and the sympathetic identification that it afforded the heroine of the novel. In the zarzuela, María la O is not presented as racially ambiguous—she is no "*mulata blanconaza.*" Most significant for this analysis is the way in which her racial attributes are immediately and explicitly announced in the *salida*. Confronting her audience boldly, María la O sings, "I am *mulata*, I don't deny it," in the opening lines of her *salida*. She goes on to recite a list of traits that will be embellished and reiterated throughout the musical number. Like the *guarachas* on which it is modeled, María la O's *salida* reveals what it means to socially and theatrically perform the *mulata* on Havana's twentieth-century stage.

María la O's *Salida*

María la O begins in the home of Caridad Almendares at a celebration honoring the Virgen de la Caridad del Cobre, Cuba's patron saint.[27] The house, the staging notes tell us, is modestly decorated, representing the living conditions of Havana's mulatto middle class. In the opening dialogue,

Caridad and her friends gossip about the romantic exploits of the zarzuela's protagonists.[28] Through their conversation, it is revealed that the Spanish shoemaker Santiago Mariño, like countless others, has fallen madly for María la O, a situation that causes Caridad considerable consternation.

"*Y, que tiene María la Os, que le fate a Caridás Armendare y de la Torre?*" she questions in her lisping accent—"And what does María la O have that Caridad Almendares y de la Torre is missing?" Her friend's answer points to the obvious truth of Cuban racial hierarchy. "*Salvo que es menos prieta que tú, ná.*"—"Other than that she's less dark than you, nothing." Later, Caridad's flirtatious conversation with Santiago Mariño reveals the basis for the zarzuela's plot: María la O is in love with Niño Fernando, unaware (it seems) that he is engaged and due to be married. José Inocente, who continues to feel unrequited love for María la O, has vowed that he will kill any man who has the nerve to do her wrong. It is with this dramatic setup that María la O enters the room, accompanied by a crowd of party guests announcing her arrival.

When the protagonist enters to the sound of the chorus in her *salida*, she is on the arm of her white lover, Fernando (Example 3.2). She makes the most of her entrance, musically as well as dramatically. As she acknowledges the chorus, María la O sings over a sustained G pedal,

Ex. 3.2

which sounds as a tremolo in the lower strings. The orchestral effect and the sustained dominant have the effect of taking her words out of "real time," adding an edge of artificiality to her delivery, which is enhanced by the overly static nature of the musical line and the self-deprecating lyrics—"A thousand thanks, I don't deserve all that I heard."[29] The resulting effect is one of musical masquerade. María la O is putting on musical airs, performing her version of upper-class (white) female behavior. Her brief, demure phrases each drop off at the end like downcast eyes, imitating graciously feigned modesty. That her first appearance is clearly a performance is not an accident. Indeed, the entire *salida* can be viewed as nothing other than a conscious performance, or rather a series of performances.

Depictions of nonwhite characters attempting to "perform" white culture had a long history in Cuban arts. In such representations, their efforts come across as comical at best and more often as ridiculous, as in, for example, Victor Patricio Landaluze's well-known nineteenth-century lithograph entitled *En la ausencia*[30] (Figure 3.1). A similar moment occurs in Villaverde's novel *Cecilia Valdés* when, in a *baile de cuna*[31] much like the one that opens *María la O*, Villaverde describes a couple dancing a minuet. In the scene, a *mulata* named Mercedes opens the dance floor for the evening by performing the aristocratic dance with another guest at the party. Villaverde writes, "The old-fashioned air was danced with considerable grace by the woman, and was enthusiastically applauded by the bystanders; but the man made a grotesque spectacle of himself."[32] Mercedes' appropriation of white culture is exposed in the mirror of her partner, who is not able to complete the act.

Similarly, while María la O herself may have had the panache to pull off her "fine lady" performance, its artificiality is exposed by the chorus, who parody her melody. Singing a whole step higher in unison octaves, with octave doubling in the orchestra, the choral response comes off as hollow and stylized. The modest downward deflections and brief pauses that characterize each of María la O's statements are completely out of sync with the syntax of the chorus's text, and the "out of time" quality achieved by María la O is replaced with a heavy-handed and ungainly melodic restatement. The entire episode is tinged with vaudevillesque camp. The chorus's mirroring of María la O reveals the performative nature of her behavior, unmasking her as inauthentic and ultimately unconvincing.

María la O reasserts control over the situation by suddenly drawing attention to the man who accompanies her, now singing over a D pedal, *"Pero está aquí el dueño de esta Reina del Manglar"*—"But here is the

Figure 3.1. Victor Patricio Landaluze, *"En la ausencia"*
*[In the absence]. (Courtesy of the Museo Nacional de Bellas
Artes, Havana, Cuba.)*

lord of this queen of the Manglar" (Example 3.3). María la O's entrance
on the arm of Fernando is dramatically problematic, for she must fulfill
dramatic expectations of the stage *mulata*, a theatrical type known for
its public persona, as well as her social obligations toward the man who
escorts her. Fernando could not be expected to tolerate a woman who
appeared to be available to other men. This predicament is mediated
by Fernando's intervention in the *salida*, a highly unusual event in the
zarzuela repertoire, allowing him to mark his territory musically. As
María la O's introduction nears its close, Fernando sings, *"Dulce amor
eres tú la reina de mi corazón"*—"Sweet love, you are the queen of my
heart." Sung a third above the melody introduced by María la O and

Ex. 3.3

over a continuing D pedal, Fernando's introduction of an F♯ tonicizes G major, which is realized in measure 65 with a lively *danza* rhythm in the orchestra.

Fernando's "interruption," and especially his apparent influence on the new key, calls special attention to his identity, the previously unknown man who had entered with María la O on his arm. Yet, while on the surface Fernando might be given credit for achieving tonal closure, declaring a sort of "ownership" over the musical conversation, a closer look reveals that María la O actually allowed him this opportunity. By deflecting the expected resolution to D major set up by the preceding

chorus entrance, María la O's repeated insistence on C♯ frames a dominant preparation, a preparation that she graciously leaves for Fernando to
complete. Fernando's outburst also provides a dramatic excuse for María
la O to break out of her public persona, and she announces in a sinewy
descending chromatic line, *"y para tí suena mi voz"*—"and for you my
voice sounds," that her voice sounds for Fernando alone. By dedicating
the performance that is to follow to her partner, María la O is able to
bridge the gap between her dramatic role as a public woman and her social responsibilities as a faithful lover.

With the same dexterity that María la O manipulates her social sur-
roundings, she also manipulates her tonal space. She easily slips out of the
G tonality "established" by Fernando, beginning her descent on a G♯ just
as the orchestra cadences decisively on the tonic. At the same time that
María la O placates Fernando with her words, she willfully shakes the
key from its tonic underpinnings and eventually leads the piece into the
new key of C major. María la O is playing Fernando, and the chromatic
line and flattering lyrics create an undeniably sultry effect. In images and
music reminiscent of the nineteenth-century stage *mulata*, María la O
introduces herself not as an individual, but as a type. She now sings a
guaracha (Example 3.4).

Ex. 3.4

In her presentation of the *guaracha*, María la O's use of performance becomes literal, for she sings directly to those present on the stage. María la O's performance of the *mulata* stereotype is a conscious decision, made clear by the calculated way in which she introduces the *guaracha*, her manipulation of key, and her deliberate switching to street dialect in the new text. Her performance exposes the multilayered complexity of stereotype, for while her performance of the *guaracha* reveals a willful and individual appropriation and manipulation of musical and theatrical conventions, it also shows María la O's inability to escape from those conventions, creating an ambivalent tension between her desire to define herself and the poverty of expressive options with which she is faced.

Otra no hay	There's no other
que se iguale a mí	who can equal me,
pues causo a los hombres	because I make the men
el frenesí.	go crazy.
Soy mulata	I'm *mulata*,
yo no lo niego;	I don't deny it;
mas tengo fuego	but I have fire
pá regalar.	to give away.
Miren tóos	All of those who wish
quien me gana a mí	to win me watch me
cuando por el Prado	when I walk down the Prado
camino así	like so.
Con mi manta voy,	I go with my wrap
que me enrosco así,	around me just so,
y me dicen tóos	and everyone says to me
al pasar, ¡Ay!	as I pass, "Ay!"

There is a marked change in María la O's music. The orchestra is dominated by the appearance of a *son* rhythm in the bass, marking the first time in the *salida* that the bass has played a prominent role in musical articulation. María la O's use of her own voice is completely different than what previously was heard. Now that she admits her race, "*Soy mulata, yo no lo niego,*" she drops the musical airs of the first section, switching into a vernacular street dialect. Her tessitura falls and she sings syllabically in the lower range of popular song. Perhaps most notable of all is the change in the melodic rhythm, as María la O leaves the languid lyricism of the opening in favor of that most Caribbean of rhythms, the *cinquillo*. María la O uses the *cinquillo* rhythm with an almost forced insistence, its effect underscored by doubling in the orchestra. The syllabic text setting relentlessly marks out the syncopated pattern, as if the music alone was proof of her mixed-race heritage.[33]

María la O's performance of the *mulata* type contrasts markedly with the music that follows, as she begins yet another charade, abandoning her own voice to sing the words of the white men who give her compliments, or *piropos*, in the street. The orchestra takes up a slow *conga/son* rhythm as María la O reverts to a more lyrical style. In the words of the white men who watch her, she sings about herself in the third person (Example 3.5). Here, María la O is not objectified merely in the sense that she describes herself as an item to be viewed; her speech is actually taken away from her, and she sings one of the most important melodies of the zarzuela in the words of a voyeur.[34]

> María la O,
> bella como flor,
> como tú en la Habana
> nunca hubo dos.
> María la O
> por gozar tu amor,
> te diera en pedazos el corazón.
> Loco por tu amor
> mulata sin par,
> tu boca de miel
> quisiera besar.
> Mírame una vez
> con ese mirar,
> que yo esa mirada
> no he de olvidar.

> María la O,
> pretty as a flower,
> in Havana there have
> never been two like you.
> María la O,
> to enjoy your love,
> I would give you my heart in pieces.
> Crazy for your love,
> *mulata* without equal,
> I want to kiss
> your mouth of honey.
> Look at me once
> with that look,
> so that I will never
> forget it.

Ex. 3.5

The stating and restating of the protagonist's name is a practice that becomes a recurring trope in zarzuela *salidas* after *María la O*; examples occur in *Cecilia Valdés, Amalia Batista, Rosa la China,* and *María Belén Chacón,* among others. While the practice of naming identifies the *mulata* as an individual, its conventional use tends to force the protagonist away from individuality and into the realm of stereotype, for in many *salida* texts it seems only the name distinguishes one *mulata* from another. Yet María la O does not succumb to generality. She does not state her name as a defensive assertion of her identity. Rather, she fulfills the convention of naming by performing an identity given to her by others. In this sense, María la O's third-person performance is not an example of musical voyeurism at all, but rather of an empowered ventriloquism. María la O behaves like a white man, stealing his speech and singing his song. She is no longer attempting to imitate white behavior, as she did in her attempt at upper-class manners at the beginning of the *salida,* but to co-opt their forms of expression. The gesture could be viewed, in itself, as a satire, a chance for María la O to critique the banality of the men's comments and their inability to resist her performance of the *mulata* stereotype expressed in the *guaracha.*

Stereotypes are powerful, however, even when they are being decon-
structed, and María la O's empowerment through satire is undercut by
the dramatic importance assumed by the "María la O" melody. Similar
to an operatic leitmotiv, the melody reappears throughout the zarzuela,
accompanying María la O's entrances in the orchestra and making a
surprise appearance near the end of the zarzuela in the confrontational
duet between herself and Fernando, as she learns that her lover means
to abandon her. In spite of María la O's willful appropriation of the voyeurs' tune, she is still ultimately defined by *their* melody—not her own.
María la O's musical identity is thus collectively shared, a reality immediately made clear in her *salida* when the chorus repeats the "María
la O" theme. Returning the voyeurs' words into the mouths of onlookers reinforces María la O's position as object, rather than subject. The
melody of the voyeurs will continue to define María la O, even after her
salida is over.

María la O's early identification with a "third person" melody also
sets up an important symmetry, for at the end of the zarzuela she will
sing about herself in the third person again, in her tragic *romanza* "Mulata infeliz." The dramatic symmetry posed by these two third-person
testimonies—María la O's triumphant entrance at the zarzuela's opening and her tragic *romanza* at the zarzuela's close—are critical reference
points. "Mulata infeliz" is sung after María la O discovers Fernando's
infidelity and makes her fateful, and ultimately self-destructive, decision
to kill him. The entire *romanza* is voiced in the third person, suggesting
that María la O herself has ceased to function as an independent subject,
joining in the voyeuristic crowd to examine the *romanza*'s pathetic object. Thus, when the second "María la O" melody appears in the latter
half of the *romanza* (Example 3.6), there is no accompanying change of
the narrating voice, affirming the *mulata*'s transformation from subject
to object.

Like the upbeat "María la O" melody that appeared in the *salida,*
the second "María la O" melody is a recurring theme in the zarzuela.
The second theme is the basis for the orchestral prelude, providing the
audience with the tune before it is given voice. When, near the zarzuela's
close, María la O finally adds the syllables of her name to the melody,
she recalls not only the melody that the audience has known since the
beginning of the zarzuela, she also recalls her first entrance—her *salida*—
and her "naming" in that performance. Just as she previously performed
the identity ascribed to her by the men in the street, she now draws the
audience into the action by singing *their* song, giving voice to the melody
by which they have identified her since the zarzuela's opening bars.

Ex. 3.6

Crucially, however, it is via the last section of the *salida* itself that we hear María la O's own voice for the first time, and not just María la O seen through the lens of the stage *mulata*. But it is a compromised and not entirely authoritative voice. Passively accepting the key dictated by Fernando, María la O lacks the spunky independence exhibited earlier in the *salida* and shows an inescapable dependence on her lover. Over a slow *tango-congo* rhythm, María la O sings of her love for Fernando and of her desperate jealousy (Example 3.7).

Ex. 3.7

Dulce bien la ilusión	Sweet illusion,
eres tú de mi amor	you are my love,
y vivir yo sin tí	and to live without you
fuera igual que morir.	would be the same as dying.
Y jamás en los brazos	And never in the arms
de otra mujer	of another woman
podría yo verte	could I see you,
pues morir es mejor	for it would be better to die
que sufrir tal dolor	than to suffer such sorrow.

The perkiness of the orchestral rhythm belies the tragic impact of María la O's melody as she sings that it would be better to die than to see her lover in the arms of another woman.[35] Yet it is Fernando's death and not María la O's that the piece foreshadows, and María la O's spoken words, "*Yo nací fatal y así he de acabar*"—"I was born fated, and fated I must meet my end," take on a chillingly prophetic edge. The earnestness of María la O's fatalistic rhetoric is expressed by her tessitura, which gradually climbs higher and higher, leaving the bodily limits of popular song to express a truth beyond the deceits and intrigues of performance. Fernando adds his voice to the aural impact of María la O's warning, doubling her line precisely at the climax of her threat.

With the *salida*, a new zarzuelistic tradition is established in *María la O*. But if the zarzuela creates one of the most interesting and complex *mulata* roles for the lyric stage, then it is the *salida* itself that has triumphed as an original musical form for the exploration of the cultural narrative such dramatic identities require.

Cecilia Valdés

Two years after the premiere of Lecuona's *María la O*, Gonzalo Roig received the permissions necessary to turn *Cecilia Valdés* into a zarzuela, and the work premiered in Havana's Teatro Martí on March 26, 1932. The libretto, written by another veteran of the Alhambra theater, Agustín Rodríguez, is remarkably faithful to Villaverde's novel, at least as far as the heterosexual romantic plot is concerned. But like *María la O*, this zarzuela also leaves behind the political message of Villaverde's novel and uses its Afrocuban characters to entertain rather than to educate.

Cecilia, like María la O, makes her first entrance at a *baile de cuna* in a private home, and her appearance is heralded by a choral fanfare in which the assembled guests proclaim her name. Prior to Cecilia's entrance, the librettist skillfully uses partygoers' gossip to fill the audience in on the earlier chapters of Villaverde's novel, drawing attention to Cecilia's illegitimate birth and insinuating Cecilia and Leonardo's shared parentage. However, neither Gonzalo Roig nor Agustín Rodríguez attempt to expose the dramatic tensions of the plot in Cecilia's *salida*, and they present none of the foreshadowing or fatalism found in María la O's entrance. In this sense, Cecilia's *salida* is much lighter fare than María la O's; the entire piece is removed from the real-time development of the plot. It is an unabashed production number.

Whereas María la O's *salida* was about the performance of the *mulata* "type," Cecilia's is a musical study of her own *mestizaje*. Clearly modeled on nineteenth-century *guarachas*, the *salida* uses physical description—and the physical response to music—to construct Cecilia's racial identity, or, better put, her "physiognomy." This approach has literary merit. Villaverde's novel obsessively documents Cecilia's racial attributes. As Cecilia is introduced as a young girl in the first scene in the novel, Villaverde goes on at length to describe her physical—and ostensibly moral—characteristics.

> Her type was that of the virgins of the most celebrated painters. Because attached to a high forehead, crowned with copious black hair, naturally wavy, there were very regular features, a straight nose that originated in between her eyebrows, and because it came a bit short, it lifted her upper lip just enough to allow one to see two arrows of tiny white teeth. Her eyebrows made an arc and further darkened her black, almond-shaped eyes, which were all movement and fire. She had a little mouth with full lips that indicated more voluptuousness than firmness of character. She had full, round cheeks and a dimple in the middle, making a pretty countenance that would be perfect if only her expression were less malicious, if not malign. . . . To what race, then, did this girl belong? It's difficult to say. Yet to a learned eye the dark line that bordered her red lips could not be hidden, nor could the fact that the illumination of her face ended in a sort of shadow that reached to where her hair began. Her blood was not pure and one could be assured that three or four generations back it was mixed with Ethiopian blood.[36]

To what race, then, did this girl belong? Picking up on the ambivalence about Cecilia's racial identity expressed in Villaverde's text, Roig's music explores the boundaries and tensions between Cecilia's white and mulatto characteristics. One of the most overt ways that Roig expresses these tensions is through the interplay of musical styles. Similar to María la O's *salida*, there is a marked difference between a lyrical, operatic style, which may be read to confer whiteness, and a more rhythmic and "Afrocuban" syllabic setting drawn from popular song.

Just as Villaverde was concerned with the minutiae of Cecilia's physical traits—the darker rim of her lips, the quality of her hairline—Roig and Rodríguez question what makes Cecilia a *mulata*. This objective is made clear by Cecilia's first words after the choral fanfare. "The blood boils in my veins," she says; "I'm of mixed blood and yet I'm not." The ambivalence inherent in that first statement flavors the rest of the *salida*, defying any attempt to label Cecilia with a clear, easily defined identity. In the opening slow section alone, Cecilia describes herself as *mestiza*, she fetishizes herself first as a voice, then as a rattle and a bell, and she identifies herself as a symbol for the Cuban spirit. The entire *salida* be-

comes a musical and poetic journey through Cecilia's varied traits, revealing an identity that seems less mixed than fractured. Roig exploits the
multisectional possibilities of the *salida* form, moving through musical
style and genre so quickly as to suggest a musical schizophrenia. Through
this musical treatment, Cecilia is revealed as a kind of shape-shifter, a
chameleon whose identity is always in flux.

The ambivalent declaration that begins the opening slow section of
the *salida* is reflected in Roig's musical setting (Example 3.8). Textur-
ally, there is a constant tension between the *habanera* rhythm in the
orchestra and the high, lyric soprano of Cecilia.

Ex. 3.8

Hierve la sangre en mis venas
Soy mestiza y no lo soy
Yo no conozco las penas
Yo siempre cantando voy.
Siento en mi alma cubana
la alegría de vivir
Soy cascabel, soy campana
Yo no sé lo que es sufrir
Yo no conozco las penas
Siento en mi alma cubana
La alegría de vivir.

Blood boils in my veins.
I'm of mixed blood and yet I'm not.
I don't know sorrows.
I go everywhere singing.
I feel in my Cuban soul
the joy of living.
I'm a rattle, I'm a bell.
I don't know what suffering is.
I don't know sorrows.
I feel in my Cuban soul
The joy of living.

Sung in her upper register, Cecilia's legato melody is replete with rubato. Her behavior is reflective of that of María la O's first entrance; the tessitura and phrasing suggest an upper-class, cultivated, and *white* self-identification. Yet just as the fragility of María la O's first self-identification was exposed by the mimicry of the chorus, a closer look at the relationship between Cecilia's opening melody and the accompaniment reveals a stronger connection to popular rhythms than the ear might first acknowledge. Cecilia herself undermines her assertion of staid, white, upper-class behavior by breaking out into syncopations on the words "mestiza," "siempre cantando," and "alegría." The orchestra, its *habanera* rhythm already undermining Cecilia's seamless rubato, further strengthens Cecilia's connection to the popular classes with its statement of the *cinquillo* rhythm just before she sings, "Siento en mi alma cubana." The sudden appearance of the rhythmic figure both strengthens her subsequent assertions of *cubanía* and draws further attention to the ambiguity of her physiological makeup—appearances can be deceiving.

In keeping with *salida* convention, the slow *habanera* opening is followed by a faster dance section. In this section, there is no longer any tension between the rhythmic aspect of the orchestration and Cecilia's vocal line. She participates in the rhythm for the first time, even leading some of the syncopations. In line with the more popular style, Cecilia sings syllabically, in the middle register, as opposed to the high operatic lyricism of the opening section (Example 3.9).

Mis amores son las flores   My loves are flowers
que perfuman mi jardín   that perfume my garden
y mi risa cristalina   and my crystalline laughter
es un eterno tin tin tin.   is an eternal *tin tin tin.*

Ex. 3.9

The chorus repeats her verse, and above them Cecilia sings an operatic countermelody (Example 3.10). The new melody abandons the shorter durations and narrow range characteristic of popular song and showcases Cecilia's voice by moving through a range of an eleventh (she reaches a high B♭ on the final "flor"), featuring sustained pitches, and even by including a birdlike warble on the word "amor."

No hay en mi jardín una sola flor
que no sea flor de amor.
Y los hombres van siempre atrás de mí
aspirando el rico olor de la flor.

There isn't a sole flower in my garden
that is not a flower of love.
And the men always follow behind me
breathing in the sweet smell of the flower.

Ex. 3.10

Cecilia's operatic, *cultivated* performance contrasts with the reference to her public persona and the attention she receives in the street. By referring to the men who follow her, Cecilia identifies herself with the stereotypical *mulata del rumbo*, an association that is confirmed in the next contrasting section—referred to in the score as *"tempo di guaracha antigua"*—a fast-paced, upbeat dance that prominently features two-against-three rhythms and a driving bass line (Example 3.11). In this "old-style" *guaracha*, Cecilia, like María la O, is concerned with how she is viewed by others. The text moves through all of the typical *mulata* clichés, identifying Cecilia as a type rather than as an individual. In one of the classic tropes of nineteenth-century *guaracha* texts, Cecilia boasts of her skills as a dancer, and her words are accompanied by an orchestral shift to a *danza* rhythm as she proclaims, "dance [*la danza*] fascinates me."[37] Throughout the *guaracha* section, Cecilia sings rhythmically, in the more popular middle register, and loses all traces of the high, operatic lyricism that we heard previously—with one exception. On the words *"algo debo de tener"*—"I must have something," Cecilia switches back to the lyric style. The emphasis on those words, "I must have something," or perhaps better put, "there must be something special about me," is a reminder of Cecilia's inner conflict to define herself and the white identity she longs for. Of course, as the zarzuela's tragedy bears out, that identity is not to be, or at least, it will not last.

> Cecilia Valdés me llaman
> me enamora un bachiller
> mis amigas me reclaman
> y algo debo de tener . . .
> Yo soy bailadora fina
> soy bailando lo major.
> La danza a mí me fascina
> soy bailando lo mejor.

> They call me Cecilia Valdés.
> A gentleman is in love with me.
> My friends all ask for me,
> and I must have something . . .
> I'm a refined dancer,
> dancing, I'm the best.
> Dance fascinates me,
> dancing, I'm the best.

Ex. 3.11

The *salida* ends with multiple repetitions of Cecilia's name. Cecilia's naming, unlike María la O's, is sung in the first person, *"Cecilia Valdés mi nombre es"*—"Cecilia Valdés is my name." Yet rather than expressing increased agency, Cecilia's insistence on repeating her name over and over, the constant self-identification, does little more than to suggest how ephemeral her identity really is. The repetition of Cecilia's name, then, becomes a vain effort to counteract her own performance, and repetition, of the *mulata* stereotype. It is only her name that distinguishes her from a bevy of beautiful and mysterious *mulatas*, each attracting attention in the street, each a natural lover, each a skilled dancer.

Amalia Batista

Unlike *María la O* and *Cecilia Valdés*, the story of Amalia Batista does not take place during Cuba's colonial years, but rather in the 1920s. Nevertheless, *Amalia Batista*'s plot and musical-dramatic structure are remarkably similar to the two earlier works', resulting in a coherent trio. If María la O is presented as a performance of the *mulata* type, and Cecilia reveals an obsession with mixed-race physiognomy, Amalia presents a study of the modern *mulata* and the harsh, judgmental, and misogynistic conditions of contemporary Havana life. The zarzuela is more than a dramatization of the tragic tale of Amalia, it is also a commentary on the mythology of the *mulata* itself.

As did its two predecessors, *Amalia Batista* begins with a large party scene. The event in question is Amalia's birthday. This is important, because it puts one of the primary tensions of the work into focus immediately: Amalia's age. Amalia is a *mulata* of a "certain age" who, over her life, has been the mistress of a series of rich white men and is currently the mistress of an older man named Don Alberto. At the party, a young guest named Julio decides that he wants Amalia for himself. Julio confronts Don Alberto, informing him that Amalia is his and that he wins her by right of his youth. Amalia leaves Don Alberto and falls passionately in love with Julio, who becomes increasingly possessive, jealous, and controlling. Gradually, Julio forces Amalia to prove her love for him by cutting herself off from all of the people in her life. Finally, isolated and alone, Amalia learns that Julio is leaving her to marry a young white woman—the daughter of her previous lover, Don Alberto. She is passed aside for youth and white skin and closes the zarzuela singing, *"Yo soy Amalia Batista, que se muere por un hombre"*—"I am Amalia Batista, who dies for a man." In spite of Amalia's fatalistic rhetoric, she does not literally die for or because of her love for the faithless Julio. Unlike Fernando and Leonardo, who pay the ultimate price for their amorous transgressions, Julio goes on to lead a life of privilege, and Amalia's life, too, goes on. Amalia is seen as the instigator of her own misfortune; the plot contrives to have her rejection of Don Alberto lead to her abandonment by Julio and the vicarious revenge of Don Alberto's daughter "stealing" Julio's love.

Amalia's *Salida*

Arguably, this more circuitous plot and murderless tragedy are prefigured in Amalia's *salida*. As she sweeps into a room full of party guests celebrating her birthday, Amalia's entrance is preceded by an orchestral introduction and a choral fanfare (Example 3.12). The music is a lively *danza*, and the chorus's articulate syncopations, doubled by the orchestra, maintain a lighthearted character as they sing:

> Ahí viene Amalia Batista
> Ahí viene Amalia Mayombe
> la mulata sandunguera
> que locos vuelve a los hombres.

> There comes Amalia Batista.
> There comes Amalia *Mayombe*,[38]
> the charming *mulata*
> that makes men crazy.

In both *María la O* and *Cecilia Valdés*'s *salidas*, the chorus announced the protagonist's entrance by identifying her by name, but they did not editorialize on her character. In the earlier examples, outside opinion was referenced rather than expressed directly, and the protagonists maintained control of such opinions at at all times, with Cecilia referring to the viewpoint of outside observers ("*Cecilia Valdés me llaman . . .*") and María la O actually taking on the voice of her critics. Of the three *salidas* discussed here, this is the first time that the chorus assumes an independent and subjective role, taking voyeuristic as well as verbal control and defining the *mulata* before she can speak. Thus, before Amalia has even sung a note, the chorus has identified her as a *mayombera*, a practitioner of herbal magic associated with the Afrocuban religious practices of *palo monte*.[39] The chorus also identifies Amalia as a femme fatale, and implicit in the juxtaposition of occult practices with feminine charm is the inference that there is something dangerously *dark* about Amalia's amorous successes.

As a result, Amalia's opening, sung in the syllabic style and low tessitura of the *mulata guarachera*, is not a personal statement but rather a

Ex. 3.12

defensive reaction to the words of the crowd (Example 3.13). She begins not by explaining what she is, but what she *isn't*. While the *salidas* of both María la O and Cecilia begin with affirmations of racial mixture (*"Soy mulata no lo niego"* and *"Hierve la sangre en mis venas, soy mestiza y no lo soy"*), Amalia begins by denying that she is a *mayombera*. The term's African origin and its associations with *palo monte*, perhaps the most maligned of the Afrocuban religions, imply blackness, rendering Amalia's statement a denial of blackness rather than an assertion of mixture. As for the chorus's claim that she is a femme fatale, Amalia does not fight the assertion, only its interpretation. Singing the alternating duple and triple divisions characteristic of the *guaracha*, Amalia claims that if men fall desperately in love with her, it's not her fault.

Ex. 3.13

A mí me dicen ma-yom-be y ma-yom-be-ra no soy___ y si_a los hom-bres a-

-ma-rro los a-ma-rro por a-mor___ tam-bién que_a los hom-bres ma-to van can-

-tan-do por a-hí___ y yo no ten-go la cul-pa de que se mue-ran por

mí___ y yo no ten-go la cul-pa de que se mue-ran por mí

Tutti

A mí me dicen mayombe
y mayombera no soy
y si a los hombres amarro
los amarro por amor
también que a los hombres mato
van cantando por ahí.
Yo no tengo la culpa
de que se mueran por mí
¡Ah!

They call me *mayombe*,
and I'm not a *mayombera*,
and if I bind men
I bind them for love.
They also go around singing
that I kill men.
It's not my fault
that they die for me.
Ah!

Amalia makes her denial clearly personal, with the earnest insistence of sustained high notes on the words *"soy"* ("I am") and *"mi"* ("me"). Not only do the higher range and sustained pitches contrast with the middle-voiced, rhythmic syllabicism characteristic of the *guaracha* style, but they also suggest, "Could a *mayombera* sing like *this?*" She offers up operaticism itself—and its accompanying white, upper-class connotations—as proof of her good intentions.

Perhaps, however, she protests too much. At the same time that her words declare her innocence, Amalia captivates—and captures—her listeners with the thrill of her voice. Her ability to insinuate herself in every gap in the choral line, embroidering an impenetrable web of denial, suggests an aural sorcery sung with the voice of the siren (Example 3.14).

Mayombera no soy   I'm not a *mayombera*,
pero placer y amor yo doy   but I give pleasure and love,
y se mueren por mí   and they die for me
cuando me ven bailar así.   when they see me dance like this.

As the chorus repeats her verse, Amalia sings a high countermelody that in its resulting texture and arching contours recalls the countermelody sung by Cecilia. In a tessitura centered nearly a fifth higher than anything she has sung up to this point, Amalia again denies her involvement in occult practices.

Ex. 3.14

Amalia's manipulation of tessitura in the above section is subtle and ironic, a raising of the aural stakes that allows her to draw her listeners in, to enchant them. The future that awaits those caught in Amalia's web is made clear in the bars that follow, where she proves that her voice can titillate as well as convince. For the first time, the melody and tessitura unite with the text to create an overtly sexual, dramatic effect as she sings, "y suelen así exclamar: Amalia me muero por tí! ¡Ah!—"and they often exclaim like this: Amalia I die for you! Ah!" The shift is first signaled by the orchestra, whose deliberate arpeggiation of the F major triad announces a change in texture (Example 3.15). The fluid triplets that had characterized Amalia's vocal line suddenly stop. The abrupt quarter-note self-restraint on the word *suelen* cannot be maintained, and the line breaks into effortful eighth notes. The textural change in Amalia's singing is made even more noticeable by the chorus's sudden stasis, their whole notes having the effect of a drum roll. The tension generated by this rapid deceleration is released in an orgasmic explosion of a high B♭ on the word *"exclamar,"* followed by the gasping *"Amalia me muero por tí."*

Amalia's mockery of her partner's short-lived self-control carries over into the next section (Example 3.16). Like both María la O and Cecilia, Amalia engages public opinion about her. However, unlike both of her predecessors, Amalia attempts to erase any rhetorical power that her onlookers may have had, by reducing their comments to trite nonsense. In a section sung as a sprightly *danzón,* Amalia pokes fun at the wavering manliness of her admirers while peppering her text with several of the most common *mulata* clichés. By mocking her admirers, and even her own behavior ("I always go sweeping about"), Amalia refuses to perform her expected role. In doing so, she undoes the stereotype of the *mulata* as performer, attempting with her mockery to assert her individual agency.

Ex. 3.15

Ex. 3.16

"Amalia Batista sí,
Amalia Batista no."
Todo el mundo me discute
y siempre arrollando voy.
"Amalia Batista sí,
Amalia Batista no,
Amalia Batista
tiene de la canela la flor."

"Amalia Batista yes,
Amalia Batista no."
The whole world talks about me
and I always go sweeping about.
"Amalia Batista yes,
Amalia Batista no,
Amalia Batista
has the flower of cinnamon."

The chorus repeats her verse, and Amalia again sings a countermelody above them, a second reference to the texture heard in Roig's composition. This time, however, the reference is more than merely textural, for Amalia repeats words sung by Cecilia: "Yo no sé sufrir." As in the case of Cecilia, those words form a dramatic challenge, for it is suffering that Amalia will learn throughout the course of the zarzuela (Example 3.17).

Yo no sé sufrir	I don't know how to suffer.
Yo no sé llorar	I don't know how to cry.
Ah sí señor	Oh, yes, sir,
Yo me sé reír	I know how to laugh,
Sí señor	yes, sir,
de los hombres y del amor	at men and at love.
Amalia Batista soy	I'm Amalia Batista,
y no tengo culpa	and it's not my fault
si algún corazón	if because of my disdain
por mi desdén	some heart
murió de amor.	died of love.

The score and libretto draw heavily on clichés of former *mulatas* because they are *meant* to recall them. The party scene in the beginning, an echo of the Saint's Day festivities that begin *María la O* and *Cecilia Valdés,* clearly references the earlier works. The twist for the informed audience is that this time it is the protagonist's birthday. This time it is she who is getting older, and it is precisely the string of love affairs in her past (or in a collective "*mulata* past") that the creators strive to recall. Amalia's suffering at the hands of Julio and her eventual abandonment are a comeuppance of sorts. Not only does she fail to attract sympathy because of her earlier abandonment of Don Alberto, but also because audiences are well informed of her checkered past.

The choice to place the story of *Amalia Batista* in the twentieth-century present reinvigorates the perceived threat that cross-racial relationships posed to social stability. The dramatic unfolding of Amalia's downfall and Julio's success also suggests that since independence, Cuban men had matured to fight that threat and that they could now see past the *mulata*'s charms and recognize her inevitable decline. The decision of the young and virile Julio and the old and wise Don Alberto to discard Amalia is seen as a sign of modernity and maturity, and with her they discard the Afrocuban culture that she represents. It is notable that among the three young lovers discussed here—Fernando, Leonardo, and Julio—only Julio emerges completely unscathed. Unlike Fernando and Leonardo, he makes the decision to marry a white woman out of desire

Ex. 3.17

rather than duty. He treats Amalia despicably, and, rather than being seen as cruel, he is rewarded at the end. Most tellingly, Julio is the only one of the three who survives. Amalia is left at the end of the zarzuela aging and alone. She has no male admirer waiting to take vengeance against her ex-lover, or to take his place. By showing the aging and downfall of Amalia, Prats and Rodríguez deny Amalia her power as a cultural icon. From the compromised voice of her *salida* to the zarzuela's conclusion, Amalia has lost the sympathy of the audience.

In *María la O, Cecilia Valdés,* and *Amalia Batista,* these three Cuban *mulatas* are presented as women who negotiate their recognizable sexual and social identities across a range of not entirely unexpected narrative twists. Yet it is in the musical and lyrical complexity of each of the trio's *salidas* that the originality of these zarzuelas is articulated. Enlisting the expectations and desires of the bourgeois Cuban audiences for whom they were intended, these zarzuelas fulfill their function as pedagogical texts, demonstrating the necessary limits of a *mulata*'s destiny. These *mulata* heroines may be exotic and "colorful," embodying the tantalizing sensuality of the racial Other, but their ability to seduce or lure white men away from their social duties is shown to have tragic consequences for the women themselves. In the decades when Cuban nationality is being ideologically tested and reformulated, the *mulata* stands in for both the promise and the social and moral collapse of racial transgression. The lesson is well understood by the new Cuba's population. Women of dubious racial heritage may be powerful as symbols of danger and temptation, but they are never powerful enough to overcome their birth or their intrinsic difference. The markers of this difference—sexual voraciousness, racial inferiority, and class marginality—are consistently restated in *María la O, Cecilia Valdés,* and *Amalia Batista.* But the story does not end with their narrative captivity and their inevitable punishment for transgression. These zarzuelas complicate the nature and potential of each *mulata* via her musical entrance, and in each case, the *salida* functions to allow more fluidity and fascination than the arc of the plot might suggest. Indeed, the *salida* does not just announce a predictable enough story that then gets played out; it actually introduces a (musical) indeterminacy that the plot and libretto are not sanctioned to match. The *salida* represents a climax that only hints at its eventual delimited resolution.

4 From the Negrito to the Negro Trágico: *The Changing Representation of Black Masculinity*

"With our faces black / from ink we'll use / no one will dare / check our bodies / to be certain whether / we are painted blacks / or blacks for real."[1]

Black bodies appeared frequently on the zarzuela stage. White actors, their faces darkened with a mixture of glycerin and charcoal, performed a parody of black behavior that included black speech patterns, dance, and music. The caricature of black masculinity was a major component of the zarzuela's success; the majority of zarzuelas produced between 1927 and 1940 include black male characters.[2] An examination of these works shows that composers and librettists followed two strategies in their representation of black men on the zarzuela stage, both of which stemmed from theatrical and literary traditions that date back to the era of slavery. The first strategy exploited the *negrito* type, which was derived from Cuban popular theater and portrayed black men as comic buffoons. The second strategy was the development of a new character type, which I have chosen to call the *negro trágico*, or "tragic black man." Focusing first on the *negrito* and then on the *negro trágico*, I discuss the historic roots of both strategies and examine the ways that these types were adapted by composers and librettists. The zarzuela's manipulation of the black masculine image evidences the profound influence of gender

politics on theatrical production, and this chapter places special emphasis on how the *negro trágico*—and his musical embodiment—served the
white female imagination.

The *negrito* and the *negro trágico* are both portrayed through the
strategies of stereotype, that is, of assigning and affirming an identity
through repetition.[3] Such repetition becomes necessary to negotiate and
define what Eric Lott, in his study of North American minstrelsy, has
called the continuing interplay between "love and theft," a Bhabhian ambivalence toward black culture and black bodies that vacillates between
fear and desire.[4] It is ambivalence, insists Bhabha, that "gives the colonial
stereotype its currency: ensures its repeatability in changing historical
and discursive conjunctures; informs its strategies of individuation and
marginalization; produces that effect of probabilistic truth and a predictability which, for the stereotype, must always be in excess of what can
be empirically proved or logically construed."[5]

Blackface theatrical practices fetishized not only the black body,
but the act of repetition itself.[6] Blackface theater allowed the repetitive
nature of stereotype to be experienced directly, for in blackface theater,
it is not only the black body that is fetishized, but the act of repetition
itself. The *process* by which actors became black was important. Audiences knew that such blackness was temporary, that the actor would
paint his face each night before ascending on the stage and, at the end of
the night, he would wipe off the makeup and leave the theater as a white
man, only to repeat the performance the following day. It was actors' familiarity with their subject, their repetitive *experience*, that made them
successful interpreters of blackface.[7] The audience, too, would return to
participate again in this parody of blackness, legitimizing—one could
say *ritualizing*—the performance of stereotype.

The history of blackface theater in Cuba illustrates that early blackface representations corresponded to "masculine" preoccupations of
politics, business, sexual dominance, and, ultimately, Cuba's emerging national identity. However, as "black" bodies crossed over from the
burlesque theaters to the sophisticated and demure venues of zarzuela,
their Otherness no longer performed the identity of (white) Cuban men,
but instead came to speak for an unlikely subject: elite white women.

History of Blackface Theater in Cuba

The first Cuban known to have blackened his face with burned cork and
personified the black man onstage was the actor Francisco Covarrubias.
Covarrubias, who was the first Cuban actor to exploit other local charac-

ter types such as the *gallego* (Spaniard)[8] and the *guajiro* (white peasant), appeared on Cuban stages in blackface as early as 1812, preceding the first American minstrel shows by thirty years.[9] No written examples of Covarrubias's comic performances in blackface survive, however, and there is no way of knowing for certain how his characters, black or white, behaved. It is thus with a Spaniard, Bartolomé Crespo y Borbón, writing under the pen name Creto Gangá, that we find the earliest example of the Cuban *negrito.*

Crespo y Borbón began writing on black themes in the late 1820s, at precisely the same time that Cuban intellectuals were beginning to struggle with increasing racial tensions that grew along with the island's slave population. Cuba did not begin the large-scale importation of African slaves until the beginning of the nineteenth century, when colonial officials seized the opportunity presented by Haiti's political unrest and entered the sugar trade.[10] In the first half of the nineteenth century, hundreds of thousands of enslaved Africans were brought to work in Cuban sugar plantations. With the growing black population came increasing fears of a slave revolt and racial violence that might echo events in Haiti.[11] A pro-Spanish businessman involved in the slave trade himself, Crespo y Borbón used his portrayals of the Afro-Cuban character Creto Gangá to reinforce the values of the slave system and stressed Cuba's dependence on Spanish governance.[12]

A comic simpleton who spoke in *bozal*, the mixture of broken Spanish and African spoken by newly arrived slaves, Creto Gangá appeared on the most powerful stages of Havana, including the Gran Teatro Tacón, where comic scenes featuring him and his *negra* girlfriend "Frasica" appeared on variety programs and between the acts of more serious works. Perhaps even more influential than his theatrical presence, Creto Gangá's comic *bozal* was a regular feature in print. The character describes his 1846 collection of décimas, titled *Laborintos y triufucas de Canavá,* as a *"veraero hitoria en veso de lo que pasá en la mácara a yo Creto Gangá y nengrita mío Frasico lucumí, cuentá po yo memo*—a true history in verse of what happened to me Creto Gangá and my black Lucumí woman Frasica at the masquerade, told by myself."[13]

Mary Cruz writes that Crespo y Borbón entered the world of literature "through the door of caricature and critique of customs."[14] Once in the door, however, his writing was prolific. Texts supposedly written by the grammatically challenged slave were popularized in conservative pro-Spanish newspapers such as *La Prensa, Diario de la Marina,* and *Faro Industrial de la Habana,* and in Crespo y Borbón's own book *Isla de Cuba pintoresca,* published in 1847. Crespo y Borbón's efforts to create an assumed Afro-Cuban dialect with its written indication of slave patois demonstrated not only an attempt to inscribe audible racial difference textually, but also the first time that the black vernacular appears in Cuban letters.[15] Although its initial intent was to denigrate its black subjects, in print, black Cuban speech acquired a textual legitimacy that realist novelists such as Villaverde would explore and that early twentieth-century poets like Guillén would later celebrate.[16] The pseudorealism of print reproductions of *bozal* was paralleled in the *costumbrismo* movement in the visual arts, which sought to represent local color and customs. The most influential exponent of this movement was painter Victor Patricio Landaluze, a Spaniard who, like Crespo y Borbón, supported Spain's right to the island colony. Landaluze's view of slaves varied between picturesque depictions of plantation life, as in his painting *El corte de la caña*, or demeaning caricature, as in his much-reproduced lithograph *Francisco besando un busto*, where a black servant puckers up next to a statue of a white woman (Figure 4.1).

The caricature of the black man, however, was not always used to stress Spanish economic, political, and cultural dominance. As tensions increased between the colony and the metropole, blackfaced comedians became a potent means of expressing *difference* from Spain. While performers continued to render inferior the black bodies upon which they built their comedy, they used those bodies as the mouthpieces of Cuban nationalism. It was their "iconic and indexical associations with the island," writes Robin Moore, that led pro-independence playwrights to use comic Afrocuban characters to promote a nationalist cause in subtle and subversive ways that might get past the Spanish government censors.[17] By 1868, with the arrival of the Bufos Madrileños,[18] the *negrito* was firmly established as one of the core characters in Cuban *teatro bufo*. The first of the wars for independence began that same year, and over the next three and a half decades of military and political struggle, theatrical representations of the *negrito* character became a voice for Cuban independence from Spain and later a critic of U.S. intervention.

The use of the *negrito* as a spokesman for liberation did not guarantee a positive, or even consistent, theatrical treatment of the black man. Strategies for the depiction of black masculinity fluctuated according to the political and social climate; at times such representations were comic and lighthearted, at other moments, frightening and violent. The *bozal*-speaking slave increasingly came to share the stage with a new representation of black masculinity: the *negro catedrático*.[19] The *negro catedrático*, or black professor, spoke with overly flowery speech using a vocabulary beyond his limited education. This character poked fun at

Figure 4.1 Victor Patricio Landaluze, "Francisco besando un busto" [Francisco kissing a bust]. (Courtesy of the Museo Nacional de Bellas Artes, Havana, Cuba.)

the growing class of black professionals, downplaying their accomplishments and belittling their ability to compete. Like Creto Gangá, the *catedrático* was a likable, good-natured sort whose comic presence rested on his linguistic failings.

In the years following abolition in 1886, the image of the benevolent *negrito* was increasingly replaced with *negros curros*,[20] *ñáñigos*,[21] and *negros brujos*,[22] marauding thugs and practitioners of witchcraft. Aline Helg documents how during this period the Cuban press was filled with sensational accounts of sacrificial murders and the theft of white children by black sorcerers.[23] By depicting blacks as dangerous savages in the press, whites laid the groundwork for new antiblack legislation.[24] The theater

also participated in this campaign, portraying black men who were examples of degeneracy rather than simple comic buffoons. Leal explains,
"Now the black man was "free," potentially equal to the white man,
and they had to find new ways to discriminate that showed his savagery
or his incapacity to fit in with the rest of the population."[25]

Early twentieth-century *negritos* entertained audiences with political satire, nonsense patter, sexually charged puns, and songs for selling
soap, hams, and ice cream. They danced stage *rumbas*, performed fan-
tastic depictions of witchcraft, and sang comic duets with the *mulata*
or the *gallego*. By the second decade of the twentieth century, *negrito*
performers such as Arquímedes Pous, Enrique "Bernabé" Arredondo,
Ramón Espigul, and Sergio Acebal were some of the most influential
players within the theatrical circuit, often founding and managing their
own troupes.[26]

The *negrito* character developed and flourished in essentially "male"
environments—political newspapers, rowdy working-class movie houses,
and the *teatro vernáculo*. On the stage of theaters like the Alhambra,
blacked-up bodies staged the fears and desires of their primarily white
male audiences. The *negrito*'s essentially masculine perspective is therefore of interest in examining how the black body is treated in a more
feminized theatrical space—the zarzuela.

The *Negrito* in the Zarzuela: *La Niña Rita*

On September 29, 1927, Cuban soprano Rita Montaner walked onto the
stage of Havana's Teatro Regina to sing the final number of the opening-
night performance of *La Niña Rita o La Habana en 1830*. The performer's
features were obscured under a mask of blackened glycerin, and her body
was clad in the tight pants, boots, and riding jacket of a coachman, or
negro calesero.[27] The audience, filled with Havana's most prominent
and fashionable women, watched from newly refurbished seats in what
had been, until recently, one of Havana's raunchiest and most notorious
burlesque theaters. Standing alongside a gilded carriage and real horse,
the blackfaced, cross-dressed actress sang the premier of Eliseo Grenet's
tango-congo, "Ay Mamá Inés."[28] The crowd went wild. Montaner's performance in *La Niña Rita* cemented "Ay Mamá Inés" as one of the classics
in the Cuban repertoire, but more important, the premiere heralded the
birth of the Cuban zarzuela, a new genre of music theater that over the
next fifteen years transformed popular entertainment on the island.

"Ay Mamá Inés" practically became a theme song for the "Rumba
Craze" that swept Europe, the United States, and Cuba itself,[29] earning

the title "the greatest of all Cuban rumbas."[30] Montaner was one of the shining stars of this movement, appearing on the stages of Paris and New York with performers such as Josephine Baker and Al Jolson, and later appearing in film. Trained as a classical singer and pianist, Montaner had the vocal prowess to take on lyrical roles such as the title role in Lecuona's *María la O.* Her greatest fame, however, came from her performance of black, lower-class characters: street food vendors, rumba dancers, and practitioners of witchcraft.

The coachman role was Montaner's first cross-dressing venture, as she revealed in an interview with *Diario de la Marina* reporter José María Herrera, the week before the show opened. "It will be the first time in my life to do it, even though I've sung a lot in public, here in Havana as well as in the United States, I've never walked out on stage as a man, moving and talking like one on the floorboards."[31]

Librettist Antonio Castells had not originally conceived of Montaner in the role. He related in an interview to the newspaper *El Mundo* that "We always assumed that the *calesero* would be interpreted by a man, but when we took the work to the Regina . . . we found that the impresario . . . didn't have, and didn't want to have a "negrito" in the company."[32] Concerned with raising the level of entertainment at the Regina above the "low" popular comedy of *teatro vernáculo* establishments, the theater's management agreed to the inclusion of Grenet's song "Ay Mamá Inés" only if performed by Rita Montaner. Montaner herself was highly ambivalent about performing the role; she later declared that it was the only thing in her career about which she had regrets.[33]

Whatever trepidation Montaner may have felt about taking on the *negro calesero* role in *La Niña Rita,* she would continue to perform comic portrayals of black masculinity throughout her career. An examination of Montaner's later recordings reveals that some of her most famous songs continue the blackface/cross-dress tradition she began with *La Niña Rita.* Songs such as "Vacúnala," "Negrito," and "El Melonero" attest to Montaner's prowess as the quintessential *negrito* of the late 1920s and 1930s.

Montaner's performance of the *negro calesero,* and the overwhelming popularity with which it was received, further complicates the meaning of blackness as it was represented and reproduced for white consumption. Not only was black skin a mask that actors donned in the performance of the *negrito,* but in this case so was the character's very sex.

The feminized portrayal of black masculinity in *La Niña Rita* must not be viewed as a comic accident but rather an intentional attack. The role played by Montaner is not the only *negro calesero* called for in the libretto. While the showstopper "Ay Mama Inés" appeared at the very end of the work, earlier in the production, audiences witnessed the appearance of another cross-dressed *negrito* dandy. Played by soprano María Ruíz and backed up by an *entire treble chorus* of cross-dressed *caleseros*, the character performed Lecuona's musical number "Los caleseros." While posterity might better remember Montaner's presentation, the day following the premiere showed a press enamored with Ruiz's performance: "Almost all of the musical numbers had to be repeated. 'La Clavelera' and 'Los Caleseros' were especially pleasing, in which the gifted soprano María Ruiz displayed her talents to good effect."[34]

The praise offered Ruíz for her performance of "Los caleseros" surprisingly comes before the reviewer even mentions the performance of Rita Montaner or that of Caridad Suárez, who played the leading lady. The piece itself is a sprightly march with the most modest of syncopations (Example 4.1). As the young coachman brags about his prowess with the ladies, the very rhetoric of the song recalls another genre—and another gender: the *guaracha*. This *mulata*-identified genre, which later forms the basis for the zarzuela *salida*, or entrance aria, is discussed in detail in Chapter 3.

> Cuando de paseo por el Prado
> voy en mi volanta o en quitrín
> todas las mulatas
> al verme tan guapo
> con zalamería me suelen decir:
>
> Calesero pinturero
> yo quisiera calesero ser tu amor
> si supiera calesero
> que sincera también fuera tu pasión

> When I go down the Prado,
> I go in my buggy or my carriage;
> all of the *mulatas*,
> seeing me so handsome,
> say to me suggestively:
>
> Coachman, so fancy,
> I would like to be your love,
> if I knew, coachman,
> that your passion were sincere.

Ex. 4.1

Cuan- do de pa - se - o   por el Pra- do   voy en mi vo-

lan- ta   o en qui - trín   to - das las mu - la-tas

"Los Caleseros" is peppered with tropes that appear in *guaracha* texts since the middle of the nineteenth century. The opening line itself, "Cuando de paseo por el Prado," instantly recalls any number of *guaracha* texts, in which the *mulata* protagonist announces her movement down Havana's central boulevard, the Prado. From this moment on, audiences would not merely have viewed the *calesero*'s performance within their expectations of the *negrito* comic type, but they would also have been comparing his behavior with that of the most feminine of racialized characters, the *mulata*. The double joke does not fail to disappoint, and the text follows the expected format of a *guaracha*, with the singer recounting the comments he receives in the street. The reworking of the *guaracha* text reverses its expected gender roles. Rather than a beautiful *mulata* receiving the admiring compliments of male onlookers, the "fancy" black man on parade receives the compliments of women, specifically aggressive *mulata* women. The coup de grâce is that this *negrito* doesn't just take on the gender role of a woman, he really is one.

Montaner and Ruíz's gender-bending portrayals of the *negrito* places their performance within the male discourse of the *teatro vernáculo* even as the rest of *La Niña Rita* attempts a new romantic and feminine sensibility. While the *sainete*'s creators experimented with pleasing a new target audience, they still relied on the *negrito*'s traditional appeal, perhaps recognizing that in order for this new "family" genre to succeed, it had to initially gain currency with (and ultimately from) both genders.

The *Negrito* in the Zarzuela: A Changing Role

While the zarzuela *negrito* entered theatrical history through the same "door of caricature" discovered by Crespo y Borbón, zarzuela librettists did not lead him down the corridor toward the political satire of the *teatro bufo*. As the zarzuela matured and developed its own gendered discourse, composers and librettists became less dependent on the *negrito* type, and while the character did not disappear, neither did it maintain the same degree of prominence that it held in *La Niña Rita*. In the zarzuela, the core comic trio of the popular theater is dismantled; the *negrito* stands outside of the major plot line of zarzuelas, and his character lacks the political poignancy of his predecessor. In this way, the subversive potential of the comic *negrito*, so important in the popular theater, is stripped away.

The *negrito* appears most frequently in zarzuelas whose main plot lines do not involve racial themes. Works in this category, such as *Lola Cruz*, *La plaza del catedral*, *Julián el gallo*, and the aforementioned *La Niña Rita*, generally involve a pair of young white lovers struggling to overcome some tragic obstacle. In such plots, the *negrito*'s parody of blackness serves as comic relief against the romantic angst of the protagonists. When the *negrito* does appear in plots that focus on race, such as the character of Tirso in Roig's *Cecilia Valdés* and Monguito in Prats's *Amalia Batista,* the character's role is diminished even further, both in the amount of time spent onstage and in the lack of musical numbers. These characters are also the most infantile and submissive *negritos* found in the repertoire.

Although no longer part of a core trio of characters, the zarzuela *negrito* remains a participant of ensemble comedy. His humor lies in his relation to other characters, not merely in his individual wit, and perhaps because of this relational characteristic, the *negrito* does not sing arias. In fact, in many zarzuelas, it is not a sung role at all.[35] While occasionally the *negrito* is given solo songs (as in the case of "Ay Mama Inés"), they are invariably topical numbers that fall outside the plot and are intended for comic relief. More commonly, the *negrito* sings with someone else, bringing the ensemble comedy of the *teatro vernáculo* to the zarzuela stage. Such numbers are frequently sung with either a black or *mulata* woman in duets rife with sexual undertones and *double entendres.*

A representative *negrito* of this type is Felo, in Ernesto Lecuona and Gustavo Sánchez Galarraga's *Julián el gallo.* A secondary character in the zarzuela, Felo is a direct descendant of the *teatro vernáculo,* and he maintains the male-oriented comedic qualities that are characteristic of that tradition. A servant on a coconut plantation, Felo speaks in *bozal,* chases women, is lazy, and casts spells. He is prone to vulgar humor. In the tradition of nineteenth-century *negritos* like Creto Gangá, Felo imparts a comic wisdom as events unfold on stage. When he spies the aptly named characters Cornelius and Taurino, both of whom know that the protagonist Julián is cheating with the other's wife, Felo wittily remarks, "This is a corral. Here the one who isn't a rooster is a bull [i.e., a cuckold]. I'm going to start singing, so they don't confuse me."[36]

Felo shares with other zarzuela *negritos* the practice of being an acute observer of all of the personal melodramas and love affairs going on around him. His habit of collecting the intimate secrets of others is considered to be, in Cuban culture, a decidedly feminine trait.[37] But unlike the gossiping *mulatas* who are a mainstay of the comic stage, the *negrito* invariably keeps his mouth shut, guarding his information carefully. Francisco, in Agustín Rodríguez's libretto *La bella cubana,* is the consummate *negrito* in this respect. He guards his knowledge and feigns ignorance when questioned. *"Negro viejo no sá ná"*—"Old black man don't know nothing."

Felo's duet with Chea fulfills popular expectations of picaresque ensemble comedy. The duet begins when Felo enters carrying a bunch of coconuts he was instructed to pick and open for the guests at his master Julián's party. Chea, a house servant, begs him to open one for her, as she is thirsty. The opening section is rhythmically and melodically simple. Both characters sing their stanzas to the same music on a staccato, disjointed melody. Felo sings to Chea, "Drink, my little *mulata*, from the coconut that for your mouth your black man has opened."[38] Chea responds by insisting that Felo hurry up and give his "water" to her, that he is making her suffer. She ends the A section by exclaiming, "*Los coquitos estos ¡Ay! ¡Qué duro son!*"—"These little coconuts, ooh! They're so hard!"[39] The explicit sexual metaphor of the duet thus laid out, the second section shifts into a spicier *tango-congo*. Here, along with the increased syncopation, the text also heats up.

> *Felo:*
> Dulce más que la miel ese coco es
> Ven acá pa beber su agua de cristal
>
> *Chea:*
> Dame ya de beber que muero de sed
> Es verdad y eso es de sabor de miel.
>
> *Felo:*
> Qué placer agujero al coco abrir
> Y poner la boca así
> y su chorro beber
>
> *Chea:*
> Quiero así mi boca negra al coco poner
> Dame ya de tu coco a beber.

> *Felo:*
> Sweeter than honey that coconut is.
> Come here to drink its crystal water.
>
> *Chea:*
> Give it to me to drink, I'm dying of thirst.
> It's true that it tastes like honey.
>
> *Felo:*
> What pleasure to pierce the coconut
> and put your mouth on it like this
> and drink from its spring.
>
> *Chea:*
> I want to put my black mouth on the coconut.
> Give me your coconut to drink.

The section comes to a close with the interchanges between Felo and Chea becoming shorter and closer together, building to a climax similar to the increasingly rapid exchanges found in the *montuno* sections of Cuban *son*. The scene ends with the two dancing until the music stops.

Characters like Felo not only provide a space for the traditional, popular *negrito* to participate on the zarzuela stage, but they also are a medium through which Afrocubanist genres reached zarzuela audiences. Pieces like Felo's duet exploited the current vogue for Afrocuban dance genres such as the *son*, at the same time offering a highly judgmental critique. The rhythmic drive and musical logic of the *son* is dismissed as primitive, ridiculous, and oversexed exotic display. Performances of stereotyped Afrocubanist numbers allowed gentrified zarzuela audiences a thrilling taste of popular trends, at the same time allowing them to maintain a sense of cultural superiority.

The *Negro Trágico*

Two years after Rita Montaner's performance of the *negro calesero*, Lecuona's *El cafetal* premiered on the same stage. The work is the first to bear all of the traits of the mature zarzuela: choruses, vocal ensembles, extended arias, and a longer, more elaborate plot. Set on a coffee plantation in the 1800s, *El cafetal* (like *La Niña Rita*) is a historical drama, and (also like *La Niña Rita*) it owed much of its success to its inclusion of a black male character. The black man in question, however, a slave named Lázaro, represents a departure from the *negrito* of the comic theater, for not only is he pivotal to the zarzuela's plot, but he is also undeniably tragic.

The plot of *El cafetal* is as follows. Lázaro has fallen in love with the daughter of the plantation owner, Niña Flor.[40] In doing so he loses interest in his girlfriend, a fellow slave named Africa who then begins to practice witchcraft to punish him. Niña Flor, for her part, falls in love and is betrothed to Niño Alberto, a wealthy *criollo*.[41] At the end of the work, Lázaro climbs up to Flor's balcony to leave her flowers as a farewell gift. Alberto shoots and kills Lázaro, thinking he was going to assault his fiancée. Lázaro dies protesting the purity of his intentions, to the dismay of Flor and the grief of Africa.

Robin Moore has suggested that relatively sympathetic representations of slaves allowed twentieth-century audiences to enjoy "serious" themes within the zarzuela while avoiding discussion of contemporary racial problems.[42] This dynamic might well explain why composers and librettists were drawn to nineteenth-century plots in general, but it does little to explain the increasing shift in the portrayal of one of Cuba's most essential stock characters.

The change in the depiction of black men might be attributed to the growing market force of the zarzuela's female audience. The *negro trágico* character developed by Lecuona and Sánchez Galarraga in *El cafetal* has its roots not in the comic theater, but in late nineteenth-century literature. Authors such as Anselmo Suárez y Romero, Gertrudis Gómez de Avellaneda, and Cirilo Villaverde popularized the antislavery narrative in their novels *Francisco*,[43] *Sab*,[44] and *Cecilia Valdés*. These authors portray slaves as noble creatures who suffer the injustice of their situation, a theme that is clearly picked up by Lecuona in *El cafetal*. Women were the primary consumers of the romantic antislavery novels produced in Cuba at the turn of the century,[45] and it stands to reason that zarzuela librettists would search for narrative models to please their target "family" audience.

Karen Hensen has observed that operatic studies of the Other have tended to focus on women and their vocality while largely ignoring the cultural work done by male bodies and voices.[46] Thus, her work on female desire, masculinity, and the depiction of male "exotics" in the French operetta contributes a welcome perspective on the importance of the feminine gaze in staged entertainment. Hensen's interest in discovering the mechanisms by which "female Orientalism" functioned and her search for the "counter-hegemonic" within such Orientalist discourse provides an important theoretical thread for this discussion.[47] The Cuban zarzuela similarly served up male exotics for its target audience. *El cafetal* marks a turning point in the theatrical representation of black masculinity, for Lázaro becomes a model for the later treatment of black men on the zarzuela stage. His portrayal as a suffering, sentimental, and ultimately sexy romantic appealed not to the validation of white public (male) identity as did the comic caricatures of the *negrito*, but to the interior dialogues and secret fantasies of the zarzuela's female spectators.

The Slave Lament

The characteristic that perhaps most distinguishes the *negro trágico* from the *negrito* is that the tragic black protagonist is, above all else, a singer. The *negro trágico* uses song as the primary expression of his dramatic conflict, and while the *negrito* used music to entertain in a performance of difference, for the *negro trágico* song becomes a lingua franca, his voice a medium for empathetic communication with his audience.

The *negro trágico*'s mode of musical expression, established by Lázaro in *El cafetal*, is a genre that becomes increasingly popular in the 1920s and early 1930s: the slave's lament. Well-known examples of the genre include Eliseo Grenet's "Lamento esclavo"[48] and Lecuona's "Canto de esclavo." Slave laments are characterized by slow or moderate tempos, *cantabile* melodies, and the frequent use of *son* or *tango-congo* rhythms in the accompaniment. Characters commonly refer to their African origins, usually *carabalí* (or *karabalí*) or *arará*.[49] Slave laments portray their protagonists as noble sufferers who long for liberty.

Lázaro's lament "Triste es ser esclavo" is distinct from music sung by the comic *negrito* both in its heartrending lyrics and in the vocal demands it placed on the performer. Written for a trained baritone voice, the melody spans a major twelfth and uses sustained pitches and legato lines to lead to soaring cadences. The text tells of the suffering of the slave and his longing for liberty. The eloquence with which Lázaro sings is striking, especially when compared with the *bozal* of a *negrito* such as Felo. More notable still is that when Lázaro speaks he uses the heavy accent and stilted grammar of a plantation slave, yet when he sings it is with perfect diction and grammar. The use of what might be called an "unnatural eloquence," that is, a departure from the quality of speech expected by lower-class Afrocuban characters, is a technique that derives from nineteenth-century literature, where such eloquence is designed to speak directly to a white audience and incite compassion.[50]

The first section of Lázaro's lament is in G minor and opens with a series of descending phrases that begin on E♭ (Example 4.2). Lázaro's first two phrases are harmonic and melodic repeats, and his Western operatic phrasing is betrayed only by the drumbeat-like setting of the word "karabalí," its emphasis on the minor third adding an air of modal "primitivism." On his third phrase, Lázaro begins again on E♭ but opens up the tessitura to a high G that extends the phrase to eight bars, ending on the same minor drumbeat rhythm that finished the first phrase.

The second half of the lament is a *tango-congo*, a genre usually used for comic or light numbers such as "Ay Mama Inés," from *La Niña Rita*[51] (Example 4.3). The eight-bar phrases that state the *tango-congo*'s theme take their melodic contour from the opening section, each phrase outlining a descent that begins from a sustained pitch. Lecuona writes over the voice part the direction "with bitterness." With the shift to the *tango-congo*, the key switches to the parallel major, the sudden sweetness of the harmony ironically emphasizing Lázaro's bitterness. Lecuona later becomes a master in using the *tango-congo* in ways that work against its traditional usage as a light, comic genre in order to invoke bittersweet or uneasy emotions.[52]

Ex. 4.3

Que triste es ser esclavo karabalí
que triste y negro si no hay en mí
¿Por qué Dios tú me abandonas en mi dolor?
¿No ves lo que sufre y llora mi corazón?

Triste es tu vida karabalí
si sueñas con amores
que no has de lograr.
Triste es nacer esclavo y ansiar
con el corazón gozoso la libertad.

How sad it is to be a *karabalí* slave,
so sad and dark that I can't explain it.
Why, God, do you abandon me in my pain?
Don't you see how my heart suffers and cries?

Sad is your life, *karabalí*,
if you dream of loves
that you cannot achieve.
It is sad to be born a slave and to desire liberty
with a joyful heart.

Black Masculinity and Unrequited Love

The emergence of the black man as a tragic, rather than comic, figure is
further codified by Lecuona in *María la O* and by Roig in *Cecilia Valdés*.
Both zarzuelas continue *El cafetal*'s treatment of the black man as a core
character in racial tragedy, and in these works, the suffering character's connection to nineteenth-century abolitionist literature is literal; both zarzuelas draw upon Cirilo Villaverde's novel *Cecilia Valdés*.[53] In terms of plot,
however, the characters of José Inocente in *María la O* and José Dolores in
Cecilia Valdés have very little in common with the doomed slave from *El
cafetal*. Neither is enslaved. The object of their affections is not a wealthy
white woman but a lower-class *mulata* and, unlike Lázaro, who dies for a
forbidden love, both José Inocente and José Dolores plan to violently stab
and kill their white rivals. Although the stories of the two Josés are quite
different than that of Lázaro, the three characters share a pivotal dramatic
function that was previously denied to black male characters. Like Lázaro,
both Josés sing laments. However, José Inocente and José Dolores do not
decry lost liberty, but rather lament their unrequited love.

Lecuona's José Inocente, the first of the Josés to appear on the stage
in 1930, revives many of the "dangerous" black stereotypes developed
in *bufo* theater after abolition.[54] A *curro* from the Manglar, José Inocente
speaks violently with a harsh street accent.[55]

Y le digo que,
si cuida su pellejo,
siga a la letra el conseijo
de reipetá a esa, amito!
Poiqué no hay poi que aclará
lo que uité sabé y yo sé;
que uité con esa mujé
tiene una deuda sagrá![56]

And I say to you,
if you value your hide,
follow my advice to the letter
to respect her, my friend!
Because there's no need to clarify
what you know and I know;
that with that woman you
have a sacred debt!

For white audiences, José represents a world that is both reviled and feared. This attitude is apparent in the fourth scene, when a coach carrying two female passengers and driven by a fainthearted *negro calesero* named Petimetre strays into the Manglar.

> *Damisela:* ¡Qué tipo tan extraño tiene!
> *Petimetre:* Parece un ñáñigo.
> *Dama:* ¡Ay, no diga usted que es un ñáñigo!
>
> *Petimetre:* Oiga, señor; ¿qué barrio es este?
> *Curro:* ¿Este? (Le mira de pies a cabeza)
> El del Manglar! (Váse)
> *Petimetre:* Ay, doña Tomasita,
> vámonos de aquí!
> *Dama:* ¿Por qué?
> *Petimetre:* ¡Porque estamos en el Manglar!
> *Dama:* ¡Ay, socorro, auxilio!

> *Damisela:* What a strange-looking man!
> *Petimetre:* He looks like a *ñáñigo.*
> *Dama:* Oh, don't say he's a *ñáñigo!*
> *Petimetre:* Hey mister, what's this neighborhood?
> *Curro:* This? (he looks him up and down)
> This is the Manglar! (he leaves)
> *Petimetre:* Oh, doña Tomasita,
> let's get out of here!
> *Dama:* Why?
> *Petimetre:* Because we're in the Manglar!
> *Dama:* Oh, help, help!

Even the streetwise *mulata* María la O is not guaranteed safety in José Inocente's world. She goes to visit José Inocente in the Manglar to tell him that he was right, that Fernando indeed has betrayed her. Both characters plot to kill Fernando. At the sound of drums, José Inocente tells María she must leave, and hurry. "Get out of here, María la O . . . the *curros* come every day to sing and play at this hour. Go, I don't want them to see you here."[57] After she rushes off, the infamous *negros curros* appear on stage. They sing a chorus with a prominent *tango-congo* rhythm and a text that undercuts their physical threat by stressing their laziness and vanity. *"No toco bongo y maruga, solo quiero mi 'sin arruga' . . . No hay nada valiente pa' este valiente."* ("I don't play drums or rasp, I only want to look good . . . There's nothing brave about this scary guy.")

José Inocente's Lament

Given the detail librettist Sánchez Galarraga and Lecuona used to paint José Inocente as a dangerous man coming from a dangerous environment, his lament is curious in that it does not portray a violent criminal but rather an amorous victim (Example 4.4). The lament comes in the fourth scene of the zarzuela, following a confrontation between the *curro*, María

Ex. 4.4

la O, and Fernando. José Inocente surprises the young couple as Fernando escorts María la O to her home in the Manglar, and he accuses Fernando of plotting to abandon her, an accusation that both Fernando and María la O hotly deny. After the two lovers exit the stage amid José Inocente's protestations that he will always love and defend María la O, the jilted *curro* laments his unrequited love.

> Un corazón herido sin piedad
> por donde va publica su dolor
> Por qué mintió con torpe afán,
> por qué se fue dejando en mi
> la pena inmensa de su traición?
>
> No puede ni podrá tener perdón
> el crimen de matar una ilusión,
> si engaño fue el amor que me juró
> irá tras él mi eterna maldición.
> Por qué mintió con torpe afán
> por qué se fué dejando en mi
> la pena inmensa de su traición?

> A heart wounded without pity
> announces its sorrow everywhere it goes.
> Why did she lie to me so easily,
> why did she go away and leave in me
> the immense pain of her betrayal?
>
> The crime of killing an illusion
> can never be pardoned;
> if her sworn love was a lie,
> my eternal curse will follow it.
> Why did she lie to me so easily,
> why did she go away and leave in me
> the immense pain of her betrayal?[58]

In "Un corazón herido sin piedad," Lecuona gives José Inocente what is arguably the most beautiful melody in the zarzuela. The role of José Inocente is written for a baritone, as are other roles of the *negro trágico* type. The accessible, romantic, and sensual depiction of black masculinity that José Inocente represents does not apply to other black male characters who appear in the zarzuela, however. While José Inocente's fellow *curros* sing production numbers that highlight Afrocuban rhythms and primitivist effects, his own lament lacks any trace of popular song, or even syncopation. The regularity of the orchestral rhythm, with its emphasis on the first and third beats and the measured eighth notes and arching phrases in José Inocente's vocal line bear no resemblance to the music typically performed by Afrocuban characters in the zarzuela. The orchestration is lush, and the upper strings richly support a *cantabile* melody that bears more resemblance to Italian opera than to the popular, coloristic settings sung by José Inocente's *negrito* predecessors. There are other characters in the zarzuela who sing in this manner, however. Indeed, the piece's most notable characteristics—the bel canto quality of the melody, the lament's song-form structure, the moderate tempo, the orchestral doubling, and the harplike arpeggiation in the introduction— connect "Un corazón herido sin piedad" with the musical rhetoric of the zarzuela's white heroines.[59]

Illusions of a Lover and a Slave: "Dulce quimera"

The baritone lament sung by José Dolores, "Dulce quimera," is one of the most famous pieces in the zarzuela repertoire written for the male voice, yet the piece is a relatively recent addition, having been added to *Cecilia Valdés* by Roig in 1954. The enshrinement of "Dulce quimera" as a classic has posed a problem for Cuban musicologists, who tend to view later additions to *Cecilia Valdés* in an unfavorable light.[60] Perhaps it is because of the piece's popularity that unsubstantiated claims of an earlier version of "Dulce quimera" appear in the scholarship.[61] The 1954 date would pose a problem for this study, as well, the sociopolitical environment of the 1950s being quite different from that of the 1930s. However, it can be unequivocally stated that "Dulce quimera" is a product of the 1930s, and its connection to the genre of the slave lament is undeniable.

The discovery of an autograph score found in the archives of the Museo Nacional de la Música Cubana proves that "Dulce quimera" premiered not in 1954 but in 1936, in the premiere of a new work entitled *El cimarrón*.[62] The zarzuela, based on a libretto by Marcelo Salinas, played for only two nights, in spite of its all-star cast including Maruja González and Miguel de Grandy and an exquisitely beautiful musical score that, aside from "Dulce quimera" included the popular *romanza* "Es mi vida tu querer." In spite of an enthusiastic press buildup in the weeks and days before the zarzuela's premiere, the papers were unnaturally quiet the day following the opening, stating only that the work would play again that evening.[63] It is difficult to say why the piece would have disappeared so quickly. Financial factors may certainly have played a part. The Roig/ Rodríguez company in the Teatro Martí was entering into its last days, being thrown out by the theater's management.[64]

Potentially, the subject matter of the work might have had something to do with its rapid disappearance. Librettist Marcelo Salinas was known for his radical politics. Earlier works highlighted the struggle of the working class, and his award-winning drama *La alma guajira* openly dealt with the question of race. Unfortunately, the libretto for *El cimarrón* is missing, and the musical score offers only partial information about the plot, leaving much of *El cimarrón* clouded in mystery. What is clear is that several factors set this zarzuela apart in its treatment of race and, in particular, the black male. The most obvious difference is the centrality of the *negro trágico;* he is undeniably the focus of the work, and there is no white male character with whom he must share the dramatic spotlight, as there is in *El cafetal, María la O,* and *Cecilia Valdés.* Roig seems to have recognized that this character was somehow different from other black male characters in the repertoire, for he composed the role for a tenor voice rather than for a baritone. This is the only tragic black role that was written to be performed by a tenor. Moreover, it was not composed for just any tenor, but for the most prominent tenor of the day, Miguel de Grandy. *El cimarrón* is thus unusual not only in that it has a black male protagonist and breaks from the convention of expressing blackness through a lower vocal range, but also because the zarzuela's title role was the only black role Miguel de Grandy is known to have played at the height of his career.[65]

Also open to speculation is the relationship between the runaway slave and his lover, Ana. The soprano role reveals a woman passionately in love with Cimarrón; it is to him that the beautiful and well-known *romanza* "Es mi vida tu querer" is dedicated. In her duet with Cimarrón, Ana begs him to explain why he is no longer interested in her, why he is leaving her. The subject of the runaway slave leaving his woman behind is part of a recurring trope in Cuban song that highlights the suffering of women in the face of black men's supposed inconsistency.[66] Beyond the confrontational duet between Cimarrón and Ana, and the *romanza,* no other information regarding Ana's character can be extracted from the musical score. It is provocative, however, that "Ana" is not a name typically used in Cuban theater of this period for black or *mulata* women and that her *romanza,* both textually and musically, has more in common with the music sung by the white ingenues of the zarzuela than with that sung by Afrocuban women characters. If the zarzuela's plot really did feature a romance between a runaway slave and a white woman, that might explain its speedy disappearance from the stage and the press's silent censorship.

José Dolores Laments

The origins of "Dulce quimera" help to explain the piece's lengthy introduction, which is unusual for the lament genre (Example 4.5).[67] Punctu-
ated by martial bursts of rhythm in the orchestral accompaniment that
sound more Spanish than Afrocuban, the introduction is unique in that
it expresses rage and frustration rather than the languid sorrow more
commonly found in laments. The introduction also allows the singer to
show off his upper range; the original version featured extended high A's.

This opening would have been a wonderful vehicle to showcase the talents of a tenor such as Miguel de Grandy, and knowing that the piece was written for him helps to explain why the version placed in *Cecilia Valdés* possesses such an awkward tessitura. Even transposed down, as it commonly is, the piece is quite "unbaritone-like" and it is difficult for many singers who are accustomed to singing the baritone repertoire.

> Callar
> debo este amor que me enajena
> debo mi pena y mi dolor callar.
> Hay un sino
> fatal que me condena
> a sufrir, a sufrir sin esperar.
> Silencio, corazón dentro del pecho,
> consúmete en tu propia desventura.
> No tienes, corazón, ni aún el derecho
> de gritar ante el mundo
> tu amargura.

> I should silence
> this love that deranges me.
> I should silence my pain and sorrow.
> There's a fatal destiny
> that condemns me
> to suffer, to suffer without hope.
> Be silent, heart within my breast,
> be consumed with your own misfortune.
> Heart, you don't even have the right
> to cry before the world
> your bitterness.

The rhythmic and melodic shift that marks the transition from the introduction to the body of José Dolores's lament is introduced by Cecilia's name[68] (Example 4.6). It is as if Cecilia herself inspires the change from angry frustration to trancelike composure, not José Dolores's own character.

The lyrics of "Dulce quimera" evidence the codification of textual tropes in the lament genre. Like José Inocente, José Dolores sings of a woman's treachery, of a shattered illusion. And, like his counterpart in Lecuona's work, José Dolores is identified by his heart. The focus on heart and soul and lofty sentiment that appears in these laments is as great a contrast to the body-oriented, physical lyrics sung by the *negrito,* as is the musical difference in their signature genres.

Ex. 4.6

Moderadamente

Ce - ci - lia trai-do-ra qui-me - ra____ de faz pla-cen-
te - ra mi al - ma for - jó.____
____ Y mi al - ma____ y mi al - ma tras de e - lla____
____ en va-na que - re - lla de a - mor se lan - zó.____ La

Cecilia
traidora quimera
de faz placentera mi alma forjó.
Y mi alma,
y mi alma tras de ella
en vana querella de amor se lanzó.
La dulce, fragante quimera
de faz hechicera que mi sueño es,
tu nombre es suave y sonoro
eres mi tesoro Cecilia Valdés.

Cecilia,
traitorous illusion
with a lovely face, is forged in my soul.
And my soul,
my soul following behind her,
launched into a futile lament of love.
The sweet, fragrant illusion
of the magic face that is my dream,
your name is soft and sonorous.
You're my treasure, Cecilia Valdés.

The equation of the *negro trágico* with sentimental emotion and the move away from rhythmic music diminishes the black man's symbolic power as a physical threat at the same time that it made his character approachable to female spectators. Much in the same way that blackface performances by women undercut black masculinity, *negro trágico* characters are represented with qualities traditionally seen as feminine—they are emotional, sentimental, and the victims of unfaithful lovers. The lament itself is a genre that is generally seen as feminine in Western culture and has historically been sung on the operatic stage by women, who were seen as more fit to express grief.[69] The psychological and musical feminization of the *negro trágico* serves to balance the threat produced by his prominent role on the stage and the violence his presence suggests (as in the case of Lázaro) or produces (as in the case of the two Josés).

Jane Tomkins, in her study of *Uncle Tom's Cabin*, shows that in North America, sentimentalist strategies for representing white women and black men were often identical.[70] The tragic representation of black men in the zarzuela, using techniques associated with operatic femininity—specifically a *white* lyric femininity—suggests a similar comparison. The discursive power generated by identifying black men with traditional qualities of white femininity in a genre that was specifically marketed to white women should not be underestimated. Fulfilling the stereotype of Afrocubans as "creatures of feeling," black male characters could be made to express emotion in ways that white female characters, held back by societal strictures, could not. White female audience members could then identify, if not with black bodies themselves, with the musical and poetic expression that those black bodies emitted. Thus the blackfaced baritone becomes the voice of white femininity; the *negro trágico* is the masked ventriloquist of white female desire.

5 Ingenues and Fallen Women: Representations of White Femininity

Although the *mulata* character is the most celebrated and prominent female protagonist in the zarzuela repertoire, white female characters also play an important role in zarzuela plots and are found in nearly every work, including those with *mulata* protagonists. Since white middle- and upper-class women were the primary audience for the zarzuela produced in Havana after 1927, the theatrical and musical representation of that social group holds special interest. How did the zarzuela's creators choose to depict the character that most closely resembled its own female spectators?

The story here is told in two parts, beginning with women of virtue and ending with those of ill repute. In zarzuela plots, class plays a major role in mapping out such moral distinctions. Women who are virtuous and innocent are generally from the upper classes, while characters who have suffered moral collapse are most typically drawn from the working poor. The social connections drawn among class, race, and virtue were the subject of considerable fascination in early twentieth-century Cuba, and they were treated by novelists and politicians as well as librettists and composers.

The literary groundwork for such treatment was laid by Martín Morua Delgado in his 1891 novel *Sofía*. The novel recounts the story of Sofía, a young woman who is the illegitimate daughter of a nobleman and a prostitute. Although Sofía is the offspring of two white parents, the social conditions of her birth actually outweigh her race. She is sold into slavery, a victim of class and the sins of her mother. *Sofía* mirrors the tragedy of Villaverde's novel *Cecilia Valdés*, while replacing the theme of miscegenation with one of class conflict and sexual transgression.[1]

Miguel de Carrión's novels *Las honradas* and *Las impuras*, published in 1918 and 1919, respectively, explore the gray space between the two poles of virtue, poles that are entrenched in and shored up by the privileges (or the disadvantages) of class. The first of the novels, *Las honradas*, tells the story of Victoria, a young woman from the Cuban bourgeoisie, whose conflicted emotions about virtue and her own sexuality lead to a miserable marriage. Ultimately, it is through Victoria's loss of virtue—an adulterous relationship—that both she and her husband find their happiness. *Las impuras* tells the story of Teresa, a prostitute struggling to make ends meet and take care of her children. The author is sympathetic to Teresa's plight and defends her right to live independently, no matter the social or moral cost. De Carrión's two protagonists, the virtuous bourgeois woman repressed by social codes and mores, and the noble and good-hearted sinner, foreshadow the theatrical representation of white femininity that will occur only a decade later on the zarzuela stage.

The Ingenue

Upper-class white women in zarzuela plots can best be referred to as ingenues. Uncomplicated and virtuous, the ingenues of the zarzuela embody beauty, modesty, and goodness and are models of proper behavior. Noble, humble, and obedient, such women are almost devoid of any interests, talents, or hobbies.[2] The zarzuela's young heroines tend to lack even the requisite skills of bourgeois female achievement; they do not play the piano, dabble in watercolors, or speak French.[3] Rather, the ingenue is a sort of eternal debutante, always dressed in pastels (or bridal white) and awaiting her coming out. The main ambition of the ingenue is marriage, and her interests, when not directly about her love life, generally turn to fashion.[4]

Frequently, ingenue characters are orphans living with distant relatives or guardians. The dramatic rupturing of the young woman's support system serves to make her vulnerable and in need of protection. The absence of familial chaperons permits the ingenue to get into dramatic and often compromising situations that, under normal circumstances, a "good girl" would not have been in. Thus, ingenue characters may end up alone onstage with a man, without a single chaperon present.[5] This departure from courtship protocol plays a role in several zarzuelas, including Lecuona's *Julian el gallo,* where Dulce María, who was happy to sing to her beloved Alberto when there was a chorus present, is frantic when she finds herself alone with him. "People might see us," she protests.[6] As she is vulnerable and alone, the ingenue's search for a husband takes on an edge of personal, as well as social, urgency, for only a husband can fully protect her virtue.

White heroines are often seen to be the agents of what today might be called a "compassionate conservatism,"[7] for it is they who recognize the evils of slavery and racism. The ingenue's orphan status works to strengthen her compassion toward black characters, because she was often raised by a black nursemaid. The maternal relation between slave women and white female children is a familiar theme in Cuban abolitionist literature,[8] and although black maternity might be presented as a powerful bond, such relationships, on the stage as well as the page, never escape the white paternalistic lens through which they are viewed.

Tula's conversation with her nurse Ña Regla in *María la O* is typical of these relationships. Tula has gone to sit at the feet of Ña Regla, who exclaims in thickly accented Spanish, "Oh this is good! The mistress on the floor and the black slave in the easy chair."[9] Tula protests, "You're not my slave, Ña Salú. You are my mother, ever since my real mother died." "A mother black as coal," muses the nurse, "with a daughter white as the snow,"[10] reflecting an enforced code of absolute racial opposites that differs sharply from the troubled liminality of the *mulata.* In spite of their compassionate feelings toward their slaves, however, none of these "white as snow" female characters (Isabel, Tula, Flor, Lola) makes any attempt to free her slaves or to change the system. Their influence seems only to ensure that the slaves will not be abused, or, as Isabel Ilincheta, the abolitionist icon from Villaverde's novel, puts it in Agustín Rodríguez's libretto adaptation, "[that] the whips will not be used in my absence." Thus, while white women show a pseudo-daughterly devotion toward their black "mothers," their attitude toward other blacks is that of a patient parent, steadfastly holding up the values of the system while rejecting its most cruel excesses.

Ingenue characters have a remarkably restricted dramatic range, appearing in zarzuelas that conform to one of two plot formulas. In the first formula, the young white woman is an ingenue character from the upper, or at least landed, class. She falls in love with a young man of the same social status. The plot revolves around the obstacles in the way of the couple's union, obstacles that usually involve simple romantic intrigues and are, in most cases, resolved. This white-on-white, class-balanced, heterosexual story is the only type of romance plot that results in happy endings in the Cuban zarzuela repertoire. Falling into this category are Lecuona's zarzuelas *Julián el gallo, La cubanita,* and *La plaza del catedral* and Gonzalo Roig's *El Clarín* and *La Habana de noche.* Lecuona's *Lola Cruz* portrays the love affair of a white, upper-class couple, but it breaks from the formula in that it does not have a happy ending.

The second plot formula also portrays a relationship between an upper-class white couple, but in this formula, the ingénue is not the female lead. In these zarzuelas, the ingenue is cast against a *mulata* protagonist in a cross-racial love triangle that propels the plot to a tragic conclusion. Zarzuelas using this plot formula include Lecuona's *El cafetal* (1929) and *María la O* (1930), Roig's *Cecilia Valdés* (1932), and *María Belén Chacón* (1934) and *Amalia Batista* (1936), both by Prats. Plots involving cross-racial romantic intrigue are usually set in the colonial era. By placing the action within a slave society, librettists could highlight race in an environment where racial boundaries, and their subsequent transgressions, seemed more clear-cut.[11] The role of the white ingenue in these racial tragedies is rarely a prominent one, for it is her *presence* that is strategic to the plot, not her actions.[12] She is merely the socially sanctioned partner who contrasts with the racial mixture and social chaos represented by the *mulata.* Representative ingenue characters from this plot type are Niña Tula in *María la O* and Carmita in *Amalia Batista,* both of whom spend the entire zarzuela waiting inside their homes for their wedding day. Neither acts independently, and they do not even appear in love scenes with their partners. The characters' lack of independent development extends to a lack of musical expression. Neither Niña Tula nor Carmita sings solo musical numbers in the original versions of the zarzuelas, although music has been given to both characters in later performances.[13]

Even Isabel Ilincheta, the self-reliant businesswoman of Villaverde's novel *Cecilia Valdés,* loses her independent spirit on the zarzuela stage. Agustín Rodríguez's libretto downplays Isabel's importance as the overseer of her family's coffee plantation, preferring to portray her as a flighty innocent of little depth.[14] Roig's score gives Isabel a more musically demanding role than that of similar ingenue characters who are cast against a *mulata* protagonist. She does, at least, sing. However, it is notable that Isabel never sings alone. She is heard only twice, once in a love duet with Leonardo, and once in a quartet with Leonardo and his friends Meneses and Solfa.

The *Romanza*

In zarzuelas where they are given a more prominent role, ingenue protagonists most often express themselves musically in the form of a *romanza*.[15] Spiritual and romantic in nature, *romanzas* occur near the beginning of the zarzuela, introducing the ingenue much as the *salida* genre introduces the *mulata*. However, while the *salida* represents a public appearance, the solo *romanza* is sung in private, allowing the ingenue to explore her feelings within a protected, private space. Expressions of romantic longing are always tempered by the constraints of virtue, and the ingenue speaks of love in metaphoric terms, using pastoral images of flowers (usually white), breezes, and little birds. Very often one of these images serves as a medium between the ingenue and her true love: the little bird will find him, or the flowers will bloom when he appears. This metaphorical distancing is a rhetorical device that relieves the ingenue of the responsibility of romantic agency.

Ingenue *romanzas* are highly melodic, usually covering a large and vocally demanding range, often up to two octaves.[16] Vocal phrases tend to be long and arching, with the melodic climax occurring in the middle of the phrase. They are always sung with legato articulation. Performed at a moderate tempo, the vocal part rarely exhibits any syncopation. The orchestral accompaniments likewise tend to be rhythmically simple, often moving in quarter notes. While the accompaniment may or may not double the vocal melody, the supporting harmonies tend to be richer, with a higher degree of chromaticism, than those found in the more rhythmic music sung by the *mulata*. There is no strict formal structure for the *romanza*, they may be written in binary or ternary form and are occasionally through-composed.

"Yo quisiera un día," Niña Flor's *romanza* from *El cafetal*, is an excellent example of the ingenue *romanza*. The second musical number in the zarzuela, following the slave chorus "¡A trabajá!," the *romanza* did not appear in the premiere of *El cafetal* but was added shortly thereafter, most likely for the performance of soprano Maruja González.[17]

The dialogue that precedes Flor's *romanza* establishes the zarzuela's plot, introducing the inhabitants of the manor house on a large coffee plantation. Through the group's conversation, it is learned that they are expecting the arrival of guests, including a young man named Alberto, whom Don Manuel sees as a good match for his daughter. Flor, who has just returned from gathering flowers, protests at her father's insinuations. When the members of the household leave the room, however, Flor finds herself alone and confesses, "If you knew how much this Alberto really interests me . . . I can't say how much . . . and how anxious I am that he arrive."[18] Thus safely alone with her fantasies, Flor begins to sing (Example 5.1).

"Yo quisiera un día" is in the style of 1920s radio-hall music. The *romanza* begins with Flor stating, "Someday I would like to feel your love in a dream."[19] Distanced from her subject matter, singing of a dream and not of herself, Niña Flor can thus sing of kisses and caresses, leading to her true desire: "Eternal love, eternal love, sublime crazy enchanter that will always live in me."[20] In the opening section, a sumptuous—and vocally difficult—melody soars over chromatic harmonies. While Flor's melody itself nearly avoids any hint of chromaticism or nondiatonic coloring, the amount of chromaticism in the accompaniment is notable, for no other character in *El cafetal* is given such a richly colored harmonic palette. Also notable is the rhythmic squareness of the *romanza*'s opening. The even quarter notes in the vocal line are reinforced by the orchestra, and Flor's dreamy attempts to swing at "y cantar un gran amor" oscillate cleanly in cut time.

> Yo quisiera un día
> sentir tu amor en sueño
> Mi dulce ideal gozar tu querer
> vivir de tus besos
> y de tus caricias
> entre las delicias
> de un amor sin fin.
> Y cantar un gran amor
> con frases llenas de pasión
> que en mi alma grabadas están
> "Amor eterno, eterno amor,
> sublime loco arrobador que
> siempre tu amor seré."

> One day I would like
> to feel your love in a dream
> my sweet ideal to enjoy your love,
> to live on your kisses
> and your caresses
> among the delights
> of a love without end.
> And to sing of a great love
> with phrases full of passion
> that are engraved in my soul:
> "Love eternal, eternal love,
> sublime crazy thief,
> I will always be your love."

Ex. 5.1

This is not a piece for an untrained voice. Ingenue roles are generally higher than other female roles, and one of the functions of the *romanza* is to showcase the ingenue's vocal virtuosity. That being said, Flor's *romanza* is high, quite high for this repertoire.[21] The tessitura of the opening section is fairly typical, lying between E and G, although it dips down as low as D♯. The second half of the *romanza*, however, features sustained singing above the staff. After climbing up to a sustained high B″, Flor sings the melody from the B section again, this time entirely above the staff. This leads into a lengthy, texted cadenza that, except for its text, is a pure bel canto vocalise (Example 5.2). Written out by the composer, the cadenza's two-octave range is replete with coloratura and staccato passages befitting a Vaccai exercise. The soprano must have the vocal fortitude to sustain a high C″ for five bars to conclude the piece. The vocal difficulty of the piece may help explain why this *romanza* is often dropped from performances of *El cafetal.*

The *Plegaría*

It seems that when the ingenue is not singing songs of love, she is often praying, and occasionally she is doing both. The other type of *romanza* most commonly sung by ingenue characters is that of the *plegaría*, or prayer to the Virgin Mary.[22] This is the case with Dulce María, the ingenue heroine of Lecuona's zarzuela *Julián el gallo.* The young, unmarried ward of the womanizing Julián, Dulce María has fallen in love with Alberto, only to learn to her horror that her guardian plans to keep her for himself. Her plaintive and rather desperate *plegaría* is illustrative of the genre.

> Virgen divina, madre de amor
> de los mortales ten compasión
> vierte en nosotros tu clara luz
> por él que ha muerto sobre la cruz.

> Divine virgin, mother of love,
> have compassion on the mortals;
> pour your clear light onto us
> for him who died on the cross.

As she devotes her prayer to the Virgin Mary, Dulce María intones with repeated pitches in a slowly ascending melodic phrase over an F major pedal. Beginning on the subdominant, Dulce María's first phrase is a long one, stretching across sixteen bars. While the phrase climbs steadily, reaching a climax of a high G ("*ten*") and quickly descending

Ex. 5.2

Cadenza (*puede hacerse en vocalise*)

A-mor, a-mor lle-gas-te al fin pa-ra con-sue-lo de mi ser a-mor e-ter-no e-ter-no a-mor sub-líme

Flauta

Clarinete

lo-co ar-ro-ba-dor feb-ríl an-he-lo yo ten-dré o-ír tus la-bios pro-nun-ciar que so-lo

yo tu a-mor se-ré A-mor, a-mor_____ a-mor a-mor_____ fe-bríl an-

he-lo yo ten-dré o-ír tus la-bios pro-nun-ciar que so-lo tu-ya se-ré

loco

with a plagal cadence to the tonic, the change of the underlying harmony to an augmented seventh chord brings the prayer back to its tonal and melodic beginnings, just as if Dulce María had passed from one rosary bead to the next. Although the text is religious rather than romantic, the musical setting portrays a passionate, even ecstatic, personality. In the second phrase, Dulce María abandons the chantlike stasis heard previously. She covers the melodic and harmonic ground of the first phrase in just seven bars, reaching the G on the word "luz" ("light") and then surpassing it. The harmony moves from the same E minor chord heard previously to a secondary dominant as the vocal line climbs to A and then resolves to G major as the melody climaxes on a high B♭.

Illustrating the blending of spiritual and romantic love that is so characteristic of the ingenue, Dulce María's religious fervor brings her in contact with her romantic feelings and she begins a love *romanza* (Example 5.3). Like Niña Flor, Dulce María distances herself from her subject matter through the pretext of a dream: "Underneath a palm tree on a night with an uncertain moon / I dreamed awake of a love / and it was your eyes and they were your lips / that I saw in my illusion."[23] With emotion already stirred from the *plegaría*, the orchestra is much more active than it would typically be at the beginning of a *romanza*, and its harplike articulation gives it an air of fluttering anticipation, as well as a pastoral quality befitting the text. When the accompaniment finally changes to the regular quarter note pattern more typical of ingenue *romanzas*, it occurs with a tempo change to *allegro molto* and a metric shift to 3/4 time (Example 5.4). Both the swift tempo and the sudden switch to triple meter serve to

Ex. 5.4   **Allegro molto**

deny the *romanza* the kind of grounded metric stability that is typically associated with an ingenue's musical romantic musings. Contributing to this lack of grounding, the orchestra doubles the vocal line and the accompaniment shifts entirely to the treble clef. The disappearance of a bass sonority seems to reflect Dulce María's feeling of loss and instability as she sings, "but my fleeting dream left with the breeze of the palm tree and the beautiful illusion died that will never return."[24]

The rhetoric of prayer and romance merge in the last section of the *romanza*. Dulce María brings back the repeated-pitch intonation of the opening, this time an entreaty not to the Virgin, but to the "dream of love." Her romantic desperation rises to the point that she actually questions her faith. "Because I know that even if my heart burns with faith, it can never bring back what has left."[25]

Musical Miscegenation

The zarzuela's manipulation of racialized musical and dramatic rhetoric served not only to define and control representations of the Other, but also to construct and defend a concept of whiteness. The white ingenue is key to this construction, because it is she who embodies the virtues of (white) social order and who, through her chaste behavior and proper marriage at the zarzuela's end, ultimately upholds that order in spite of the philandering of her male counterpart.

Ironically, while the ingenue served as a symbol of whiteness, as the zarzuela's conventions solidified in the early 1930s her character was increasingly relegated to secondary roles, with nonwhite and lower-class characters taking center stage. As the popularity of exotic and afrocubanist compositional styles spread, the ingenue's musical behavior—lyrical *romanzas*, long legato lines, high tessitura, romantic texts—does not represent the standard, but the exception. The ingenue's vocal expression contrasts sharply with the *guarachas, tango-congos,* and stage *rumbas* that filled zarzuela scores.[26] Indeed, the hegemonic musical discourse of the zarzuela was not European lyricism, but Afrocubanism.

At the same time that the appropriation by whites of black cultural forms allowed for the redefinition of blackness in white terms, the line that separated *white difference* from the Afrocuban majority began to blur.[27] The appropriated music, adapted to its new environment, began to define the parameters of white Cuban cultural identity. Thus, in the zarzuela repertoire, the characters that define the musical parameters and establish rhetorical symbolism are the nonwhite characters, especially the *mulata*. Audiences desired and expected to see female protagonists perform the kind of public spectacle popularized in *María la O* and *Cecilia Valdés*, and, while ingenue characters continued to maintain their class status and personal propriety, such roles were increasingly defined not by the dramatic and musical attributes of their whiteness, but rather *against* the heavily gendered and racialized poetic and musical attributes of the *mulata*. By 1930, nearly all female protagonists, regardless of race, performed genres and musical forms that were previously associated with blackness. Thus the musical genres most associated with the *mulata*—the *salida* and the tragic *tango-congo*—gradually are reworked and adapted to be sung by the white ingenue.[28]

The establishment of the *salida* as a convention of performance for white, as well as *mulata*, protagonists was not an easy fit. Unlike other "nonwhite" genres that fully crossed over into white Cuban culture and eventually lost their racialized connotations, such as the *danzón*,[29] the *salida* did not lose its strong associations with race and sexuality. Indeed, the opinion of a newspaper critic, regarding the once scurrilous *danzón*, that "dances do not make people decent, instead, decent people make decent all dances,"[30] appears not to have been the case in dramatic portrayals of white women who perform *salidas*. Composers and librettists had to go to extra lengths to frame the genre in such a way as to protect the ingenue's virtue. In spite of these lingering associations and their dramatic and musical consequences, however, the *salida* genre gradually became a necessary convention for all female protagonists, *mulata* or white.

To reflect, the *salida* represents a *public* entrance. It is sung with the aid of a chorus of onlookers, who repeat the protagonist's *guaracha*-inspired text as she sings of walking in the street alone and proudly draws attention to her physical attributes. How could this genre, so connected to public sensuality and male desire, be sung by a symbol of chaste female virtue, and to what end?

Lola Cruz

The most interesting use of ostensibly nonwhite musical genres by white female characters occurs in Lecuona and Sánchez Galarraga's 1935 zarzuela, *Lola Cruz*. The zarzuela takes place in December, 1878, at the end of the Ten Years War.[31] Lola Cruz is the twenty-year-old granddaughter and only living relative of Mama Trina and Niño Quico, elderly and wealthy Havana residents who own many slaves. Before the story begins, Lola's brother José María has been killed in a brawl while studying in Paris. His killer, a fellow Cuban student named Ricardo Chacón, comes to the family's house to make amends. When he sees Lola, however, he is instantly smitten and conceals his true identity by giving her the false name of Alberto Alarcón. The young couple has fallen deeply in love when Concha Cuesta, the former girlfriend of Lola's dead brother, learns of the matter. She recognizes Chacón's true identity and vengefully plots to expose him and destroy his happiness. Concha is successful in her efforts. Lola renounces "Alberto," and Chacón, having nothing more to lose, goes off to join the revolutionary fighters, known as *mambises*, in their war for independence.

Lola herself is pure ingenue. She fulfills all of the requirements of her type: she is beautiful, rich, orphaned, kind, and compassionate. These demure characteristics alone, however, are not enough to create a viable and engaging protagonist. Moreover, the convention of titling a zarzuela after its female lead carried particular expectations. Not only were protagonist-titled works unwaveringly tragic, almost all of them had *mulata* protagonists.[32] By naming *Lola Cruz* after its heroine, the authors set expectations for how she would be treated musically and dramatically. They were thus faced with the challenge of making Lola fulfill the demands of a genre that required not only a tragic ending, but also that the protagonist sing the musical genres associated with the stage persona of the *mulata*, particularly the *salida*.

The *Salida* of Lola Cruz

Lola's *salida* is a marvel. In it, Lecuona manages to fulfill all of the clichéd expectations of the genre while allowing Lola to be a model of female virtue. The foremost dramatic obstacle that this staging presents is the "public" aspect of the *salida*. Such a public spectacle would be unacceptable for an unattached upper-class young woman in a nineteenth-century plot. A girl's reputation could be easily ruined during this period; even formal courtship had the power to ruin a reputation.[33] Therefore, for an ingenue character like Lola, the uncontrolled public display and suggested sexual availability associated with *salida* performances were out of the question. Lecuona's librettist, Sánchez Galarraga, resolves the dilemma by staging a party for Lola and her girlfriends. The scene takes place in Lola's house, and the privacy of the domestic space counteracts the element of public spectacle so inherent in the *salida* genre. Protected inside the walls of her home with a crowd of giggling virgins as her audience, Lola can behave as "publicly" as she wants, and there is no stain upon her honor.

Lola's entrance begins with her naming. If there was any question that librettist and composer were going to fully embrace the performative tropes of the *mulata*, Lola's entrance lays such doubts to rest. She announces her presence in a move that recalls Cecilia Valdés's entrance, singing high above her girlfriends, "Yo soy Lola Cruz." Her girlfriends, too, take part in the masquerade, calling her the "Reina de amor," yet another poetic trope commonly associated with the *mulata* (one need only recall María la O's designation as the "Reina del Manglar," for example).

Lola modestly deflects her friends' praise (like María la O), but her melody is surprisingly energetic, enthusiastically bouncing along over a marching vamp in the orchestra (Example 5.5). Her exuberance gives the impression that she is only playing, engaging with her friends in a kind of musical "dress-up," trying on the genre for size.

Ex. 5.5

La Salida de Lola Cruz

Beatriz y Amigas
Vienen aquí, de cabalgar,
estas damiselas
que son la flor de la ciudad

Aurelia y Beatriz
La flor gentil

Todas
Galán gentil todos al par
Nos proclaman sí
Cual mejor no la hay
mas de la sociedad
es Lola Cruz la flor
Y es reina del amor

Lola
Yo soy Lola Cruz.
Dicen que yo provoco admiración
Y me llaman la gloria del salón
Pero yo no he creido eso jamás
Pues todo eso es lisonja
Y nada más.

Todas (Repeat Lola's Text with Subject Change)

Lola
Y en la agitación alegre del vals
Mientras danzo así con algún galán

Todas
Mientras danza así
con algún galán
como una nostalgia
inmensa de amor

Lola
Ay, no sé que siento
en mi corazón
como una nostalgia
inmensa de amor

(Vals)

Lola
Sueño divino de una ilusión
hecha de besos y de pasión
Ven a mi vida que ansiosa está
Del dulce encanto de tu llegar.

Todas
Donde te escondes, sombra sutil
florida y bella como un abril
Ven que se muere mi corazón

Lola
Con la nostalgia de tu pasión

Todas
Eres la reina tú del salón
Como tú, Lola, no existen dos

Todas	*Lola*
Por esa reina	Esos halagos
Ya te llamamos	los agradezco
Lola divina	aunque me llenan
A tí, de amor	ay, de rubor.

Todas
Sueño divino de una ilusión
hecha de besos y de pasión
Ven a mi vida que ansiosa está
del dulce encanto de tu llegar.

Lola
¿Dónde te escondes, sombra sutil
bella y florida como un abril?
Ven que se muere mi corazón.

Todas
Con la nostalgia de tu pasión
De tu amor
Tu amor . . .

Beatriz y Amigas
They come here on horseback,
these girls
that are the flower of the city.

Aurelia y Beatriz
The gentle flower

Girls
Peerless gentle lover,
they tell us
that there is no one better,
but in society,
Lola Cruz is the flower
and she is the queen of love.

Lola
I am Lola Cruz.
They say that I provoke admiration
and they call me the glory of the salon.
But I've never believed that,
because it's all flattery
and nothing more.

Girls (Repeat Lola's Text with Subject Change)

Lola
And in the happy agitation of the waltz
while I dance like this with some gentleman

Girls
While she dances like this
with some gentleman,
with a nostalgia
immense with love

Lola
Oh, I don't know what I feel
in my heart,
like a nostalgia
immense with love.

(Waltz)

Lola
Divine dream of an illusion
made of kisses and of passion,
come into my life, for it is anxious
for the sweet enchantment of your arrival.

Girls
Where do you hide, subtle shade
blooming and beautiful as April?
Come or my heart will die.

Lola
With the nostalgia of your passion

Girls
You are the queen of the salon.
Like you, Lola, two don't exist.

Girls	*Lola*
For that queen	Those praises
we call you	I appreciate
divine Lola	though they fill me,
to you, with love	ay, with embarrassment

Girls
Divine dream of an illusion
made of kisses and of passion,
come into my life, for it is anxious
for the sweet enchantment of your arrival.

Lola
Where do you hide, subtle shadow,
beautiful and blooming as April?
Come, or my heart will die.

Girls
With the nostalgia of your passion
of your love
your love . . .

Fitting her ingenue image, Lola is looking for love, not a man. Like Niña Flor, she approaches her desire for love through a dream metaphor, allowing her to merge the conventions of the ingenue *romanza* with those of the *salida*. Lola's use of imagery that recalls the *romanza* genre occurs in the dance portion of her *salida*, the section most associated with the body and sexuality. The use of a spiritual and romantic text at precisely the moment of the *salida's* greatest physicality mediates the *salida's* potential sensuality and reinforces the ingenue's virtue at a critical moment. This mediation is not only textual, but rhythmic, as well. Where a typical *salida* would move into a *guaracha* or *tango-congo* dance rhythm, Lola bends convention and sings a waltz (Example 5.6).

Ex. 5.6

Thus, a rhythm associated with street culture and Afrocuban percussion is supplanted by one associated with European culture, high society, and string orchestras.

Lola Laments

The *salida* is not the only time that Lola reinterprets the musical norm established by the *mulata*. Later in the zarzuela, after learning the true identity of "Alberto," Lola sings a tragic *romanza* in the tradition of the *mulata fatal*. The extent to which racialized language and metaphors permeate the *romanza* is striking and illustrates that the zarzuela's manipulation of racially coded musical genres was no accident of convention or convenience.

> *La Romanza de Lola Cruz*
> Junto a un amor florecer
> blancas flores vi ayer
> su blancor era de nieve
> trocada en flor
> En soledad vuelve el alma hoy
> a ver blanquear esas flores de ayer
> mas me hablan hoy de nostalgias
> de nostalgias de amor.
>
> Lola Cruz todo ayer fue alegría
> pero hoy ya tu vida toda es dolor
> Olvidar corazón tu quisieras
> mas ansiar y querer olvidar vano es.
> Lola Cruz que ilusión te alumbraba
> pero ya que tiniebla ahora ves
> Oh fatal soñadora de un loco amor
> Lola Cruz se fué tu ilusión.
>
> (hablado) Blancas flores
> que vieron mi dicha,
> ven hoy mi dolor
> Florecieron bajo tiernas promesas
> de un tierno amor
> y hoy no pueden
> sus pétalos blancos
> a mi lado ver,
> al que ayer,
> junto a mí,
> las veía también florecer.

Lola Cruz, qué cruel es la suerte
Tu ilusión ideal
te dejó sin tornar
Negra noche ya tu vida será
pues tu sueño no volverá.

Together with a flowering love,
yesterday I saw white flowers;
their whiteness was of snow
turned into flower.
The soul returns today in loneliness
to see the whitening of yesterday's flowers,
but today they speak to me of nostalgias,
of the nostalgias of love.

Lola Cruz, yesterday everything was joy,
but today your life is all sorrow.
Heart, as much as you would like
to, it is vain to try to forget.
Lola Cruz, what an illusion shone on you,
but you already see it darkening,
oh, cursed dreamer of a crazy love.
Lola Cruz, your illusion has gone.

(spoken) White flowers
that saw my happiness
today see my pain.
They flowered under tender promises
of a tender love,
and today
their white petals can't be seen
at my side,
the ones that yesterday,
together with me,
I also saw blooming.

Lola Cruz, luck is cruel.
Your ideal illusion
left you without return.
Your life will be a black night,
for your dream will not return.

Throughout the zarzuela, the texts of Lola's music have contained images of whiteness. Her first *romanza*, "Los aguinaldos blancos," told the story of an ill-fated love that takes place among the white flowers of Christmastide. Now, torn apart by the discovery of her lover's betrayal,

Lola again sings of whiteness, but of a whiteness lost. "Together with a flowering love / yesterday I saw white flowers / their whiteness was of snow turned into flower / The soul returns today in loneliness / to see the whitening (fading) of yesterday's flowers."

The repeated textual references to whiteness in the introduction highlight a tension between Lola's own racial identification and the non-white characteristics of the music she is singing. This tension is not only expressed through the *romanza's* text, but through its music, as well (Example 5.7). The *habanera* rhythm in the accompaniment is masked by the shape of the vocal line. The long, arching phrases transform and refine the rhythm into one of fluid motion, an effect that is emphasized by the tonal stasis of the line, the two-bar pauses on "ayer" and "flor," and the consistently upward motion of the pitch. Rather than reaching the much-anticipated C, however, the melody spins off downward in a descending motivic sequence from the high A♭ ("En soledad vuelve el alma"). Eight bars later, the melody finally settles on the desired tonic ("amor"), albeit an octave lower, and the key moves to the parallel major.

With the change to the parallel major, the rhythm changes to the slow *tango-congo* so familiar from laments sung by the *mulata* and the *negro trágico*. The phrase "Lola Cruz, todo ayer fue alegría" establishes the melodic theme on which the *tango-congo* portion of the *romanza* is based. Lola's use of the third person to sing about her pain further ties her performance to the convention of the *mulata fatal*; the textual similarity to other tragic *romanzas* sung by *mulata* (or other morally compromised) protagonists is striking, for in each tragic *tango-congo*, the protagonist begins with her name, followed by some fatalistic pronouncement. "María la O, todo se acabó"; "Amalia Batista, tú al amor jugaste"; "María Belén Chacón, no podrás ya cantar"; "Rosa la China, por que soñaste, ave sin nido, rama sin flor."[34]

That Lola undergoes a generic, if not genetic, darkening in her performance of a *tango-congo* is further supported by the images in the sung portion of the text. After she begins the *tango-congo*, there are no further references to whiteness. Instead, Lola begins to speak of herself in darker images. "Lola Cruz, what an illusion shone on you, but you already see it darkening . . . Your life will be a black night because your dream will not come back."[35] Lola's newfound darkness is further emphasized by the placement of the adjective *"negra"* in front of the noun it modifies, breaking with standard grammatical convention. The emphasis on blackness at the end of the *romanza* creates a dialectic symmetry with the introduction and shows that Lola's identity, once couched entirely in white terms, has darkened. Stripped of her constructions of white

Jun-to a u-na a-mor flo-re-cer blan-cas flo-res vi a - yer___

su blan-cor e-ra de nie-ve tro-ca-da en flor___ En so-le-dad vuelve el

al- ma hoy a ver blan-que-ar es-as flo-res de a - yer mas me ha-blan hoy de nos-

-tal- gias___ de nos-tal-gias de a - mor___ Lo-la Cruz to-do a - yer fué a-le-

-gri - a___ pe-ro hoy ya tu vi - da to-da es do-lor___ ol-vi-

feminine identity—innocence, purity, gaiety—Lola can no longer define herself in white terms. To understand her tragedy, Lola self-consciously appropriates racially coded constructions of the Other, finding her new identity in the attributes of the *mulata fatal.*

The Case of Concha Cuesta

It is a common ploy in Lecuona's zarzuelas to contrast two numbers of the same musical genre in order to highlight the difference between the two performances and between the performers themselves. Typically, the desired effect is a comic one, with nonwhite characters bearing the brunt of the joke. The matched duets of Dulce María/Eugenio (love duet) and Felo/Chea (comic duet) in *Julián el gallo* are an example of this type of genre pairing. Successive musical numbers, the two duets, make use of the same poetic imagery, and while the young white lovers' "thirst" references a spiritual love, with the black servants it becomes an unveiled sexual innuendo.[36]

Sánchez Galarraga and Lecuona show their skill at manipulating conventional genres and their meaning by contrasting Lola with her bereaved friend Concha Cuesta, who also sings a *salida.* With Concha's entrance, Sánchez Galarraga and Lecuona confront the same conventions, with very different results.

As already mentioned, Concha was the fiancée of Lola's brother before he was killed in Paris, and she has never recovered from her loss. Concha's desire for vengeance causes her to expose Ricardo's true identity to Lola, and while the libretto does portray her, rather unflatteringly, as an embittered soul, there is also a notably judgmental aspect to her portrayal, as if she were a fallen woman. Perhaps, in some sense, she might have been considered to be so. Eileen J. Suárez Findlay, describing courtship patterns in the Spanish Caribbean, writes that a woman's reputation could be stained by engaging in a formal courtship with a man and then, for whatever reason, having that courtship end. There was a "frequent presumption that women were no longer virgins once they had established a public relationship with a man. Courting, then, for 'respectable' white women was a serious business; it usually meant closing off the possibility of marrying anyone else."[37] By this mode of reasoning, Concha's honor had been in the hands of her betrothed. The circumstances of his death, his involvement in gambling and drink, cast a bad light on Concha herself, for ungentlemanly behavior of her fiancé suggested that she had made a poor choice, a choice that put her own virtue in question, as well.

Concha's *salida*, like Lola's, contains textual markers that point out her upper-class status. She is the "honor and elegant light of the salon."[38] However, Concha's interpretation and performance of *salida* conventions makes it evident that she is not a "good girl" like Lola. First and foremost, her *salida* is not sung with her girlfriends, but with several young men. Her opening line refers directly to her male companions, giving them a *piropo*, or flirtatious compliment. "Concha Cuesta has arrived, with the cream and the flower of the gentlemen that are the glory of the salon." This very subtle transgression of gender roles, the woman giving the compliment, the men modestly deflecting, allows Concha to move into the more masculine, public space normally inhabited by the *mulata*.

La Salida de Concha Cuesta

Victor y Amigos
Concha Cuesta viene aquí
que es hermosa como flor
y es prez y gala deslumbrante
del salón

Victor and Friends
Concha Cuesta comes here,
who is pretty like a flower
and is the honor and elegant light
of the salon.

Concha
Concha Cuesta aquí llegó,
Con la crema y con la flor
de los galanes que son la gloria
del salón

Concha
Concha Cuesta has arrived
with the cream and the flower
of the men who are the glory
of the salon.

Victor
Gracias te da la juventud
pero la flor, Concha,
eres tú

Victor
The youth thank you,
but the flower, Concha,
is you.

Amigos
Eres gala del salón
mas la flor, Concha,
eres tú.

Friends
You're the pride of the salon,
but the flower, Concha,
is you.

Concha
Cuando surjo en el salón
Con mi gracia y con mi *chic*
Todos me dicen:
No se iguala la otra a mí.

Concha
When I appear in the salon
with my grace and my chic,
they all say to me:
there's not another equal to me.

Amigos
Verdad Concha, es así

Friends
Yes, Concha, that's right.

Victor
Cuando vas en el quitrín
por el Prado o por Tacón,
cuantos te miran
quedan presos en tu amor

Victor
When you go in the carriage
down the Prado or to the Tacón,
everyone who looks at you
is held captive in your love.

Amigos	Friends
Es el quitrín tu trono real	The carriage is your royal throne.

Concha	Concha
Pero a pesar de que yo triunfo por doquiera encierro un pesar.	But even though I triumph wherever I want, I carry a weight within me.

Although the text calls up many of the poetic tropes of the classic *mulata* type, an immediate musical connection to the *mulata* persona cannot be found in Concha's opening theme. Concha's entrance does not reference the popular dance rhythms commonly found in *mulatas' salidas*; the accompaniment reassuringly marks the first and third beats, and both Concha and her male friends sing a rather repetitive, circular vocal melody that pedantically fills in the beats without syncopation. Concha's opening music is so square, in fact, that it acts as an aural denial of mixture, a statement for Concha's racial, if not moral, purity.

The music's efforts, however, are undermined by the text. Unlike Lola, Concha makes no effort to mitigate the now-familiar poetic tropes of the *mulata's salida*. Unchaperoned in the company of two young men, Concha is unabashedly self-confident. She sings of her public exploits not within the social sanctity of the salon, but in the street. Although Concha does not travel on foot but in a carriage, as befits her class, she describes the experience in clearly exhibitionist terms, and her words "Todos me dicen: no se iguala la otra a mí" clearly reference the text of María la O's well-known *salida*: "Otra no hay que se igaule a mí." Thus, while Concha may still *sound* like a white girl, her words betray an uncanny familiarity with the *mulata's* rhetoric. Likewise, Victor's words echo the nineteenth-century *guaracha* text quoted in Chapter 3, "Mulata santa te quiero yo / Doy media vuelta y me queda preso / En las varillas del malecó," with the new text exchanging the scene of the low-class public bathhouses for the upper-class, refined mobility of the *quitrín*, or carriage.

Concha's choice of musical expression in the next section further distances her from Lola's cautious manipulation of the *salida* format and allies her more closely with the *mulata* persona. She goes into a "dark section" much like the fatalistic *tango-congo* that ended the *salida* of María la O (Example 5.8). Unlike María la O, however, Concha expresses her fatalism and resignation without syncopation. She sings elided eight-bar phrases over an accompaniment that emphasizes the weaker second and fourth beats, with much the same flavor as a Cole Porter ballad. The melody itself is based on an eighth-note figure on the pitches G–A–G, or its variation, which consistently leads to a sustained pitch. The consistency with which this gesture is used recalls to the listener's memory the "sueño de amor" ("dream of love") theme from the waltz section of Lola's *salida*. The waltz's melody also makes use of an eighth-note figure, this time without the pickup, on the pitches A–G. The gesture likewise leads to a sustained pitch, with a tendency to hover on C. The melodic recollection of Lola's waltz alludes to Concha's lost innocence; her manipulation of Lola's motive shows the decadent transformation of the once gay, hopeful waltz, now changed by the realities of life.

Concha sings, "My laugh is a mask, it already laughs on its own. In the end I will laugh without a laugh of pain." By saying that her laugh, not her face, is a mask, Concha draws a connection between her oral expression and her identity. In this sense, her choice of the mask metaphor is apt, for Concha is engaging in what might be considered musical blackface, taking on the musical persona of a nonwhite character. On the other hand, perhaps it is Concha's whiteness that is the mask, and she is, by nature, a *mulata del rumbo*.

> Rio jovial, pero un dolor
> y un hondo dejo de rencor
> esconden en mí que ya perdí
> mi único anhelo y dulce amor
> Tuve la dicha junto a mí
> soñé con besos de ilusión
> y con el ciego frenesí
> y el loco afán de la pasión.
>
> Es mi risa un antifaz
> ya tan solo así
> siempre mi boca reirá.
> Al fin reiré sin risa de dolor.
> Mi vida es ya un loco
> y constante carnaval,
>
> Rio jovial, pero un dolor
> y un hondo dejo de rencor
> esconden en mí que ya perdí
> mi único anhelo y dulce amor, etc.

> I laugh jovially, but a pain
> and a strong aftertaste of resentment
> hide in me, for I've already lost
> my only desire and sweet love.
> I had happiness next to me.
> I dreamed of kisses of illusion
> and of the blind frenzy
> and the crazy zeal of passion.

My laugh is a mask;
already by itself
my mouth will always laugh.
In the end I will laugh without a laugh of pain.
My life is already a crazy
and constant carnival.

I laugh jovially, but a pain
and a strong taste of resentment
hide in me, for I've already lost
my only desire and sweet love, etc.

Ex. 5.8

While white and upper-class, Concha Cuesta may be considered one of the zarzuela's fallen women. She does not achieve such a reputation merely because of her unladylike desire for vengeance and her lack of concern for hurting Lola, for which she repents, and achieves absolution, at the zarzuela's end. Rather, her performance of music that contrasts so sharply with Lola's exposes Concha's moral slippage and makes the ethical distance between the two women clear.

Fallen Women and the *"Gente de Mal Vivir"*[39]

Concha Cuesta's upper-class status sets her apart from the typical zarzuela bad girl, for the majority of the genre's fallen women are drawn not from Cuba's bourgeoisie but rather from Cuba's poor whites, both urban and rural. Struggling to survive on their own, these lower-class women, like the ingenue, lack the protection of family members. Unprotected and alone, they have slipped through the cracks of society to fall into a state of "mal vivir," literally, "bad living." Such a life is commonly associated with the Havana underworld, an environment filled with theft, violence, and prostitution. "Fallen women" zarzuelas are nearly always set in the Republican period. They represent a contemporary concern—and fascination—with women of the night.

Republican Cuba offered ready material for such fascination, for prostitution flourished in the tumultuous economic and political climate of the 1920s, protected by organized crime and the complicity of powerful Havana politicians and businessmen. Both the government and emerging women's groups attacked the existence of prostitution as a scourge on Cuban society, although there was no consensus on how the problem should be dealt with. Women's groups focused their attention on the problem of illicit sexual relationships and the children they produced. The rehabilitation of women who "by nature" were unable to help themselves was a heated topic of discussion in the women's conferences of 1923 and 1925.[40] While some conservative women attacked prostitution as a moral outrage that weakened the Cuban family, more and more women began to view prostitution "not . . . like a sin but like a social phenomenon or pathology that should be cured instead of condemned."[41]

Rather than focusing on rehabilitation, however, the official reaction was to arrest and imprison sex workers and to stage periodic raids on neighborhoods where prostitution flourished. Focusing their arrests on women, officials largely ignored the role of men as both purveyors and consumers in the prostitution trade.[42] Both the desire to eliminate prostitution and the frustration felt by social critics can be seen in the following excerpt from the *Diario de la Marina*.

An energetic moral campaign, an extensive raid of all the outermost neighborhoods of the city, against the "people of the bad life" that are offending public morals, with detriment to good manners. The moral action will be carried out by the Supernumerary of Public Order, Octavio Cánovas Martínez, who by his personal orders has been realizing a wide investigation that has already produced an enormous list of women that lead unholy lives . . . In Matanzas there have been other raids of this type . . . always resulting in similar cases, in which it is always the most unhappy and defenseless of that class that have been victims, those that start and foment vice at the upper levels, the madams of brothels and well-known pimps, have continued to enjoy the greatest impunity in the population.[43]

Prostitution and the Theater

The lives of prostitutes and their relationship with their pimps was a frequent subject of the popular theater produced in the 1910s and early 1920s. The tone of these works was generally comic and frequently vulgar. *La busca-bulla*,[44] a musical comedy produced for the notorious Molino Rojo theater in 1916 with music by a young Gonzalo Roig, shows the length to which prostitution comedy could go. The comedy also illustrates that the theme of redemption, which would be so important in zarzuela representations of fallen women, was already making an appearance on the popular stage.

The action takes place in a tenement (*solar*). The piece opens with two of the building's "professional" residents engaging in a catfight with Rosa, the protagonist.[45] The two prostitutes, Caridad and Trina, are trying to kick Rosa out of the *solar* because she has attracted the attention of José Luis, a handsome mechanic that the two women have their eyes on. The fight is broken up by Don Jaime, who is the landlord of the *solar*. One suspects that Don Jaime may profit from activities that occur on his property, for he is constantly lapsing into French, a snide allusion to the French control of Havana's prostitution racket.

Rosa herself is never openly depicted as being a prostitute, although her lines certainly betray a familiarity with the picaresque. Rather, she is portrayed as an unfortunate who wishes for a better life. In her *romanza* she dreams of finding a respectable and well-dressed man and sings of leaving behind her ironing to wear white and promenade with a man in "yellow pants." Rosa is secretly in love with José Luis but has refused his romantic overtures, determined not to get involved with any man without a firm commitment. Rosa's dreams of a better life never materialize, however. Upon learning that neighborhood thugs plan to ambush José Luis at a *rumba* party (a jab at the perceived threat posed by black Cubans, their music, and their gatherings), Rosa goes to the *rumba* to warn him of the ambush. In his defense, she ends up stabbing one of José Luis's attackers to death. As she faces prison rather than the prospect of a church wedding, Rosa's dreams of a reformed life through hard work and arduous selection of romantic partners are thus dashed.

La busca-bulla is unusual in that such unhappy endings are rare for the popular theater of its time. Both its tragic ending and its representation of character types foreshadow later zarzuela plots. Lecuona and Sánchez Galarraga's *Rosa la China*, which will be discussed later in this chapter, bears an especially uncanny similarity to the plot of *La busca-bulla*. However, the 1916 comedy also contains burlesque elements that distinguish it from later zarzuelas and that firmly place it in the realm of male-oriented popular theater. One such scene occurs between the two prostitutes and their pimps "Merengue" and "Mongo," played by comic actors Alberto Garrido and Juan Gilberto. The scene's dialogue shows the extent to which Havana's popular theater could descend into pornography.

> *Caridad:* No vengan Uds. ahora a salar . . .
>   todavía no hemos hecho ni un kilo . . .
> *Trina:* La noche está de perro . . .
> *Merengue:* Mira, Caridad, dejate de obras y venga la harina . . .
> *Mongo:* Lo mismo te digo . . .
> *Caridad:* La harina! Para mí que Uds. se creen que todavía estamos en
>   tiempo de la esclavitud
> *Merengue:* Caridad! Que me caliento y te rompo la cara . . .
> *Trina:* Tu! Eres muy poco hombre.
> *Mongo:* Ud. se calla . . .
> *Trina:* No me da la gana.
> *Merengue:* Déjala . . .
>   Ya en el cuarto nos la pagarán . . .
>   Venga la harina . . .
> *Caridad:* Ya te he dicho que no tengo.
> *Merengue:* No tienes . . .
>   Y los chinos que entraron en la posada con Uds.?
> *Trina:* Nos dieron mico
> *Merengue:* Mira, Trina . . . Nosotros vimos perfectamente cuando tú,
>   al salir, le distes el dinero a esa . . .
>   Ella lo tiene . . .
> *Caridad:* Regístrame si quieres
> *Mongo:* Regístrala, Merengue.

Merengue: A ver . . . En el seno, no tiene nada ni en las medias
    tampoco . . . ni en los zapatos . . .
    O está escondido la harina en alguna parte o nosotros hemos visto
    visiones . . .
Mongo: Parece mentira que seas chulo veterano. Yo sé donde esta
    desprestigiada tiene el dinero. Dile que abra las piernas y brinque.
Caridad: Yo no soy chiva para brincar!
Merengue: Ya caigo! A ver . . . brinque!
Caridad: Pero—Merengue . . .
Trina: Deja a la pobre mujer . . .
Merengue: Que brinque le he dicho! O de lo contrario le empujo un
    leñazo.
Caridad: Ya que te empeñas . . . Vaya. (Brinca estrechando las piernas)
Merengue: Así no. Abra las piernas.
Trina: Este hombre está loco.
Mongo: Ud. se calla . . .
Merengue: Mujer! Abre las piernas más y brinca porque si no por
    mí madre que te hago picadillo. (la hace brincar con las piernas
    abiertas cayendole de entre las faldas varias monedas de un peso.)
Mongo: Ya te lo decía yo.
Merengue: Esta es una sinvergüenza. Oye! y que los pesos esos huelen
    a bacalao!

Caridad: Don't come here to bother us . . .
    We still haven't made a cent . . .
Trina: This night is for the dogs . . .
Merengue: Look, Caridad, stop fooling around and bring the dough
Mongo: I say the same to you . . .
Caridad: The dough! It seems to me that you believe that we are still
    in the time of slavery
Merengue: Caridad! I'm getting angry and I'll break your face . . .
Trina: You! You're not much of a man.
Mongo: You shut up . . .
Trina: I don't feel like it.
Merengue: Leave her . . .
    They'll pay for it later in the room . . .
    Hand over the dough . . .
Caridad: I already told you that I don't have it
Merengue: You don't have it . . . And the Chinese men that went into
    the room with you?
Trina: They didn't give us anything
Merengue: Look, Trina . . . We saw perfectly when you, on leaving,
    gave the money to her . . .
    She has it . . .
Caridad: Search me if you want

Mongo: Search her, Merengue

Merengue: Let's see . . . in her breasts, she has nothing or in her
    stockings . . . or in her shoes . . .
    Either the dough's hidden somewhere else or we've been seeing
    things . . .

Mongo: It seems a lie that you're a veteran pimp. I know where this
    disgrace has the money. Tell her to open her legs and jump.

Caridad: I'm not a goat to jump!

Merengue: That's enough! Now . . . jump!

Caridad: But—Merengue . . .

Trina: Leave the poor woman . . .

Merengue: I told you to jump! Or I'll club you if you don't.

Caridad: Well, since you insist . . . Fine. (She jumps with her legs
    together)

Merengue: Not like that. Open your legs.

Trina: This man is crazy.

Mongo: You shut up . . .

Merengue: Woman! Open your legs more and jump, because if you
    don't, on my mother, I'll turn you into chopped meat. (He makes
    her jump with her legs open, and several peso coins fall out.)

Mongo: I told you so.

Merengue: She's shameless. Hey! And these pesos smell like fish!

Rosa la China

Such tawdry scenes would not appear in the more family-oriented librettos of zarzuelas, although prostitution would remain a theme of interest. *Rosa la China*, by Sánchez Galarraga and Lecuona, is the best known of these prostitution zarzuelas. The work, as previously mentioned, bears a strong resemblance to *La busca-bulla* and suggests that the representation of the fallen woman character had become as fixed as that of the ingenue or the *mulata*. The zarzuela's *solar*-dwelling protagonist is also named Rosa and, like her picaresque predecessor, she falls in love with a young mechanic whose name is José. The story similarly ends in tragedy when, after dreaming of a better life, Rosa kills to protect her man.

As with the protagonist of *La busca-bulla*, Sánchez Galarraga's libretto never says directly that Rosa is a prostitute, although the description of the cast that appears at the beginning of the libretto describes her marriage to the unpleasant bully Dulzura in the following manner: "[Dulzura] is the husband of Rosa la China, he lives off of her, because he makes her live a life that Rosa detests, in a word: he has put Rosa in the "gay life," in order to exploit her."[46] He appears to be, in short, a pimp.[47]

Rosa's earnings, however gained, appear to be enough to humbly support both herself and her husband. The couple shares a small room in one of Havana's infamous *solares*, and their goings-on (and everyone else's) are the subject of acutely accurate courtyard gossip. The tenor hero, José, also rents a room in the *solar*. A mechanic by trade, José represents the virtues of hard work and moral living, and his serious self-discipline contrasts sharply with the behavior of other residents of the *solar*. Doña Tana and Doña Calixta play the lottery and gossip. The girl Greta idly dreams of becoming a star in "Joligú"—Hollywood—and the other young men who live in the building are amiable loiterers.

The zarzuela's protagonist has little doubt about her moral peril, and her desire to reform her life provides the impetus for the entire plot. It is Rosa's search for redemption, rather than mere romantic interest, that causes events to unfold in the zarzuela, and it is that desire for self-betterment that sets the piece off from a typical love-triangle drama. Thus, José is much more than Rosa's love interest. José is both an ideal and a means to an end; he is the agent that will convert Rosa into a virtuous, morally upright woman; he represents the path to redemption.

Rosa and José provide an odd reversal of gender roles. While Rosa lives and works in the public sphere, José represents an almost Victorian womanhood. He is the keeper of the moral flame, and, most important, the imagined caretaker of that unattainable piece of domestic bliss that Rosa dreams of. Rosa's husband, Dulzura, is also portrayed as outside the norms of male gender roles. He does not appear to work, but remains closeted in their room most of the time and lives off the money that Rosa brings home. Both Dulzura and José remain tangential to the zarzuela's action; while they may threaten, they do not act. The character who acts is Rosa. She openly declares her love to José. She stabs and kills Dulzura, to prevent José from confronting Dulzura himself, thus protecting not only José's life but his moral purity. When José finds Rosa on the bridge and realizes that she has just killed Dulzura, he asks her why she did it. "Por salvarte, José mio," she responds.

The morality and redemption sought by Rosa prove to be illusive. On stabbing Dulzura, Rosa's watch is dragged off by the knife and falls with the body into the water under the bridge. The watch is engraved with a dedication from her husband, making it easy for authorities to identify Rosa as the murderer. Although Rosa and José briefly elude the police by obscuring themselves in the chaotic frenzy of a Carnival parade passing through the streets of Havana's Chinatown, capture is imminent. The zarzuela closes as police lead Rosa off to jail, where, she promises, she will eventually emerge from her cell a reformed woman.

Rosa's Music

In a move that is fitting of Rosa's class status and, perhaps, her role as a "public" woman, she is introduced to the audience through the performance of a *salida*. Little more than an introduction followed by a sprightly setting of a *guaracha*-inspired text, what is most remarkable about Rosa's *salida* is its brevity. Indeed, Rosa's *salida* seems a compositional exercise in getting through a convention as quickly as possible. After a fourteen-bar introduction by Rosa's friends Paciente and Preciosillo, Rosa begins the *guaracha*, which she maintains without any variations of tempo or style.[48] In its lack of musical diversity, the piece barely fulfills the formal requirements of the *salida* genre. Furthermore, unlike the tragic *salidas* examined in Chapter 3, Rosa's *salida* does not foreshadow the zarzuela's latent tragedy. There is no unveiling of the soul, no exploration of Rosa's identity or her desires, or of the circumstances that will lead to her downfall. In fact, apart from the *salida*'s brevity, its description of Rosa as a brunette rather than a *mulata*,[49] and the fact that she is accompanied only by two young male neighbors rather than by a large public crowd, Rosa's *salida* is rather unremarkable.

Although the *salida* does not lay the groundwork for the ensuing drama, the following musical number, a duet between Rosa and José, does. The duet reveals the zarzuela's central conflict, not as a foreboding prognostication, but rather as a violent and passionate confrontation. The dramatic placement of Rosa's confrontation with José, so close to the zarzuela's beginning, sets *Rosa la China* apart from other operatic models of ill-fated love affairs between respectable men and women of low reputation. *Carmen* and *La Traviata*, for example,[50] showcase couples who come together at the works' beginnings and, throwing caution to the wind, ignore the differences of class and vocation that doom their relation from the start. This plot formula is also found in the race-based plots of zarzuelas like *María la O* and *Amalia Batista*, where, as with the operatic examples, the works' dramatic logic depends on a growing tension resulting from the disparity in the lovers' social situations and each results in a climactic confrontation: Carmen's rejection of José, Alfredo tossing the money in Violetta's face, the violent duet between María and Fernando, Julio's rejection of Amalia. *Rosa la China* is not a drama about the results of class/race disparity, however. It is a drama about moral transgression and the struggle for redemption.

Sung at the zarzuela's outset, Rosa and José's duet fulfills, in many ways, much of the function of the *"mulata fatal"* section that concluded the *salidas* of María la O and Concha Cuesta. While Rosa's own *salida* offered us not a glimmer of her personal character, the words she sings to herself at the opening of the duet provide the fatalistic rhetoric that we have come to expect and that the *salida* so disappointingly failed to deliver. Alone in her room, unseen by the audience, Rosa begins to sing, and José, in his own room, echoes her (Example 5.9).

> "La que nace para el mal
> cae en la boca de la cárcel
> por huír del lupanar."
> Qué bien dice esa canción
> que yo a todas hora
> llevo clavada en el corazón
> "La que nace para el mal . . ."

> "She who is born to be bad
> will fall into the mouth of prison
> to escape from the brothel."
> How well that song says it,
> the one that I at all times
> carry nailed to my heart.
> "She who is born to be bad . . ."

Musically, Rosa's melody could not contrast more sharply with the *guaracha* that preceded it. Unlike the music in her *salida*, the melody that opens the duet has an almost tuneless quality that is exaggerated by the rapid manner in which Rosa moves through the octave, the indirect motion of the vocal line, and her tendency to return to the pitch where she began and start the gesture all over again. The tune's stability is further undermined by the fact that Rosa begins all of her gestures on the second beat, regardless of whether the length of that gesture has changed. Yet while the melody is not particularly tuneful, its rambling nature and jutting agogic accents ably communicate the text, and the ear is drawn to the words "mal" and "lupanar," each sung on an extended high note. As the couple is drawn "by some mysterious force"[51] out of their rooms and toward each other, José concludes this introductory section with a final echo of "La que nace para el mal," firmly establishing the zarzuela's central conflict.

Once they are together, José refuses to even look at Rosa, expressing disgust for her lifestyle. She beseeches him to listen to her and begins an *agitato* section that rises in pitch and intensity. As her pleading becomes ever more frantic, harmonic tension builds as the key modulates up a third to F on the words "no es Rosa la China ninguna maldá" and finally

to A as she concludes, "Yo soy solamente una desgracia" (Example 5.10).
José maintains Rosa's A major frenzy and spits back with a cruel sarcasm
that recalls Alfredo's actions in *La Traviata,* "Desgracia te llamas, yo
no sé porque, si vives rodando por los cabaret y cuando alguien necio te
invita a pasear en buenos billetes te haces pagar."

Ex. 5.10

Rosa:
José, escúchame por Dios!
¿Por qúe no me oyes siquiera una vez?
¿Por qué me desprecies con esa altivez?
No es Rosa la China ninguna malvá
Yo soy solamente una desgracia!

José:
Desgraciá te llamas, yo no sé porqué,
si vives rodando por los cabaret
y cuando algun necio te invita a pasear
en buenos billetes te haces pagar.

Rosa:
Oh, Dios mio que vergüenza tan horrible para mí!

Rosa:
José, listen to me for God's sake!
Why won't you listen to me just once?
Why do you despise me so?
Rosa la China is not evil.
I'm only a disgrace!

José:
A disgrace you call yourself, I don't know why,
if you're always around the cabarets,
and when some idiot invites you out,
you make him pay you in big bills.

Rosa:
Oh, my God, what a horrible shame for me!

José's words cut Rosa to the quick, and while she may not collapse on stage like a consumptive Violetta, her vocal line does the melodic equivalent. Rosa's anguished exclamation "Oh Dios mio que vergüenza tan horrible para mí," outlines a descending diminished seven chord that suggests the D tonality of the opening. Rosa ends by sustaining the seventh of the chord on the word "mí," a move that makes her precariously vulnerable and, as the orchestra arpeggiates the A seventh chord lower and lower, she seems even more isolated and alone.

The couple begin to speak over the orchestra, which remains stuck in a harmonic stasis, having moved on from the V/D cadence with which Rosa cried out to an even tenser vii°7/D. Just as the orchestra's harmonic tension shows no sign of abating, Rosa and José are at an impasse. Rosa begs, "José, no me ofendas por la gloria de tu madre—José, don't offend me, for the glory of your mother." Rosa's invocation of José's mother has no effect. "Qué culpa tengo yo si decir lo que tu haces sea una ofensa para tí?"—"What fault is it of mine if what you do offends you?" he snipes back.

At impasse they might be, but it is at this moment that the orchestra finally resolves the tension, beginning a soft *son/bolero* rhythm in which, both the musical autograph and the libretto specify, the sound of the *bongo* drum should be heard, very softly (Example 5.11). Here, Rosa sings the same syncopated rhythm as in the *guaracha* portion of her *salida*, but it could not be interpreted more differently. Where once the rhythmic pattern had been sprightly and coy, at the new, slower tempo and over the anticipated bass and percussion patterns it becomes sultry, seductive, and, for José, irresistible. He is lost. With her new rhetorical and musical power, in just one stanza Rosa convinces José to at least reconsider her moral state, and he confesses immediately that he is in love with her.

Rosa:	*Rosa:*
Ay, quien pudiera morirse,	Ay, if one could die
por no sufrir lo que	to not have to suffer what I am
sufro	suffering,
Rosa la China no es mala	Rosa la China is not bad.
por mi madre te lo juro	On my mother I swear it.

José:	*José:*
Si no dijeras mentiras	If you were not lying
ni engañaran tus palabras	nor your words deceiving,
yo por tu amor te daría	I, for your love, would give you
la vida entera y el alma.	life itself and my soul.

Rosa:	*Rosa:*
No estás jugando.	You're not joking.

José:	*José:*
No sé mentir.	I don't know how to lie.

Rosa:	*Rosa:*
¿Tú me querías?	You would love me?

José:	*José:*
¡Con frenesí!	With passion!

Together:	*Together:*
Ah!	Ah!

Rosa:	*Rosa:*
Oye José de mi alma	Listen, José of my soul,
lo que yo supe esconder	to what I knew to hide
mientras vivía en silencio	while I lived in silence
soñando con tu querer.	dreaming of your love.

Rosa, growing confident in José's feelings, reveals that she, too, has a confession to make. "*Dime*—tell me," urges José expectantly on the dominant (Example 5.12). Her confession, now comfortably back in the D major of her *salida,* is one of the most revealing moments in the zarzuela.

Yo viví soñando en un cuartito	I lived dreaming of a little room,
un cuartito que luz bañara,	a little room bathed in light,
donde yo pudiera ser buena	where I could be good
y donde me amparara	and where I'd be protected by
tu amor que siempre ansié.	your love that I always yearned for.

Ex. 5.12

Here, Rosa draws a connection between her moral failures and her lack of domestic space. What she dreams of, in short, is "a room of her own."[52] Her assertion that the *cuartico* would allow her to be "good" suggests that it is not the personal privacy that the room she seeks offers (although that certainly would have been a welcome respite from the openness of the *solar*) but a kind of protected, *feminine,* domestic privacy, the same kind of privacy that protects the virtue of Lola Cruz. Rosa desires to leave behind her public street persona, her "business," even her free mobility, in order to become enclosed and protected.

Rosa's dream of a light-filled "*cuartico*" is also a rhetorical strategy making the cell a symbol that then frames the entire zarzuela. At the end of the work, what was foreshadowed will come to pass, and Rosa will go to jail for the murder of Dulzura. While her cell may not be "bathed in light," there is the promise that she will emerge a reformed woman.

The formulaic redemption tragedy of *Rosa la China* and the early Rosa seen in *La busca-bulla* is played out again and again. The story of Charo, a lady of the evening in Lecuona's *La de Jesús María* (*The Woman from Jesús María*),[53] is a similar tale of thwarted redemption. The zarzuela takes place in the Jesús María district, exploiting the poverty of one of the poorest areas of Havana. Like Rosa, Charo falls in love with a virtuous mechanic, a revolutionary named Andrés.[54] Like Rosa, Charo also vows to change her life, but she is discarded with contempt by Andrés, who fans the flames of his moral judgment with leftist zeal.

> *Charo:*
> Te juro que te ayudaré en tu causa.
>
> *Andrés:*
> No, esas joyas que luces,
> son el producto del sudor del pueblo.
>
> *Charo:*
> Las arrojaré al mar.
>
> *Andrés:*
> Mejor a los pobres.
> Pero . . . adios.

> *Charo:*
> I swear that I will help you in your cause.
>
> *Andrés:*
> No, those jewels you wear
> are the product of the sweat of the people.
>
> *Charo:*
> I'll throw them to the sea.
>
> *Andrés:*
> Better to the poor.
> But . . . good-bye.

Undaunted by Andrés's criticism, Charo gives up her flamboyant lifestyle and gets a job working as a seamstress. However, she learns that he has married someone else, and, furious, she goes to his house to kill him. She is unable to complete the act, however, for after arriving at the house, she looks in the window and sees Andrés's wife cooking and caring for their little daughter. It is the power of the domestic space, and the stability and respectability that it represents, that stops Charo's vengeance. Seeing the infant daughter of Andrés, so well cared for within protected domesticity, Charo realizes that the child has the possibility for a life that she could never have. Rather than cause the child to suffer a life without a father and a probable fate similar to her own, Charo kills herself instead.[55]

Zarzuelas such as *Rosa la China* and *La de Jesús María* inform audiences that a fallen woman can never truly be restored to grace. In this sense they are nothing new, merely additions to a long stream of "bad girls pay" dramas. However, at a time when Cuba's economy was being squeezed to the breaking point, the urban bourgeoisie began to see the economic barriers separating them from the working classes slip away. Zarzuelas that focused on prostitution and poverty established the moral superiority of theater audiences over the underclass.

Women characters who engaged in "honest" wage labor fared little better on the zarzuela stage. Working (white) women were a frequent source of ridicule, and it was precisely their sexual virtue that was suspect. In Gonzalo Roig's *La hija del sol* (1933), the shopgirls sing a suggestive chorus, "Guaracha-fox de las modistas," in which they discuss the hard work of selling lingerie all day. The shopgirls protest their virtue and denounce the low opinion men in the street have of them.

> Pobre pepillito que por bonito
> quieres de mí triunfar.
> A la dependiente
> que hace la venta
> quieres amor comprar.
> Esa mercancía que tú me pides
> no puedo darla
> Compra chucherías
> porque en mis días
> no venderé placer

> Poor fashionable boy, who, so handsome,
> wants to triumph over me.
> From the clerk
> who makes the sale
> you want to buy love.
> That merchandise that you ask of me
> I can't give.
> Buy some trifles,
> because in my days
> I will not sell pleasure.

It should be noted that librettists Agustín Rodríguez and Aurelio Riancho pointedly omit any mention of what the shopgirls do by night![56]

The representation of lower- and working-class characters in the zarzu-ela is much more than a venture into exoticism. While audiences may have experienced a type of exotic thrill upon entering a *solar,* or ob-serving the lives of characters from neighborhoods in which they never set foot, such social tourism is only tangential to the central pleasure relayed by such works—an unwavering defense, and even glorification, of class privilege. Class-based redemption tragedies demonstrate lower-class women's lack of fitness for upward mobility by using representa-tions of the fallen woman to suggest an innate moral deficiency. While it might be argued that in these zarzuelas there do exist morally upright characters who come from the lower classes, such characters are consis-tently men. These plots reinforced conventional wisdom that the lower classes could not be saved if women, the nurturers of the children, were not morally sound.

6 Ambivalent Heroes and Sensual Peasants: The Galán and the Criollo

> "You people are inferior, dedicating yourselves in a morbid manner to just one woman. Just like the Poet I say: past girls with their cups empty, in them we put a little love. The hours passed, the days flew . . . Bring me new cups, with new liqueur."
>
> —Leon, in *El olvido de la canción*[1]

The character types discussed so far in this book—the *mulata*, the black man, the ingenue, and the fallen women—all represent, in one way or another, the fantasies of patriarchy. These characters' inability to supersede their social limitations is the foundation of the zarzuela's tragic ethos, an ethos that is performed not only by characters' struggles to improve their situation or to realize their desires, but also by their expressive restriction to particular musical genres.

Throughout the zarzuela repertoire, white male protagonists inhabit an expressive world as constrained by social constructions of identity as that inhabited by the *mulata*, ingenue, or *negrito*. Similar to the portrayal of white women, class and social status are as important as race in the representation of white men on the zarzuela stage. Two major types of white men appear in the repertoire. The first type, known as the *galán*, is urban, wealthy, and educated. The second type, the *criollo*, is rural, uneducated, and generally poor.

The *Galán*

If the black man, the *mulata,* and even the white ingenue are all characters with limited options, the character of the young white male, or *galán,* represents the other side of the equation of power. More than any other character in the zarzuela, the *galán* stands for the Cuban patriarchal establishment, for he is white, educated, and upper-class. In zarzuela plots that take place in the nineteenth century, the *galán* is frequently the owner of slaves; in the twentieth century, he is the employer of (black) house servants. Frequently, these characters are university students studying law or medicine.[2]

As the character that best represents the status quo, we might expect the *galán* to be portrayed in a way that positively supports ideals of masculine control and patriarchal power. Ironically, while zarzuela composers and librettists never actively undercut white male privilege, they often present the *galán* in a light that can at best be called ambivalent, if not outright negative. The zarzuela's white male protagonists are a motley group of two-faced, lazy, spoiled womanizers. Leonardo, Fernando, and Julio, from *Cecilia Valdés, María la O,* and *Amalia Batista,* respectively, are notorious womanizers who maintain a *mulata* mistress while courting the white woman they wish to marry. Niño Alberto, in *El cafetal,* is spoiled, jealous, and insipid. *Lola Cruz's* Ricardo Chacón conceals his identity as the murderer of Lola's brother in order to woo her. The soldier protagonist in Rodrigo Prats's *Soledad* seduces a young country girl, takes her to Havana, and then abandons her. Narciso, the appropriately named *galán* from *La carrera del amor,* is a good-for-nothing living off his family's money who has begun five or six university majors and has yet to complete one of them. So imperfect are the majority of these personalities, that, while they might have been able to win the affection of the female protagonist on the stage, it is difficult to believe that they would have caused female theatergoers to swoon, or even to support them in their conquest.[3]

The role of the *galán* is invariably sung by a tenor. This showcasing of the tenor voice is a significant factor differentiating Cuban and Spanish zarzuelas, as Spanish zarzuelas demonstrate a preference for baritone protagonists. In Spanish zarzuelas, such baritone roles have an extended upper range, so that the protagonist's high notes carry extra weight, producing an exciting and more "manly" sound.[4] The lyric tenor casting of Cuban zarzuela protagonists, by contrast, lends an entirely different character to his musical expression. In a clearly operatic gesture, the *galán's* voice distinguishes him from other character types who communicate in more popular styles, and especially from nonwhite male characters, who typically are baritones. Vocal range thus carries associations with race and class, with the lower, baritone roles reserved for Afrocubans and high tenor roles for elite white men. While the Cuban zarzuela interprets the "bodily" sound of the baritone voice as yet another attribute of the black male character's sensual physicality, the *galán* is portrayed as a creature of artifice. His manners, habits, and rational knowledge are the products of learning, not of nature. The *galán*'s use of the detached, unnatural sound of the tenor voice is a reflection of his mannered education, and at the same time, his vocal artifice is also suggestive of a lack of engagement and emotional commitment.

Unlike the other character types discussed here, the *galán* is not strongly identified with any particular musical genre. Rather, the *galán* has a palette of generic possibilities that include student songs, love serenades, and duets. Although it may appear that he has a wider array of options, the *galán*'s music has a fairly limited range of thematic and expressive possibilities, singing either of his youthful prowess or his desire for amorous union. The solo numbers sung by white male characters are rarely dramatic musical soliloquies. Hardly ever is the *galán* heard questioning or regretting his decisions, or lamenting life's consequences.[5]

The Student Song

When the *galán* is given a solo number, it is most often of a light, topical nature, with a chorus at least physically, and usually vocally, present. Most often these pieces are based on upbeat march or *habanera* rhythms. The most popular version of this genre is the university student song, which reveals the *galán* as a charming rogue at the same time that it alludes to his social status as a student of law or medicine. Student songs draw from the Spanish tradition of *tunas estudiantiles*, musical groups made up of male students who wander the streets singing songs of love and country.[6] Although the *galán* and his companions lack the guitars and capes of organized *tuna* ensembles, student songs are always recognized as performances within the dramatic action onstage.

An example of the *canción estudiantil*, or "student song," is the "March of the Students and Song to Havana" from *Cecilia Valdés*. Here, Leonardo and a few of his classmates are accompanied by a chorus of young women who are clearly unimpressed with the example set by the students. The piece begins with a choral introduction leading into a vigorous march, and its text makes conflict between the genders its first priority.

El estudiante de la capital
pasea por La Habana en su quitrín.
Y es su ideal
engañar con palabritas a las niñas mas bonitas
que le miran con buen fin; ay, qué pillín!

The student from the capital
roams through Havana in his carriage.
And it's his ideal
to use little words to deceive the prettiest girls
who look upon him with interest; what a scamp!

The woman's chorus quickly denounces the students' claim that they can be so easily seduced.

Por tener noviecito estudiante,
ni una pena, chica, yo daré.
Pues nunca nos habla de casar,
mucha miel gasta él
y el tunante del amor nos habla solo por hablar.

To have a student boyfriend,
girl, I wouldn't give anything.
Because he never talks to us of marriage,
he wastes a lot of honey,and the rascal's talk of love is only talk.

The women's rhetoric against the students quickly heats up. "I know well that there's no passion in his heart / I don't want the love of a seducer who follows after me / With great frenzy and trickery he'll say sweet things to you without passion in his heart / and I don't want the love of a student, no!" In the face of such criticism, Leonardo simply changes the subject to one about which the group cannot disagree. He launches into a tribute to the city of Havana. In praising the beauty of the city, Leonardo's singing is full of macho bravura. Held-out high notes combine with aggressive, minor-key *habanera* syncopations in the orchestra, leading to a military band–style march. The female chorus, their complaints forgotten, joins Leonardo and the students in praising the spirit of their city.

In some zarzuelas, the university song is converted into a mere song of youth, most famously seen in Julio's song "Juventud" ("Youth") from *Amalia Batista*.[7] The same lighthearted protagonist/chorus format is also sometimes used to express not youthful vigor, but youthful love. This is the case with Niño Alberto's "Canción de la Flor" ("Song of the Flower")

from *El cafetal* (Example 6.1). In the piece, Alberto appears with a group
of slave women, who offer him a flower on his arrival to the coffee plantation. Their text, which follows here, is notable in its exaggerated use
of *bozal* slave speech. Alberto, in turn, makes use of the play on words
and sings a tribute to Niña Flor.

Negritas
> Niño viene acá
> Coge eta fló
> Ha nasío para uté
> Rico e su oló
> Niño coge ya eta fló
> der cafetá

Niño Alberto
> Venid con la flor gentil
> que me dais y esa flor
> he de besar

Negritas
> Boy, come here.
> Take this flower.
> It was born for you.
> Its scent is lovely.
> Boy take this flower
> from the coffee plantation.

Niño Alberto
> Come with the gentle flower
> that you give me, that flower
> I have to kiss.

In this piece, composer and librettist play an intricate semiotic game that informs the audience about several important aspects of Niño Alberto's character. It is notable that rather than introducing himself onstage, Alberto is introduced by the slave women in a manner similar to the way the *mulata* is introduced by the chorus in the *salida* genre. Not only do the slave women introduce Alberto to the audience, but they also introduce the melodic material that Alberto will adopt when he begins to sing. This early equation of Alberto with black women and their modes of musical expression is significant, for it foreshadows the zarzuela's later pairing of Alberto and the slave Africa, with whom he will destroy Lázaro.

Just as Alberto is marked with a kind of musical Otherness through his association with and imitation of the slave women, the language he uses also distances him from the Cuban audiences who would come to see him onstage. From his very first word, "venid," Alberto uses the Spanish *vosotros* conjugation to refer to the slave women, rather than the *ustedes* form more commonly used in Cuba. Just as black characters are set apart by their *bozal* patois, Alberto's speech marks him as an outsider, more Spanish than *criollo*, more foreign than Cuban.

Alberto maintains the singsong melodic quality established by the *negrita* chorus, moving rapidly through a surprising array of harmonies before arriving on the dominant on the word "besar." Two bars later, however, he independently changes course and begins a serenade (Example 6.2). The repeated rocking bass brings the harmonic rhythm to a crawl after the frenzied chord changes in Alberto's introduction, and the accompaniment is reduced to a heartbeat-like pulse. The melody, which previously had moved in two bar units, now spins out eight-bar phrases.

Ex. 6.2

Flor, rosa del abril	Flor, rose of April,
fuego de pasión	fire of passion,
roja como un vivo corazón.	red like a living heart.
Es gloria floreal	It is flowering glory
que ama el colibrí	that the hummingbird loves
cuando se abre el sol.	when the sun opens.
Ven que mi corazón ansia	Come, for my heart is anxious
saber	to know
cuando el dulce amor	when sweet love
llegará hasta él.	will arrive.
Sed tengo de encontrar	I am thirsty to find
esa tierna rosa del abril	that tender rose of April,
triunfo del vergel	the triumph of the garden.

The serenade's text borrows poetic tropes established in the ingenue's *romanza,* such as hummingbirds, gardens, and the metaphoric distancing of love. Alberto's choice to communicate in an established feminine discourse suggests that he is prone to behave in other ways that were associated with the feminine, particularly emotionality and irrational behavior, a supposition that is borne out during the course of the zarzuela.

Immediately after Alberto finishes his serenade, the *negritas* interrupt, breaking the tranquil mood (Example 6.3). Shifting to the relative minor of E minor, the women sing a *tango-congo* that converts the phrase structure from Alberto's languid eight-bar crooning to one repeated eight-bar phrase that has been broken up into choppy rhythmic cells of only a bar and a half.

Negritas
> Ahora agüete mi niño
> como baila la negrita
> eta negrita que tiene
> cuando baila jiribilla

Niño Alberto
> Flor ardiente de abril,
> oh Flor
> siempre serás flor de pasión

Negritas
> Now, look, my boy,
> how the black girl dances.
> That black girl's got it
> when she dances with movement.

Niño Alberto
> Burning flower of April,
> oh, Flor,
> you will always be the flower of passion.

The interruption is jarring, not only because it abruptly ends Alberto's lyricism, but also because it falls completely out of context. The *negritas* have gone from being Alberto's welcoming party to being mere bodies on display. Yet it is this display of dancing black bodies that arouses Alberto to his most passionate moment in the entire piece, *"siempre serás flor de pasión."* Alberto recapitulates his serenade, but it is no longer the bland, pretty tune it once was. Another side of Alberto's personality has been exposed, a passionate, emotional, physical side, and it will be that side

Ex. 6.3

of Alberto's personality, here mirrored by the black women, that will bring about *El cafetal*'s tragic conclusion.

The Duet

The duet is the most prominent of the musical genres that the *galán* performs. Even in zarzuelas where he is given no solo repertoire, the *galán* invariably sings a duet with the female protagonist. Such duets are most frequently romantic, but they may also be angry confrontations. It is often in duets between the *galán* and a female protagonist that the zarzuela's strongest statements on gender relations can be found.

In *El cafetal*, Alberto sings two duets, one of love, the other of vengeance. The first duet, between Alberto and Flor, shows remarkably unequal participation between the two characters. Befitting her passive role as a virtuous ingenue, Flor's involvement is limited. Alberto enters first, and his words, "my heart is yours, you are my only love," carry with them his previous contact with the erotically dancing *negritas*, for he begins with a highly syncopated rhythm that Flor, rightly, takes to be a bit fresh. "*¡Calla por favor!*"—"Be quiet, please!" she protests. Alberto calms himself down to straight eighth notes and begins to sing to her. Still, he cannot quite control himself and, as the text moves from talking about Flor as his "*niña ideal*—ideal girl" to mentioning her physical characteristics, Alberto begins to lose control. The tempo accelerates to an allegro scherzando, and the melody begins to move in large leaps. The meter changes from 6/8 to 12/8 to 3/4 in rapid succession. Regaining control and finishing his proposal in a steady duple meter, Alberto finally succeeds in winning Flor over. Only then, and only after allowing Alberto to set the melody and the tempo, does Flor sing of her willingness to love him. The duet closes with Alberto serenading Flor with the theme from the "Canción de la Flor," giving a sense of unity for the entire opening scene.[8]

An even clearer example of the prescribed gender balance between the *galán* and his ingenue can be found in the duet between Leonardo and Isabel in *Cecilia Valdés*. An ingenue in the model of Bizet's Micaela, Isabel is an exemplar of bourgeois female sensibility. She is portrayed throughout the zarzuela as a young woman fulfilling her duty, both as a daughter and as a fiancée. Thus, it is not surprising that the duet between Leonardo and Isabel reinforces a relationship in which Leonardo clearly holds the reins.

The duet begins with a two-phrase introduction in which Leonardo proclaims that Isabel brings him tranquility and Isabel responds that he is her happiness. The introduction makes it clear that this duet is not a seduction scene, but the reinforcement of an already established relationship. What is most surprising about the interaction between the couple is that after their brief eight-bar exchange in the introduction, almost the entire duet is sung in parallel thirds (Example 6.4). Such parallel textures are unusual in a zarzuela love duet; it is much more common for the couple to sing alternating phrases, with parallel singing occurring only at the duet's climax. Thus, the emphasis on the parallel texture is notable and is made even more so because of the incessant consistency with which it is applied. Furthermore, throughout the piece, Isabel does not sing the top line, as is typical for the *tiple,* or soprano, in zarzuela duets where parallel voicing is used. Rather, Isabel fulfills her role as Leonardo's complement.

She sings the lower third, always supporting Leonardo's melody. Only at the very end does the complementary texture briefly shift, with Isabel embroidering Leonardo's sustained high notes at the duet's close.

While love duets between the *galán* and the ingenue illustrate the proper nature of courtship, confrontational—or rage—duets (the other type of duet in which the *galán* regularly participates) demonstrate the results of subverted social norms. These "dysfunction" duets are often paired with love duets between the ingénue and the *galán,* the contrast between the two serving as a lesson on how relationships should be conducted. Thus, Leonardo's love duet with Isabel is paired with his "Gran Duo" with Cecilia, a duet that, rather than showing an idealized and harmonious relationship between the genders, highlights romantic conflict. The "Gran Duo" begins much the same as the duet with Isabel, with Leonardo singing sweet nothings to Cecilia and expecting her to respond in kind. Cecilia, however, is having none of it. "I knew that one day your lips would win my disdain and my bitterness," she proclaims.

"Gran Duo" Between Leonardo and Cecilia
(Introductory Section)

Leonardo:
Yo sabía vida mía
que esa puerta la abriría
la firmeza de mi amor.

Leonardo:
I knew, my life
that the strength of my love
would open that door.

Cecilia:
Yo sabía que algún día
con su labia vencería
mi dispecho y mi rencor.

Cecilia:
I knew that one day
with your eloquence you would win
my disdain and my bitterness.

Leonardo:
¿Rencor?

Leonardo:
Bitterness?

Cecilia:
¡Rencor!

Cecilia:
Bitterness!

Leonardo:
No hables así
pues sólo amor siento
por tí
tan sólo a tí
quiero en la vida
no viviría lejos de tí.
El corazón hacia tí
me guía
y el corazón
no sabe mentir

Leonardo:
Don't speak like that,
for I only feel love
for you.
I only want you
in my life.
I couldn't live far from you.
My heart guides me
to you,
and my heart
doesn't know how to lie.

The duet, set up at the beginning to follow a standard love duet formula, veers widely off course. The two characters sing overlapping musical lines, with Cecilia accusing Leonardo of infidelity and Leonardo proclaiming his innocence. As the duet nears its close, Leonardo attempts to calm Cecilia: "You will always have my love and my help. The world can hate us but it will never be able to separate us."[9] Leonardo's manipulative lie causes Cecilia to lose her confidence and her resolve. "Tell me you don't love her. Swear to me you won't see her. Swear to me that you only belong to your Cecilia Valdés"[10] (Example 6.5). Cecilia's music shows the depth of her self-doubt, for these pleading words are voiced with the opening melody from her *salida*. A melody that had previously represented her self-confidence and autonomous identity is now nothing more than a weak plea that Leonardo see some worth in her.

As mentioned previously, Alberto also sings a rage duet in *El cafetal*.[11] The duet is sung with Africa, a slave woman who is in love with Lázaro. Embittered because Lázaro has ceased to love her, Africa, overcome with jealousy, informs Alberto that Lázaro is in love with Flor. Africa knows

Ex. 6.5

full well what the result of her treason will be, that it can end only in Lázaro's destruction, but her rage has consumed her, and it will soon take over Alberto, as well.

The duet is marked as unstable from the outset. The accompaniment features an insistent eighth-note pattern that converts the compound meter into a driving machine. It is Africa, not Alberto, who impels the duet. She instigates each musical phrase, and Alberto, while singing alongside—but not *with* her—repeats her motives (Example 6.6).

> *Africa:*
> Quiero que sufra él
>
> *Alberto:*
> No he visto ofensa igual
>
> *Africa:*
> Que sufra como sufro yo
>
> *Alberto:*
> Tamaña ofensa
> he de castigar
> pasión indigna
>
> *Africa:*
> Como sufro yo

> *Africa:*
> I want him to suffer
>
> *Alberto:*
> I've never seen such offense
>
> *Africa:*
> that he may suffer as I suffer
>
> *Alberto:*
> a huge offense
> I must punish
> despicable passion
>
> *Africa:*
> as I suffer

In his first statement, "No he visto ofensa igual," Alberto not only repeats Africa's motivic gesture, but also her harmonic progression, moving from ii to V. However, Alberto quickly masters Africa's style and assumes control of it. He grounds his second entrance firmly in the tonic,

Ex. 6.6

the first time that F major has been stated clearly, in root position, since the duet began. While his melodic gesture begins by mirroring Africa, in the next bar he opens up the tessitura to a high G, rather than the E established by Africa. Alberto's melodic expansion allows him to break the four-bar phrase pattern established by Africa, and his control over the direction and shape of the phrase displaces Africa from her former leadership role. Her following entrance, "como sufro yo," is nothing more than a supportive echo—Africa cannot meet Alberto's raised stakes, nor has she anything new to add textually.

Although they develop their melodic material to different degrees and sing different texts, the jagged melody of Africa and Alberto's jealousy *sounds* the same, showing an expressive empathy between the two characters. Since the beginning of the zarzuela, there has been a connection drawn between Alberto and black female characters and the unstable passions that they are made to represent. In the next section of the duet, that affinity is further stressed; now Africa and Alberto's vocal lines not only resemble each other, but they are joined in parallel harmonies (Example 6.7).

> *Alberto:*
> Y no podré olvidar
> esa mancha vil.
> Yo he de castigar
> al esclavo infiel traidor.
>
> *Africa:*
> Quiero que sufra,
> quiero que llore,
> quiero que muera
> y que padezca como yo.
>
> ———————————
>
> *Alberto:*
> And I will never be able to forget
> that vile stain.
> I have to punish
> the faithless traitorous slave.
>
> *Africa:*
> I want him to suffer.
> I want him to cry.
> I want him to die
> And to suffer like me.

Ex. 6.7

Just as the influence of the *negritas* seemed to incite Alberto to greater passion in the "Canción de la Flor," singing in parallel with Africa brings him to new heights of ire. As he sings with Africa of the "traitorous infidel," Alberto's vocal line climbs to a high C, the agogic climax of the entire piece. The passionate fury of Africa and Alberto's parallel thirds leads to the last section of the duet, where, for the first time, Alberto introduces a melodic motive (Example 6.8).

> Quiero que padezca el infiel
> y sabré castigar con la muerte
> al esclavo implacable

> I want the infidel to suffer,
> and I will know to punish
> the implacable slave with death.

Ex. 6.8

With his death threat, Alberto switches to a highly syncopated rhythm. The change in rhythm is exaggerated by the "maestoso" marking in the orchestra and by the orchestra's octave doubling of the voice. The frantic quality of the vocal line and the orchestral emphasis draw attention to Alberto's words and the specific threat that he has made. Alberto's introduction of this new syncopated material, brought into even sharper relief by the orchestral doubling, suggests that in giving over to his jealousy, Alberto is behaving musically in a manner associated with nonwhite characters. His outburst connects him especially with vengeful *mulatas* like *María la O*, who plot to avenge their loss to the syncopated beat of the *tango-congo*.

In the bars that follow, Alberto and Africa watch together as Lázaro appears carrying flowers meant as a farewell gift to leave at Flor's window. Alberto takes out his pistol and fires, claiming that Lázaro was going to violate his fiancé. Lázaro is left on the ground, gasping out his dying words. Throughout this entire sequence, the orchestra has played a continuous, gentle *son/tango-congo* rhythm. The rhythm thus becomes the soundtrack for repeating tragedy; it is both the premonition of Lázaro's death and the accompaniment to it, and its continual presence renders the result less tragic. The music, so conventional, so *expected*, distances the listener from the horror of the murder itself. The predictability of the musical dramaturgy leads the listener to accept that such endings are conventional and expected, as well. Thus defined by formula and convention, everyone is just *"cumpliendo su papel"*—playing his part.

The Rural *Criollo*

Not all white male protagonists are university-educated *galanes* who are primarily identified through their relationships with women. The second major type of white men showcased by the zarzuela are rural white peasants who, while they may also be involved in a love affair (or more than one), are primarily identified with the Cuban countryside itself. These characters belong to a traditional character type that has its roots in the early nineteenth-century popular theater of Francisco Covarrubias: the *criollo*.[12]

Written for urban audiences, zarzuelas that portray Cuban country life emphasize a deep connection to the land and its riches. Part of this was surely meant to invoke the nostalgia of cement-trapped *habaneros* for palm trees and rolling green hills. Zarzuela librettos impart an almost spiritual quality to Cubans who work the land, and one suspects that the nationalistic homage to the peasant might also be an allusion to the threat posed by the rapid investment of foreign companies in Cuba's natural resources. However, at the same time that the zarzuela librettos spin this nationalist web, they also portray rural people as primitive, instinctual, and incapable of making their own decisions.

One such rural zarzuela is Lecuona and Sánchez Galarraga's *Julián el gallo*. The work actually has two important roles for white men. The first, Eugenio, is a typical tenor *galán*. In love with Dulce María, he woos her with a series of love duets but is denied the object of his desire when Julián, Dulce María's guardian, jealously refuses to consent to the match. Julián, in contrast, is a true incarnation of the *criollo* type. The owner of a coconut plantation, Julián is married to a maternal figure named Generosa, who has recently given birth to their child. Throughout the zarzuela, Generosa represents motherhood, fertility, and the maternal aspect of nation building, while Julián's character relates pride in Cuba, its land, and its productivity.

The role of Julián is one of the few lyric roles in the Cuban zarzuela repertoire that is written for a high baritone. In Cuba, as mentioned earlier, male leads are usually lyric tenor roles. Thus, the aggressive, "manly" edge of Julián's high notes is notable within the Cuban repertoire and a stark contrast against the dreamy quality of lyric tenors like Eugenio. In many ways, *Julián el gallo* serves as the Cuban response to Arrieta's extremely popular zarzuela *Los gavilanes*. Both zarzuelas feature free-spirited middle-aged baritone protagonists who attempt to impede the union of young lovers out of a misguided desire for the ingenue.[13]

The case of Julián is fascinating, for while his vocal style is more "manly," his actions—and his music—portray him in a way that crosses the boundaries of gender identity. Julián is portrayed as an overtly sexual being who cannot control his own behavior, and he has strong spiritual and emotional ties to the earth that are reinforced with constant animist metaphors: rooster, bull, coconut grove, palm tree, et cetera. At the beginning of the zarzuela, an old woman named Bibiana relates to the village priest, Padre Chucho, that Julián is honest, simple, and hospitable and takes care of his family, but that he is too much of a womanizer. The Father responds that Julián is instinct made flesh and adds, *"Modo de ser de hombre de campo, de campo criollo, donde todo convida a la sensualidad!"* ("That's what it is to be a man from the country, from the Cuban countryside, where everything invites sensuality!") The strategy of relating Julián with the land and sensuality is a potent one, as these are images that were most often seen as feminine and were strongly associated in popular and literary discourse with the *mulata* stereotype.

Julián's connection with the *mulata* is a musical as well as a textual one, for he is one of the few, if not the only, male characters to sing a true *salida*. While zarzuela composers typically used the *salida* to reference the sexuality and waywardness of the *mulata,* in Julián's singing of the genre the creators reach beyond the obvious reference to Julián's sexuality to a second layer of signification, calling up the *mulata*'s representational connection to the land and to Cuban nationalism.

The *Criollo* Gone Wild: *El Clarín*

El Clarín, by Gonzalo Roig and Agustín Rodríguez, plays on similar animist images to those found in *Julián el gallo.* The hero of the story, known by his nickname El Clarín, is a peasant in the Cuban country-side, and the zarzuela continues the theme previously seen in *Julián el gallo* of connecting the figure of the peasant with Cuban nationalism. In establishing this earthy, rooted sense of Cuban identity, Roig turns to the agenda promoted by composer and social critic Eduardo Sánchez de Fuentes, which praised the Spanish-derived peasant music genres such as the *décima* or *"punto guajiro"*[14] as the authentic musical expression of Cuban nationalism. So it is that we first meet El Clarín singing a styl-ized version of a *punto* (Example 6.9). In this opening number, Roig and Rodríguez deftly link the protagonist with the Cuban homeland, nature, bodily experience (his voice), and folk music. He sings, "in the remote confines of the Cuban countryside, in the mountains and the savanna, El Clarín sings his song."[15] He then sings a cappella in the tremulous melis-matic style of Spanish folk music, "the bird sings, the river sings, and the palm sings as well [repeat], and if you love me, my dear, then my heart will sing happily."[16] The orchestral accompaniment enters only between El Clarín's vocal phrases, in the same way that instruments such as the *laúd* or the *trés* would play between verses of a folk *décima.*

El Clarín's voice is the most prominent aspect of his character, a prominence alluded to even in the zarzuela's title, for his (nick)name, "El Clarín," means "The Bugle." In his love duet with Azucena, he reveals the importance of his vocal expression in *décima* form. He sings,

No traigo ricos presentes	I don't bring fine presents
guardados en áureas cajas	packaged in lovely boxes,
ni puedo brindarte alhajas	nor can I give to you
de piedras resplandecientes.	jewels of precious stones.
Yo traigo cosas mejores,	I bring better things.
traigo flores,	I bring flowers,
traigo pájaros cantores	I bring singing birds
ocultos en mi garganta	hidden in my throat,
y cada pájaro canta	and each bird sings
la canción de mis amores.	the song of my love.

Ex. 6.9

Easily the most difficult tenor role in the zarzuela repertory, the role of El Clarín not only requires the singer to negotiate a tessitura that frequently soars above the staff, but also to produce both full-lyric, sustained singing and melismatic coloratura. Additionally, the role demands tremendous stamina, as its use of the chorus is minimal and the secondary characters' musical participation is also minimal. The entire score is a string of difficult *romanzas* and duets, and the soprano role of Azucena, El Clarín's love interest, is equally difficult.[17]

In the characters of the *galán* and the *criollo*, the zarzuela offers no heroes, no strength, no sense of security, and—most surprisingly—little romantic fantasy. The juvenile singers of university songs, the gamblers, womanizers, and self-entitled heirs of the zarzuela are not the stuff of fantasy, but an exaggerated reflection of reality. Of all the character types found on the zarzuela stage, the *galán* and the *criollo* are the only characters who consistently create problems faced in everyday life—infidelity, deceitfulness, lack of familial responsibility. Zarzuela plots' tolerance, and ultimately their sanction, of this bad behavior reflects contemporary social attitudes toward marriage and the discouragement of divorce. In short, while the zarzuela exposes the white male protagonist's failings, it also teaches the necessity of having to learn to live with him.

However shallow the *galán* or *criollo* might be, however unfaithful, spoiled, or jealous, he is also inevitable. The zarzuela does not offer romantic fantasy. In the end, the young ingenue will not escape a future of domestic tediousness. She will end up married to an unfeeling patriarch who, the audience already knows, will spend his evenings in the arms of another woman. The zarzuela offers no dashing and honorable rogues to rescue the ingenue (or the *mulata*, for that matter) from a life of acceptable predictability. The white boy gets the girl in the end, and in the end she goes willingly to her fate, with all the pomp and circumstance of opera.

In spite of the zarzuela's ties to nineteenth-century romanticism, its musical conservatism, its trite and often shallow plots, the message sent by composers and librettists in their presentation of white men is one of modernist realism. Zarzuela audiences could revel in the open sensuality of the stage *mulata* or allow themselves to be seduced by the sultry baritone voice and beautiful melody of the ill-fated black man. In the end, however, marriage with the bland and philandering *galán* was inevitable. The zarzuela's creators neither romanticize the outcome nor provide escapist alternatives. Of all the repeating tropes found on the zarzuela stage, marriage between the upper-class white protagonists is the one nearly inescapable certainty, a realist constant that is neither lamented nor celebrated—and is never challenged.

Epilogue: El Teatro Se Va: The Cuban Zarzuela and Its Destiny

The production of new zarzuelas dropped off sharply in the 1940s, owing to both the economic hardships brought on by World War II and the increasing popularity of cinematic entertainment. In spite of the lack of new works produced during the period, zarzuela performances continued in the late 1940s and throughout the decade of the 1950s. These performances showcased the fraction of the original zarzuela output that gradually became enshrined as classics, including *Cecilia Valdés, María la O, Rosa la China, Amalia Batista, El cafetal,* and *María Belén Chacón.* Throughout the turbulent years of the Batista dictatorship, these zarzuelas were continually revived as part of a repertoire that included Spanish zarzuelas such as *Luisa Fernanda, La leyenda del beso, La verbena de la paloma, Los gavilanes,* and *Molinos del viento* and the Spanish translation of Franz Lehar's popular operetta *La viuda alegre (The Merry Widow).*

The zarzuela's successful transition from a premiere-based genre to a revival phenomenon was perhaps due to the enormous pool of talent available in Cuba in the decade and a half before the revolution. Some of the important names during this period had been part of zarzuela history since the beginning, among them Miguel de Grandy, Maruja González, Caridad Suarez, and Pedrito Fernández. Other talents, including Marta Pérez, Rosa Elena Miró, Esther Borja, Sarita Escarpenter, Gladys Puig,

Mimi Cal, Francisco Naya, Pedro Gómez, and Rosita Fornés, added new life—and new glamour—to the genre. Ernesto Lecuona, Gonzalo Roig, and Rodrigo Prats actively conducted their works during this period, often augmenting existing works with new *romanzas* or duets.

Technology had an inevitable effect on the establishment of a zarzuela canon. As recording technology became increasingly available, many popular numbers from zarzuelas were recorded on compilation albums. It would not be until 1948, however, when Gonzalo Roig directed the first recording of *Cecilia Valdés*, that full-length zarzuelas began to be recorded. The cast of the 1948 recording included Marta Pérez in the title role, along with Francisco Naya and Puerto Rican singers Aida Pujol and Ruth Fernández. The recording itself was the brainchild of Fernando Montilla, whose Puerto Rico–based record label, Montilla, recorded not only that early recording of *Cecilia Valdés*, but subsequent recordings of other zarzuelas, as well. In 1955, *Rosa la China, El cafetal,* and *María la O* were recorded by Montilla in Spain under the baton of Félix Guerrero. The Montilla recordings of *Rosa la China* and *El cafetal* continue to be the only available recordings and are still marketed today, while other versions of *Cecilia Valdés* and *María la O* were recorded after the revolution, both in Cuba and abroad.[1]

The recordings were widely distributed in Cuba and had a significant impact on the zarzuela's international exposure, as well. Roig's personal correspondence shows a number of letters from interested conductors and directors who had heard the recording of Cecilia Valdés and wanted to learn where they could obtain a musical score.[2] In 1950, television service was established in Cuba, the second country in the world after the United States to establish such service. Beginning in 1952, Cuban television began presenting full-length zarzuelas, with the different channels competing to present the best productions with the most impressive singing talents.[3]

Although new zarzuelas were no longer being regularly produced in Cuba, popular works were gaining increasing international exposure. In 1943, Ernesto Lecuona brought singer Esther Borja to New York, where she debuted in Steinway Hall to great acclaim. So popular was her performance of zarzuela excerpts and other light lyric music that impresario Sigmund Romberg offered her a contract on the spot and Borja spent the next five years performing for Romberg in America's most important theaters.[4] After successful tours in Mexico, with more than fifty performances, *María la O* and *El cafetal* premiered in Spain in 1953.[5] Lecuona's lengthy tenures in Spain in the 1950s and in the years following the Cuban Revolution increased his music's international exposure. Some of the most important holdings of Lecuona's music reside in Spain, a result of his close ties with that country.[6]

The 1959 Revolution had the unintended consequence of increasing the zarzuela's international exposure. The zarzuela's bourgeois status rendered it suspect under the emerging cultural program of the new government. Discomfort over the government's nationalization of theaters, the recording industry, and music publishing, as well as concern over stars' ability to set their own wages, control copyright, or accumulate property, led a large number of performers and musicians to leave the island.[7] The departure of Ernesto Lecuona and some of the zarzuela's most significant stars, especially Miguel de Grandy and Marta Pérez, was a significant blow to lyric theater performance in the 1960s and 1970s. Once abroad, many performers established new theatrical companies in their adoptive countries. Perhaps the most significant of these early companies was Pro-Arte Grateli, a Miami-based zarzuela troupe founded by Marta Pérez, Miguel de Grandy, and Pili de la Rosa. The fledgling company was soon filled with much of the same talent that had graced the stages of Havana; along with Pérez and de Grandy appeared Julita Muñoz, Zoraida Marrero, Armondo Pico, Blanca Varela, José Le Matt, and Francisco Naya.[8]

The exodus of so many of the zarzuela's most important talents has also had its effect on the historical record. Singers abandoning Cuba for political reasons were not allowed to carry much with them. Many scores and librettos were left behind and often thrown out by the people who relocated into abandoned apartments. Even the belongings of a personality as important as Ernesto Lecuona were not safe. Living in Spain, Lecuona had left his personal collection of scores, playbills, recordings, and photographs in the home of his mother. Upon her death, new families moved into the apartment, and a few days later his former assistant Pedrito Fernández received a frantic call reporting that Lecuona's personal belongings were being thrown out of the window into the street. While some of the materials were ultimately salvaged, it is impossible to know how much was lost.[9]

Ideological issues aside, economic and material constraints made the high cost of producing lyric theater impractical. As a result of both cultural upheaval and limited resources, there was little incentive to preserve much of the material record of zarzuela performance from the 1950s. Recordings from radio performances and television productions have largely disappeared. Many tapes were simply destroyed in the years immediately after the revolution, in an effort to purge the country of a perceived bourgeois influence, or to erase the artistic record of musicians who had left the country. Often the motivation was more pragmatic than ideological, however; state-run television and radio stations erased much of the filmed and recorded record in order to reuse the scarce magnetic tape.[10]

After its initial ambivalence regarding the zarzuela's role in a revolutionary society, the Cuban state began to have a positive impact on lyric theater. In 1962, the Teatro Lírico Nacional de Cuba was founded, and the government organized competitions to locate the best talent to fill its ranks.[11] The organization's mission was to produce zarzuelas and operas not only for the island's urban population, but for rural workers, as well. Productions traveled to the farthest corners of the island, and free performances were held for cane cutters, fishermen, and road builders as part of the revolution's educational project. After initial clashes with the government,[12] Gonzalo Roig became increasingly involved in postrevolutionary cultural production, earning himself the moniker "the father of Cuban music," by the time of his death in 1970. The state recording industry, EGREM, produced a recording of *Cecilia Valdés*, with soprano Alina Sánchez replacing Marta Pérez, for island listeners, as the quintessential voice of the popular character.

The Zarzuela Today

There is little disagreement that the zarzuela today is in crisis. Fully staged zarzuelas are rarely produced in Cuba now, largely because of the severity of the current economic situation. Costly to produce, zarzuela performance is not a huge draw for the foreign tourist, whose hard currency is much courted on all levels of the Cuban tourist economy. Visiting tourists' desires for performances of salsa, Tropicana-style floor shows, and anything related to recent cinematic blockbusters, such as Wim Wender's *Buena Vista Social Club* (2000) or Benito Zambrano's account of Havana's alternative popular music scene, *Habana Blues* (2005), put the performance of genres such as the zarzuela on the bottom of the state-run entertainment industry's priority list. The performances that do take place tend to borrow as much glitz as possible from the cabaret entertainment popular with tourists.

In contemporary zarzuela performances, the omission of the libretto is an increasingly frequent phenomenon. The language of zarzuela librettos often seems dated to contemporary audiences, leading to efforts to rewrite the zarzuela's spoken dialogue to make it sound more modern or more compatible with contemporary social values. Such experiments have had varying degrees of success. While Miguel de Grandy's 1962 libretto of *Cecilia Valdés* is regarded by many as an improvement to the original, changes made to *Amalia Batista, El cafetal,* and *Rosa la China* have been much less well received.[13]

Another change in zarzuela performance since the revolution has been the inclusion of performances by Afrocuban folkloric ensembles, performing music and dance not included in the original musical score or libretto. The insertion of folkloric Afrocuban production numbers has been increasingly popular since the 1980s. The success of Cuba's plan to nationalize its folklore, exemplified by the 1962 founding of the Conjunto Folklórico Nacional, provided theater directors with a corps of dancers and musicians that could participate in zarzuela production. By presenting a more authentic portrayal of Afrocuban cultural forms, it was hoped that the original racial caricature found in many zarzuelas could be shed in favor of a genre that served as a symbol of national pride, both white and black.[14] Program notes from the 1990 Festival de la Zarzuela state that the decision to add extensive folkloric material to *El cafetal* was based on "an attempt to analyze passions and situations with a certain ethical focus, bringing a social validity to the genre that will help to destroy the false image of the Cuban zarzuela as a socially intransigent genre."[15]

The merging of folkloric culture with the convention of the musical production number is not without its dangers. There is a risk that the new musical material could merely become an update of the blackface *comparsas* of the 1930s, an "authentic" addition of exotic local color.[16] This type of cultural exploitation has already taken hold within Cuba's tourist industry, which regularly uses kitsched-up, folkloric floor shows and cabaret acts to attract foreign tourists—and their hard currency.

Whether or not lyric theater continues to be a vital part of Cuban identity remains to be seen. It is clear, however, that the zarzuela participated in a vibrant conversation regarding the formation of social identity among Cuba's upper classes, even as it contributed to and enhanced the construction of that identity. The key to further understanding the zarzuela's role in such a construction lies in the present. Much work remains to be done. Issues of source studies need to be addressed. Scores and recordings are disappearing from archives, because of the ravages of time and climate, as well as the ravages of economic necessity—theft. The role of lyric theater and how it changed under the Batista dictatorship is not well understood. Such a study will require Cuban cultural institutions to end their silence on the history of the Batista years and make such information more available to scholars, both Cuban and foreign, and ultimately, the cooperation of Cubans on both sides of the Florida Straits will be required. In many ways, the documentation of the zarzuela's history is a race against time, not only because of the degradation of material resources, but also because surviving singers and audience members of the zarzuela's golden age are becoming more and more scarce.

In the 1920s, 1930s, and 1940s, zarzuela scores were invested with an intricate musical hermeneutics of race, class, and gender that audiences were well positioned to understand. I would suggest that many of the same meanings associated with a particular rhythm, poetic trope, or melodic style are still part of Cuban music today. Implicit to this study is the suggestion that the same type of musical and textual analyses might be applied to contemporary musical forms such as *timba, nueva trova,* and rap and that an awareness of musical meaning in the past might help us to better understand the musical culture of the present.

APPENDIX

Chronologies of Lyric Works by Ernesto Lecuona, Gonzalo Roig, and Rodrigo Prats

Ernesto Lecuona

1919

Mar. 9.   Teatro Martí. *Domingo de piñata.* (*Revista.*) Libretto by Mario Vitoria.

May 16.   Teatro Martí. *El recluta del amor.* (*Cuento lírico.*) Libretto by Gustavo Sánchez Galarraga.

Jun. 13.   Teatro Martí. *La caravana.* (Zarzuela in one act and three scenes.) Libretto by Gustavo Sánchez Galarraga and Valeriano Ruíz París.

Aug. 15.   Teatro Martí. *La liga de los naciones.* (*Revista.*) Libretto by Mario Vitorio.

Aug. 22.   Teatro Martí. *El triunfo de Virulilla.* (*Juguete lírico.*) Libretto by Rafael Medina and Mario Vitorio. Music in collaboration with Manuel Banueco.

Dec. 31.   Teatro Martí. *El 20 . . . el de la suerte.* (*Revista.*) Libretto by Joaquín González Pastor.

1920

Feb. 2.   Teatro Martí. *El portafolio del amor.* (*Revista.*) Libretto by J. G. Pastor.

1922

Mar. 10.   Teatro Martí. *Diabluras y fantasías.* (*Revista.*) Libretto by Carlos Primelles.

1924

Sept. 26.   Teatro Ruzafa (Valencia, Spain). *Al caer la nieve.* (*Opereta.*) Libretto by M. Marino and Antonio Paso.

Oct. 23.   Teatro Martín (Madrid, Spain). *Levántate y anda.* (*Revista.*) Libretto by Francisco de Torres and Aurelio Varela.

1925

Mar. 18.   Teatro Apolo (Madrid, Spain). *Radiomanía.* (*Revista.*) Libretto by Mario Vitorio.

1926

s.f.   Teatro Esclava de Madrid, Spain. (*Revista.*) *La revista sin trajes.* Libretto by Tomás Borrás.

1927

Sept. 29.   Teatro Regina. Inauguration of the theater with *Niña Rita o La Habana en 1830.* (*Sainete lírico* in one act and five scenes.) Libretto by Aurelio Riancho and Antonio Castells. Music in collaboration with Eliseo Grenet.

Sept. 29.   Teatro Regina. *La tierra de Venus.* (*Revista.*) Libretto by Carlos Primelles.

Oct. 6.   Teatro Regina. *La carrera del amor.* (*Pasatiempo cómico lírico bailable.*) Libretto by Carlos Prime lles. Music in collaboration with Eliseo Grenet.

Oct. 14.   Teatro Regina. *Es mucha Habana.* (*Revista.*) Libretto by José López Ruíz.

Oct. 27.   Teatro Regina. *Chauffeur al Regina.* (*Revista.*) Libretto by Aurelio Riancho. Music in collaboration with Eliseo Grenet.

Dec. 8.   Teatro Regina. *La liga de las señoras.* (*Revista.*) Libretto by Castells.

Dec. 13.   Teatro Pavón (Madrid, Spain). *Rosalina.* (*Opereta.*) Libretto by Antonio Paso.

Dec. 21.   Teatro Regina. *Cuadros nacionales.* (*Revista.*) Libretto by Antonio Castells and Aurelio Riancho. Music in collaboration with Eliseo Grenet.

1928

Nov. 3.   Teatro Martí. *La despalilladora.* (*Sainete.*) Libretto by Gustavo Sánchez Galarraga.

Nov. 8.   Teatro Martí. Cuban premiere of *Rosalina.*

1929

Feb. 15.   Teatro Regina. *Alma de raza.* (*Revista fantástica.*) Libretto by Gustavo Sánchez Galarraga and Elías Ferrer.

Mar. 1.   Teatro Regina. *El cafetal.* (Zarzuela in one act and three scenes.) Libretto by Gustavo Sánchez Galarraga.

Apr. 18.   Teatro Regina. *El batey.* (Zarzuela in one act and five scenes.) Libretto by Gustavo Sánchez Galarraga.

May 15.   Teatro Auditorium. *La flor del sitio.* (Zarzuela in one act and three scenes.) Libretto by Gustavo Sánchez Galarraga.

Jul. 12.   Teatro Payret. *El amor del guarachero.* (Zarzuela in one act and three scenes.) Libretto by Gustavo Sánchez Galarraga.

Jul. 16.   Teatro Payret. *La mujer de nadie.* (Zarzuela in one act and four scenes.) Libretto by Gustavo Sánchez Galarraga.

1930

Mar. 1.   Teatro Payret. *María la O.* [Zarzuela in one act and five
              scenes.] Libretto by Gustavo Sánchez Galarraga.
March 7.   Teatro Payret. *El maizal.* [Zarzuela in one act and three
              scenes.] Libretto by Gustavo Sánchez Galarraga.
Mar. 15.   Teatro Payret. *El calesero.* [Zarzuela in one act and three
              scenes.] Libretto by Gustavo Sánchez Galarraga.

1932

March 11.   Teatro Principal de la Comedia. *La guaracha musulmana.*
              [*Opereta bufa.*] Libretto by Gustavo Sánchez Galarraga.
May 27.   Teatro Martí. *Rosa la China.* [*Sainete lírico.*] Libretto Gustavo
              Sánchez Galarraga.

1934

May 22.   Teatro Felipe Currillo Puerto [Veracruz, Mexico]. *Julián el
              gallo.* [Zarzuela in one act and six scenes.] Libretto by Gustavo
              Sánchez Galarraga.
June 20.   Teatro Auditorium. Cuban premiere of *Julián el gallo.*
Nov. 8.   Teatro Principal de la Comedia. *El torrente.* [Zarzuela in one
              act and five scenes.] Libretto by Victor Reyes.

1935

Sept. 13.   Teatro Auditorium. *Lola Cruz.* [*Opereta revista.*] Posthumous
              libretto by Gustavo Sánchez Galarraga.
Oct. 26.   Teatro Principal de la Comedia. *La revista sin trajes.* [*Revista.*]
              Libretto by Álvaro Suárez.

1937

Apr. 28.   Teatro Auditorium. Premiere of *Sor Inés.* [Comedia lírica.]
              Libretto by Antonio Castells and Francisco Meluzá Otero.

1941

Oct. 3.   Teatro Principal de la Comedia. *La de Jesús María.* [*Sainete
              lírico.*] Libretto by Agustín Rodríguez.

1942

March 27.   Teatro Principal de la Comedia. *Cuando la Habana era inglesa.*
              [*Opereta.*] Libretto by Antonio Castells and Francisco Meluzá
              Otero.
Apr. 25.   Teatro Principal de la Comedia. *La cubanita.* [*Comedia
              musical.*] Libretto by Agustín Rodríguez.

1944

Mar. 10.   Teatro Nacional. *La plaza de la catedral.* (*Comedia lírica.*)
            Libretto by Francisco Meluzá Otero.

1946

Dec. 20.   Teatro Nacional. *Mujeres.* (*Opereta.*) Libretto by Agustín
            Rodríguez.
Mar. 22.   *Serenata del caribe.* (*Revista musical.*)
May 16.   Teatro América. *Un viaje a la luna.* (*Fantasía lírica.*)

1957

            Teatro Cómico (Barcelona). The Tropicana Show opens.
            July Lecuona works on his last work, *El sombrero de Yarey,*
            without premiering it.

Gonzalo Roig

1913

            El Baratillero. (Zarzuela.)

1914

            Las ventajas del fotingo. (Zarzuela.)
            Las musas americanas. (*Revista musical.*)

1915

            La lámpara maravillosa o Danza del opio. (Zarzuela.)

1916

            A la Habana me voy. (Zarzuela.)
            Teatro Molino Rojo. *La busca-bulla.* (*Sainete.*)
            Teatro Molino Rojo. *La revista del aire.* (*Revista.*)
            La paz mundial. (*Revista musical.*)
            Molde de suegras. (*Juguete cómico.*)

1917

            Teatro Molino Rojo. Havana premiere of *Las ventajas del
            fotingo.* (Zarzuela.)
            Teatro Molino Rojo. *La lámpara maravillosa o Danza del opio.*
            (Zarzuela.)
            El rey del descaro o Cosas del país. (Zarzuela.)
            El servicio militar obligatorio. (Zarzuela.)
            Teatro Molino Rojo. *El número fatal.* (Zarzuela.)

1919

> *El rey de la barra.* (Zarzuela.)

1924

> *Amor vencedor.* (Zarzuela.)

1931

Aug. 7.	Teatro Martí. *Los madugadores.* (Zarzuela.)
Aug. 10.	Teatro Martí. *La mujer fatal.* (Zarzuela.)
	Teatro Martí. *La mulata.* (Zarzuela.)
Nov. 13.	Teatro Martí. *Frivolina.*

1932

	Tinta rápida. (Zarzuela.)
Mar. 26.	Teatro Martí. *Cecilia Valdés.* (*Zarzuela.*) Libretto by Agustín Rodríguez.
Jun. 24.	Teatro Martí. *El voto femenino.* (Zarzuela.)
Jul. 15.	Teatro Martí. *El jibarito.* (Zarzuela.)
Jul. 22 .	Teatro Martí. *El impuesto a los solteros.*
Aug. 23.	Teatro Martí. *Los médicos en huelga.*
Oct. 4.	Teatro Martí. *En el aire.* (Zarzuela.)
Nov. 18.	Teatro Martí. *El Clarín.* (Zarzuela.) Libretto by Agustín Rodríguez.

1933

Jan. 24.	Teatro Martí. *Julita y Julito.* (Zarzuela.)
Apr. 18.	Teatro Martí. *El patio de los tulipanes.* (Zarzuela.)
Apr. 21.	Teatro Martí. *La moratoria.*
May 5.	Teatro Martí. *La guayabera.* (Zarzuela.)
Jun. 16.	Teatro Martí. *Sevilla-Habana.* (Zarzuela.)
Jun. 27.	Teatro Martí. *Sueño azul.* (Zarzuela.)
Nov. 24.	Teatro Martí. *La hija del sol.* (Zarzuela.)

1934

May 15.	Teatro Martí. *Volando hacia la Habana o El principe.* (Zarzuela.)
Jul. 25.	Teatro Martí. *Carmiña.* (Zarzuela.) Music in collaboration with José Guede.

1935

> *Perlas.* (*Revista musical.*)

1936

Jan. 17.   Teatro Martí. *La Habana de noche.* (Zarzuela.)
Oct. 14.   Teatro Martí. *El cimarrón.* (Zarzuela.) Libretto by Marcelo
                 Salinas.

1938

                 La veguerita. (Zarzuela.)
s.f.
Album de postales
Balance del año
De Paris a la Habana
El futuro de la niña
Los cubanos en Paris
Verdún la inespugnable

Rodrigo Prats

1927

                 Teatro Molino Rojo. *La danza de las guatacas.*

1928

                 Teatro Payret. *Cantos de Cuba.* (*Revista.*) Libretto by
                 Mario Sorondo and Gustavo Sánchez Galarraga. Music in
                 collaboration with Jaime Prats.

1929

                 Teatro Actualidades. *En tierra de Marte.* (*Revista.*) Libretto by
                 J. T. Miranda. Music in collaboration with Jaime Prats.

1930

                 Teatro Payret. *La peligrosa.* Libretto by Mas y López.
                 Teatro Alhambra. *El cuarto no. 13.* (*Juguete cómico lírico.*)
                 Libretto by Víctor Reyes.

1931

                 Teatro Martí. *La perla del caribe.* (*Revista histórica.*) Libretto
                 by José Sánchez Arcilla.

1932

                 Teatro Martí. *Soledad.* (*Sainete.*) Libretto by Miguel Macau.

1933

Teatro Martí. *El pirata.* (*Novela escénica.*) Libretto by Agustín Rodríguez and José Sánchez Arcilla.

1934

Teatro Martí. *María Belén Chacón.* (Zarzuela.) Libretto by José Sánchez Arcilla.

1936

Teatro Martí. *Guamá.* Libretto by Federico Villoch.
Teatro Martí. *Amalia Batista.* (Zarzuela.) Libretto by Agustín Rodríguez.
Teatro Martí. *El teatro se va.* (*Revista.*)
Teatro Martí. *Don Juan Mortuorio.* (*Revista.*)
Teatro Martí. *Don Juan Jutía.* (*Revista.*)

NOTES

Introduction

1. In Cuba, the term *criollo* pertains to one of two things. As an adjective it denotes a specifically local Cuban culture. As a noun, it refers to a person born in Cuba rather than someone who immigrated to the island.

2. "Nuestra campaña a favor del teatro cubano, del teatro criollo plantea este problema: ¿Debe el criollismo mantenerse, tratándose en sainete, revistas y zarzuelas dentro de un ambiente de baja moralidad y grosería patente?

"La respuesta, evidentemente, es negativa.

"El teatro criollo o podrá adquirir posición entre los de los otros países de América en tanto no se despoje de ciertos convencionalismos que se mantienen por un grave error de óptica y de apreciación de los propios autores." Quoted in Rio Prado, *La Venus de bronce,* 56.

3. Feminine allegories for Cuban nationalism were used not only by Cuban revolutionaries during the Wars for Independence, but by North American and Spanish media, as well. Images of both the maiden warrior as well as the supportive and maternal helpmate helped to fuel pro-independence rhetoric during the more than three decades of revolutionary conflict. The most famous embodiment of the latter figure was Mariana Grajales, the mother of Antonio Maceo, who followed her husband, and later her sons, to the battlefield, exhorting them to fight for Cuban independence. Both Spanish and U.S. propaganda portrayed Cuba as a helpless female victim in need of armed, male (military) intervention. In the U.S. portrayals, Cuba's maiden virtue was threatened by lascivious and murderous Spain. Spanish representations tended to show the nubile heroine under threat of violence by an unkempt Afrocuban mob. An excellent collection of these images of racist propaganda can be found in *La gráfica política del 98,* a catalog produced by the Junta de Extremadura as part of a joint exhibition held at the Casa de las Americas in Havana in 1998. See also the images reproduced in Jules Benjamin, *The United States and the Origins of the Cuban Revolution.*

4. See Heller, *Emblems of Eloquence;* Abbate, *Unsung Voices;* Hadlock, *Mad Loves;* Smart, *Siren Songs;* Hunter, *The Culture of Opera Buffa in Mozart's Vienna;* Allenbrook, *Rythmic Gesture in Mozart;* McClary, *Georges Bizet, "Carmen";* and Clément, *Opera, or the Undoing of Women.*

5. See Radano and Bohlman, eds., *Music and the Racial Imagination,* and Bellman, *The Exotic in Western Music.*

6. Lane, *Blackface Cuba.*

7. Lipsitz, *The Possessive Investment in Whiteness.*

8. While complete scores were never published, individual songs were. A proliferation of sheet music attests to the popularity of particular songs and to Lecuona and Roig's influence on the Cuban music publishing industry.

9. The correspondence of Roig and Lecuona archived in the Museo Nacional de la Música Cubana show a sagacity in business, as well as a jealous control over their creative property. Roig was particularly careful with *Cecilia Valdés,* brushing aside the interest of impresarios outside Cuba who wanted to produce or publish the work.

10. Several of these reorchestrations (all anonymous) can be found in the archives of the Museo Nacional de la Música Cubana.

11. Félix Guerrero, personal communication.

12. The difference in the way popular hand percussion and Western orchestral percussion instruments are treated evidences an interesting split in the performance practice and suggests a simultaneous interaction between "literate" and oral music traditions. It was beyond the scope of this study to investigate percussion performance practice in greater detail, but such a study would be valuable, not merely for coming to a better understanding of the zarzuela's performance practice, but also in helping to understand the process of musical change and transmission in the first half of the twentieth century.

13. A great deal of music is held in private collections, and for many Cubans, this intellectual property is a potentially valuable resource, leading to the hoarding of material.

14. There are notable exceptions in the younger generation of Cuban music scholars, of whom Ramón Fajardo Estrada, Enrique Rio Prado, José Ruiz Elcoro, and Gisela de la Guardia stand out for having continued to research and write about lyric theater under very difficult conditions.

15. Several institutions have begun to take steps to remedy problems in archival security and preservation. The Museo Nacional de la Música Cubana now has a much stricter procedure for gaining access to original sources, and the National Library recently implemented rigid admission requirements.

16. Pedrito Fernández's collection was donated to the Museo Nacional de la Música Cubana upon his death in 1998. The entire collection had not been inventoried and catalogued to be made available to the public at the time that this book was written. I am grateful to Museo director Jesus Gómez Cairo for giving me access to this material. The Museo also holds its own large collection of librettos, particularly those of works by Gonzalo Roig, and several librettos can be found in the Biblioteca Nacional, as well.

17. I feel a very special debt to Pedrito Fernández, whom I had the good fortune to meet and interview the summer before his death in October of 1998. Early in my research I purchased a number of used books at a stall in Havana's Plaza de Armas. All of them had been the property of the same owner and included a number of handwritten annotations, corrections, and critiques. Some of the books even included newspaper clippings of contemporary reviews and obituaries of performers. It was only after I began going through his personal archives after his death that I came to recognize that the handwriting in the books I had purchased was that of Pedrito Fernández.

Chapter 1: Cuban Lyric Theater in Context

1. "Nuestros personajes teatralizados son exclusivamente 'nuestros', los hallamos alguna vez en la existencia cotidiana habanera, pero serían exóticos e incomprensibles en otros medios, en lugares distintos. Su convencionalismo carece de posible universalidad. Nada dirían a un español en España, o un francés en Francia, o uno cualquiera de nuestros iberoamericanos en su país respectivo, si no conocen La Habana, si no han vivido aquí durante tiempo bastante para estar en contacto con 'nuestra' mulata de solar, alegre y casquivana, nuestro negrito burlón y guarachero, nuestros policías . . . y el español acriollado que siente y vive 'en cubano' y se asimila nuestros malos hábitos hampones."

2. The reciprocal nature of Cuban and Spanish musical influence is discussed in Linares and Nuñez, *La música entre Cuba y España: La ida, la vuelta*, and in Eli and de los Angeles Alfonso, *La música entre Cuba y España: Tradición e innovación*. The trading of musical influences between Cuban and North American musicians has been of great interest to scholars of jazz and popular music. See Acosta, *Descarga cubana*, and Roberts, *The Latin Tinge*.

3. See Stein, *Songs of Mortals, Dialogues of the Gods*.

4. Ibid., 297.

5. Felipe V was king from 1700 to 1746. The two married in 1701.

6. Regidor Arribas, *Aquellas zarzuelas*, 15.

7. Ibid., 16, and Le Duc, "Los orígenes de la zarzuela moderna," 3. See also Vásquez, "The Quest for National Opera in Spain."

8. That same year, the Real Conservatorio presented the first nineteenth-century zarzuela in celebration of a royal birth. The creators of *Los enredos de un curioso* titled their work a "melodrama," but several music historians have rejected that designation, preferring to call it a zarzuela. José Subirá claims that perhaps the work was called a melodrama because the term *zarzuela* had fallen out of use or was considered passé. He writes, "They gave it the title 'melodrama' because the word 'zarzuela' seemed inappropriate, or it was considered inopportune, or it had fallen into disuse, perhaps." ("La apellidaron 'melodrama' porque la palabra 'zarzuela' parecía inpropia, o se consideraba inoportuna o había caído en pleno olvido quizás.") Subirá, *Historia de la música teatral en España*, 172. See also Encima Cortizo's discussion of the work, "La zarzuela romántica," 25.

9. Le Duc, "Los orígenes de la zarzuela moderna," 6–8.

10. Regidor Arribas, *Aquellas zarzuelas*, 17.

11. *Costumbrismo* was a literary and artistic movement that sought to represent local customs. The movement took root in Cuba in the 1830s. Scholars who have examined the connections between the Spanish zarzuela and nationalism include Roland Vázquez, Luis G. Iberni, Serge Salaün, and María José Corredor Alvarez.

12. See Le Duc, "Los orígenes de la zarzuela moderna," 12. A fascination with poverty is especially evident in the work of Charles Dickens and Victor Hugo, where sympathetic realist strategies can often be looked at as escapist voyeurism, with the poor as its object. Anne J. Cruz looks at the origin of this literary trend in Spain in her monograph *Discourses of Poverty: Social Reform and the Picaresque Novel in Early Modern Spain*.

13. The construction of the Teatro Tacón illustrates that Cuban theater was intimately tied up in a web of sugar, slavery, and economic advancement. Governor Miguel Tacón's desire to construct a world-class theater in Havana led him to impose a seventeen-peso tax on every slave imported to the island. The tax raised so much money that Tacón was able to erect the largest, most luxurious theater in the New World, with money to spare. Tacón used the leftover proceeds to fund the construction of the first railroad linking Havana with the sugar plantations (vital for establishing Cuba's primacy as a sugar-producing nation) and to install drinking fountains in the capital. See Knapp Jones, *Behind Spanish American Footlights*, 394.

14. The first season of opera opened in 1851 with a company brought by Catalán impresario José Robreño. While operas had been performed in Cuba well before this date (the earliest known performance of an opera dates back to 1796, with a performance of an anonymous work titled *Didone abbandonata*), they were isolated events and not available to a large public. González, *La composición operística en Cuba*, 9–10. It is provocative to speculate that the appearance of commercially available opera and zarzuela at nearly the same historical moment might have made Cuban composers and librettists, less entrenched in the tradition of each genre, more willing to "cross-pollinate" between genres.

15. González,"Establecimiento y desarrollo de la zarzuela en La Habana durante el siglo XIX," 7.

16. Rine Leal, having discovered the libretto for *El industrial de nuevo cuño*, relates that "The zarzuela takes place outside the walls of the city, on Salud Street, and offers a real mix of Irish, blacks, [Canary] islanders, Catalans, ticket vendors, bartenders, peasants, popular Cuban music, dances, and local humor." ("La zarzuela transcurre en extramuros de la ciudad, en la calle de Salud y ofrece una verdadera ensalada de irlandeses, negros, isleños, catalanes, billeteros, baratilleros, guajiros, música popular cubana, bailes y gracejo vernáculo.") Leal, *La selva oscura*, v. 1, 254.

17. Cuban blackface theater practices are discussed in Chapter 4.

18. Teurbe Tolón, *Teatro lírico popular de Cuba*, 11. ". . .figura extraordinaria en nuestra historia teatral, artista genial y fundador del teatro popular cubano y del nacionalismo en nuestras artes."

19. Weiss, ed., *Latin American Popular Theater*, 121.

20. Versényi, *Theater in Latin America*, 19.

21. For example, Lope de Vega's play *The Discovery of the New World by Christopher Columbus* features a seductive Moorish girl named Zara who sings and dances for the men on stage.

22. Stevenson, "The Afro-American Musical Legacy to 1800," 496–97.

23. Subirá, *La tonadilla escénica*, 41–53.

24. The most valuable resource for these early works of popular theater is the first volume of Leal's *La selva oscura*.

25. Casares, "Historia del teatro de los bufos," 74–76.

26. Ibid., 74–76.

27. Ibid., 77.

28. Ibid., 79.

29. Ibid..

30. Leal, *La selva oscura*, v. 2, 26.

31. Leal describes both the political and comic content of the Cuban *bufos* in the first chapter of *La selva oscura*, v. 2, 15–67. Other scholars who have described nineteenth-century *bufo* theater in Cuba include Cristobal Díaz Ayala, Laurie Aleen Frederik, Jill Lane, Robin Moore, Eduardo Robreño, and Judith Weiss.

32. Díaz Ayala, *Del areyto a la nueva trova*, 63. Leal claims there were eight. *La selva oscura*, v. 2, 26.

33. Leal, *La selva oscura*, v. 2, 15–16. It should not be understood that this was the first time that Cuban themes were treated on the lyric stage, as the information available on the 1853 zarzuela season makes clear. The difference lies in the fact that these musical elements of local "color" are now central to the work itself and showcased musics of various local groups increasingly become viewed not as "their music," but as "our music." Robin Moore views the late nineteenth-century comic theater as crucial to the formation of a new Cuban identity and as a forerunner to the *afrocubanismo* movement of the 1920s and 1930s. He writes, "the *teatro vernáculo* might be theorized as a forum of symbolic negotiation, a bounded artistic terrain in which concepts of self, nation, and *cubanidad* were slowly defined in the national consciousness in relation to Hispanic- and African-derived cultural influences, as well as others from Europe and the United States." Moore, *Nationalizing Blackness*, 41–42.

34. The Irijoa became the Teatro Martí in 1900. It would become a key space for the Cuban zarzuela from August 7, 1931, until November 26, 1936, when Gonzalo Roig, Manuel Suárez, and Agustín Rodríguez maintained a company there.

35. Arredondo, Robreño, and Leal all provide accounts of the types of repertoire performed in these theaters.

36. The building's roof collapsed on February 18, 1935, ending the longest theatrical run in Cuba's history. The collapse occurred after the house had cleared at the end of the night and, miraculously, no one was hurt.

37. Eduardo Robreño, . . . *Y escrito en este papel . . .*, 28–29.

38. Nono Noriega would later become the stage designer for the Roig/Rodríguez company in the Teatro Martí, where many of his innovations were applied to the zarzuela. Robreño, "Prologo," 13–14.

39. Robreño paints an unrealistically rosy view of the "genteel" crowd made up of laborers, professionals, and men of power. "Prologo," 15.

40. Robreño, *Historia del teatro popular*, 51–79, "Prologo," 10–12, and Arredondo, *La vida de un comediante*, 119–22.

41. Examples include *La carretera central*, which dealt with the construction of the new national highway, a piece on the World War I titled *America en la guerra* (*America in the War*), and perhaps two of the best-known Alhambra works, *La casita criolla* (*The Creole House*) and *La isla de las cotorras* (*The Island of the Parrots*), which deal with corruption in the Menocal regime and the United States' efforts to annex the Isle of Pines, respectively. For more detailed discussion of the political works presented in the Alhambra during the Republic, see Robreño, *Historia del teatro popular cubano*, 69–70.

42. Eduardo Robreño admits that the Alhambra did receive its share of criticism, although he protests that the majority of its critics were "autores fracasados, cómicos resentidos y algún que otro intelectualoide que no podía comprender aquello" ("failed authors, resentful comedians, and other "wannabe" intellectuals who couldn't understand it"). *Como lo pienso lo digo*, 127–28.

43. Alhambra productions grew more sordid during the years of what Eduardo Robreño terms the theater's "decadence," during the last decade of the theater's existence. *Historia del teatro popular cubano,* 20. These were difficult years for theater; Cuba was suffering through the turbulent years of the Machado regime, audiences were scarce, and actors poorly paid. Curiously, these were also the same years that the zarzuela reached its height.

44. The Gran Teatro Nacional of the Republican era should not be confused with the contemporary Teatro Nacional de Cuba, located on Plaza de la Revolución. The Gran Teatro Nacional, erected on the site of the former Teatro Talón, opened in 1915 under the auspices of the Centro Gallego.

45. Robreño claims that "not even a comma was added or taken away" in the presentation of risqué Alhambra works for family audiences, a claim that is likely an exaggeration but perhaps not far from the truth, as Enrique Arredondo also asserts that such changes were minimal and that the suggestive nature of the humor remained in place, to the delight of the audience. Robreño, *Historia del teatro popular cubano,* 69; and Arredondo, *La vida de un comediante,* 29.

46. While the film has been responsible for rekindling interest in Cuban theater history, and filmmakers went to great lengths to achieve visual authenticity, the film has been criticized for inconsistencies in the repertoire selected and its performance practice (José Ruiz Elcoro, personal communication).

47. Rine Leal, *En primera persona,* 150.

48. A large collection of Anckermann's scores was held in the archive of the Centro Odilio Urfé. The Centro has since merged with the Museo Nacional de la Música Cubana, which has yet to catalogue and make available the Anckermann holdings. Musicologist José Ruiz Elcoro has completed a detailed chronology of all of Anckermann's works, and it awaits publication. Recordings by the company of Regino López were produced by both Victor and Columbia Records in the first two decades of the twentieth century. I am indebted to José Ruiz Elcoro for allowing me access to his personal archive of historic recordings.

49. *América en la guerra* premiered November 18, 1918.

50. Sergio Acebal, one of Cuba's most celebrated *negrito* performers, is the most striking example of this, yet Enrique Arredondo insists that lack of singing ability was not the norm. "Todos los negritos del teatro cubano tenían que cantar y bailar." ("All of the *negritos* from Cuban theater had to sing and dance.") Arredondo, *La vida de un comediante,* 118. While the *negrito* role itself is generally less vocally demanding than other stock roles, *negrito* performers were frequently required to perform comic duets with other actors or solo numbers such as *pregones,* where in language rich in double entendres the *negrito* acted as a street vendor trying to sell tamales, melons, ice cream, or soap.

51. Characters named Cecilia and Leonardo, clearly derived from Villaverde's novel *Cecilia Valdés* (see Chapter 3), appear in a 1918 Alhambra production, and a character named María la O appears in other popular theater productions, including a *guaracha* by Jorge Anckermann called "Y ñamo María la O." A woman named María la O also appears in Villaverde's novel, sentenced to death for the murder of her husband.

52. Visiting Italian opera companies advertised themselves as "di primo cartello," even if they weren't. Well-known impresarios Manuel García and Max Maretzek, in particular, made Cuba a regular stop on their New World tours.

53. See Rio Prado, *La música italiana a Cuba*. The book is a valuable resource for understanding Cuban spectatorship in the nineteenth and early twentieth centuries. Contemporary journals of culture, such as *Musicalia, Pro-Arte Musical*, and *Germinal* are also important sources for an understanding of spectatorship in Republican Cuba.

54. Hubert de Blanck, born in Utrecht, Holland, in 1865, moved to Cuba in 1882 and became a committed *independista*. He founded Cuba's first national music conservatory in 1885. See Tolón and González, *La opera en Cuba*, xiii–xxxii.

55. The *habanera*, for example, already associated with racial exoticism after operas such as Bizet's *Carmen*, becomes a metaphor for the racial fraternity thought to be experienced by the multiracial independence army. Faustino Núñez provides an interesting discussion of the international role of the *habanera* and its importance in Spanish music. Núñez and Linares, *La música entre Cuba y España*, 187–205.

56. See, for example, Zoila Lapique Becali's scathing critique, "Figura musical de Eduardo Sánchez de Fuentes." Moore reserves some of his harshest criticism for the composer, in *Nationalizing Blackness*, 134. Examples of Sánchez de Fuentes's racist philosophy can be seen in his own writings, "Influencia de los ritmos africanos en nuestro cancionero" and "Panorama actual de la música cubana."

57. Sánchez de Fuentes's means of combating that growing influence was to write Afrocubans out of Cuban history and thereby negate their influence in shaping Cuban identity. Moore discusses this strategy at length. *Nationalizing Blackness*, 127–32.

58. Also called *siboneyismo*, after "Siboney," the name given to Cuba by the island's native inhabitants.

59. It should be pointed out, however, that Sánchez de Fuentes's interest in indigenous themes began years before his published attacks on Afrocuban music.

60. The first was *Colón en Cuba*, written by Italian composer Giovanni Bottesini during his 1848 visit to Cuba. See González, *La composición operística en Cuba*, 59–67.

61. Clemente Vázquez, "Una ópera cubana," in *El Fígaro*, Nov. 9, 1898. Quoted in González, *La composición opererística en Cuba*, 310. González describes the opera in detail in the same volume, 306–46. See also Tolón and González, *La opera en Cuba*, 285–301.

62. "Los bailables . . . ofrecen un ritmo extraño que se dice ser auténtico y perteneciente a los diversos que los taínos empleaban e sus areítos y [son] lo mejor de la obra." González, *La composición operística en Cuba*, 430.

63. The work was composed in 1918 but premiered in Havana's Teatro Nacional in 1921.

64. Robin Moore examines Ortíz's own shifting ambivalence in his study "Representations of Afrocuban Expressive Culture in the Writings of Fernando Ortiz," 32–54.

65. On poetry, see Vitier, *Lo cubano en la poesía*. José Seoane Gallo's biography of artist Eduardo Abela, *Eduardo Abela: Cerca del cerco*, is a particularly useful source for understanding the creative currents in the visual arts community. For a wider, historical approach to the visual arts, see Martínez, *Cuban Art and National Identity*. Núñez Jiménez provides a concise biography of Wilfredo Lam, as well as some insightful analyses, in *Wilfredo Lam*. Composers Roldán and Caturla

are both the subjects of recent scholarly interest. See Piñeiro and Henríquez, eds., *Amadeo Roldán: Testimonios,* and Henríquez, *Alejandro García Caturla.*

66. This is not unlike the spread of jazz to white audiences in the United States via dance bands such as that of Paul Whiteman. (Whiteman's band, incidentally, enjoyed considerable popularity in Havana.)

67. Moore, *Nationalizing Blackness,* 95–97.

68. Ibid., 135.

69. During the colonial period, the term *curros* referred to free blacks from Havana's underclass who wore distinctive clothing and were suspected by whites of involvement in crime, violence, and witchcraft. The theatrical character type most likely shares a lineage with the Spanish *majo.*

70. Published as sheet music by Ediciones Roig, Havana, 1932.

71. The *mulata,* and the music with which she is identified, is the subject of Chapter 3.

72. This tendency to use the term *zarzuela* abstractly appears to have been adopted from the Spanish, who, Janet Sturman notes, have had a historical tendency to use the word indiscriminately for Spanish-language music theater. Sturman, *Zarzuela,* 14.

73. *La Niña Rita* (discussed in both Chapter 2 and Chapter 4) is not itself considered to be a zarzuela, because of its length, but rather a *sainete.* The work premiered in the Teatro Regina, September 29, 1927. Music by Eliseo Grenet and Ernesto Lecuona and libretto by Antonio Castells and Aurelio Riancho. This work will be discussed in Chapter 1.

74. The first evidence I have found of a composer's attention to generic classification occurs in a 1975 interview with Rodrigo Prats. Pols, "Rodrigo Prats," 29.

75. Lecuona did eventually succeed in writing an opera. The work, *El sombrero de Yarey,* was written in New York in 1946. Cuban composers were not the first to conceive of converting a zarzuela into an opera, which was perhaps most famously done by Spanish composer Emilio Arrieta with his zarzuela *Marina* (1871). Neither Roig nor Prats ever finished the revisions of *Cecilia Valdés* or *Amalia Batista.* Ironically, recent performances of *Cecilia Valdés* show what their authors might have considered an evolutionary "regression." Stripped entirely of the spoken libretto, and in many cases of any sense of plot, performances string together the show's "hits" without any sense of dramatic cohesiveness. These performances typically rely heavily on dance numbers, drawing particularly on the current vogue of folkloric dance. I viewed such a performance on September 9, 2000, when members of the Pro-Arte Lírico performed *Cecilia Valdés* in the open-air Amfiteatro de La Habana. There was no orchestra, and singers were accompanied by a recording of the orchestra made during Roig's lifetime, with the composer conducting. Due to the acoustical challenges of the performance space, and the technical limitations of the company, the vocal performances were dubbed, with the singers lip-synching to their own recorded performances. All of the dialogue had been removed and a number of folkloric production numbers had been added. It was remarked by a disgruntled elderly audience member, "Pobre Roig, quería tanto convertirla en opera, y ahora está reducida a una revista." ("Poor Roig, he wanted so much to convert it into an opera, and now it's reduced to a *revista.*")

76. See Leal, *La selva oscura*, v. 2; Robreño, *Historia del teatro popular cubana;* Tolón, *Teatro lírico popular de Cuba;* and José Juan Arróm, *Historia de la literatura dramática cubana.*

77. Musicologist Ángel Vázquez Millares discusses this problem in his article "De la zarzuela española a la zarzuela cubana: Vida del género en Cuba."

78. Sturman, *Zarzuela,* 19.

79. Cuban *solares* generally feature individual rooms opening off a communal courtyard. Amenities such as kitchens, bathrooms, and areas for washing clothes are shared. Such circumstances make personal privacy nearly impossible. The social conditions of tenement living were not only of interest to middle-class Cubans during the early twentieth century. North Americans, too, shared a fascination in the lives of the black underclass, as Gershwin's attention to the tenement in his opera *Porgy and Bess* illustrates. Examples of lengthier works with developed musical scores that receive the label "*sainete*" include *Rosa la China, La de Jesús María,* and *María la O,* all by Lecuona and Sánchez Galarraga and all of which deal with lower-class characters.

80. Following the U.S. intervention, several theaters changed their venues to appeal to North American tastes. The Teatro Alhambra was briefly renamed the Café Americano and its repertoire changed to American-style vaudeville and reviews.

81. Barce, "La revista: Aproximación a una definición formal."

82. Machado's downfall, and the performance of this *revista,* happened at the height of the zarzuela's popularity.

83. Pols, "Entrevistas: Rodrigo Prats," 32. "El día del estreno no pasó nada, pero a la función siguiente se creó tremendo problema. Al parecer, alguien le llevó el chisme a las autoridades de lo que pasaba en la obra y por la noche el teatro se llenó; cosa extraña, porque la pieza no era para tanto público. Lo que ignorábamos era la canalla que habia entrado! De ahí que cuando empiezo a tocar la conocida pieza popular y en la escena un actor imitaba a Grau, comienzan a llover, desde el público, tomates, papas, piedras y un grupo de policías vestidos de civil inician un tiroteo. Fué necesario tirar el telón, si no matan a los actores. A la vez comienzo a dirigir el Himno pero ní con eso calmaba aquellos energúmenos. Al final me quedé solo con el trompeta, porque toda la orquesta también puso 'pies polvorosa.'"

84. The *romanza* is the zarzuela equivalent of the aria. The *lamento* genre began as a stylized slave lament, but by the 1930s it could also be used to lament unrequited love. See Chapter 4. The type of duo being referred to here is not the comic duet, so prevalent in Cuban popular theater, although the comic duet also maintains a foothold in the zarzuela, but rather the dramatic duo. Such music numbers may be love duets, confrontations, or two characters singing simultaneously (but not to each other) during a moment of crisis.

85. Titled *La viuda alegre* in Spanish. Janet Sturman discusses the European operetta's popularity in Sturman, *Zarzuela,* 111–12.

86. Such as Lecuona's *La guaracha musulmana,* an *opereta bufa* that premiered in 1932 in the Teatro Principal de la Comedia in Havana.

87. Lecuona's *Lola Cruz* is a prime example of this phenomenon.

88. In this sense, the *opereta cubana* is sort of the antithesis of the *sainete.*

89. Bordman, *American Operetta,* 6.

Chapter 2: Eminently Feminine

1. Called the "fat cow" years, the period 1913–20 saw the price of Cuban sugar rise dramatically, owing to the destruction of the European sugar beet crop during World War I. By 1919, Cuba was producing over one quarter of the world's sugar. See Cantón Navarro, *Historia de Cuba*, 95. Cubans would pay a high price for their single crop dependency, however, and the crash in sugar prices in 1920 led to a national economic crisis. For a discussion of the economic crisis of the sugar crash, and its causes, see Pérez, *Cuba*, 224–28.

2. Machado's political career is discussed by writers Cairo, *La Revolución del 30 en la narrativa y el testimonio cubanos*; Ibarra, *Un análisis psicosocial del cubano: 1898–1925*; Roa, *Retorno a la alborada*; and Pérez, *Cuba*, Chapter 9, 229–75. Stoner analyses the political consequences of the constitutional assembly in her monograph *From the House to the Streets*.

3. The politically motivated killings were so numerous, and the dictator so hated, that in 1933, immediately following Machado's fall from power, Carlos Peraza was able to publish a lengthy book detailing the assassinations of Machado's victims. Written in concise, journalistic prose, the book is startlingly emotional, serving to recount and name each of the regime's victims. Peraza, *Machado: Crímenes y horrors*.

4. From 1930, a series of massive worker strikes propelled the country in the direction of revolution. Cuban historians argue about when the true struggle against Machado began; some scholars see the economic revolt to be as critical as the violent one in 1933. See le Riverand, *La República: Dependencia y revolución*, 257–78.

5. Batista helped to lead the 1933 revolt against President Gerardo Machado and subsequently headed the movement to oust Machado's replacement, Carlos Manuel de Cespedes, from power. Installing himself in the highly influential position of army chief of staff, Batista oversaw and directed much of government and military policy from behind the scenes, persevering through a chain of short-lived presidencies (Ramón Grau San Martín [100 days], Carlos Mendieta y Montefur [11 months], José Barnet y Vinajeras [5 months], and Miguel Gómez y Arias [7 months]), as well as Federico Laredo Bru's full-term presidency, before assuming the office for himself in 1940. For a concise history of the changing administrations during this period and their political implications, see Cantón Navarro, *Historia de Cuba*.

6. Pérez, *Cuba*, 284.

7. McClintock, "Family Feuds: Gender, Nationalism and the Family."

8. García, "La zarzuela en Cuba," 24.

9. Undated playbill (1940s) for performances of *Rosa la China* and *María la O*. Private collection of Pedrito Fernández.

10. Stoner, *From the House to the Streets*, 59.

11. Ibid., 75–77. A tendency by historians to associate the entire women's movement as complicit in Machado's dictatorship has resulted in the movement's underrepresentation in the literature, a deficit that Stoner's book begins to address.

12. Machado's response was to subdue women activists through sexual humiliation, having them stripped naked in the street by his secret police. The women's

groups responded by sending out male protesters dressed as women, who then surprised and beat back their attackers. Stoner, *From the House to the Streets*, 120.

13. Limited suffrage was achieved in 1934.

14. Women's participation in charities and moral causes in colonial Cuba is discussed by the Countess of Merlin in her memoirs. See Méndez Rodenas, *Gender and Nationalism in Colonial Cuba*, 87.

15. Muñoz de Quevedo, "Una Mujer."

16. Stoner discusses the role of women in the group, in *From the House to the Streets*, 90, For general information about the Minoristas, see Cairo, *El grupo minorista y su tiempo*; and Moore, *Nationalizing Blackness*, Chapter 7.

17. Stoner, *From the House to the Streets*, 89.

18. Sánchez Galarraga was the first president of the Sociedad "Teatro Cubano." A playwright who wrote for the Alhambra theater, he later became Ernesto Lecuona's preferred librettist.

19. Carbonell, *Las bellas artes en Cuba*, 74.

20. Leal, *La selva oscura*, v. 1, 166–67.

21. Teurbe Tolón, *Historia del teatro en la Habana*, 24. This is the first sign of a relationship between politics, public policy, and the entertainment industry in Cuba. It would not be the last.

22. Leal points out that there has been some discrepancy on whether the theater opened in 1775 or 1776, but his discovery of a document stating that the theater was ready to present a play in celebration of the king's birthday, January 20, 1775, resolves the issue. Leal, *La selva oscura*, v. 1, 173.

23. Martínez-Fernández, *Fighting Slavery in the Caribbean*, 67.

24. Ibid., 69–70.

25. See Martínez-Fernández's discussion of theatrical space. *Fighting Slavery in the Caribbean*, 102–4.

26. Leal, *Breve historia*, 68.

27. Built by the Pro-Arte Musical in 1928, largely because of the insistence of Teresa García Montes, the Auditorium served primarily as a concert house. Now called Teatro Amadeo Roldán, the building was badly damaged by an arson attack in the 1980s and reopened in 1999.

28. Discussed in Chapter 1.

29. "A las diez tomamos nuestro chocolate y nos acostamos después de rezar. Y a las seis de prisa nos levantamos y vamos a misa sin desayunar."

30. An obsession with fashion among young female characters can be seen in both *María la O* and *Cecilia Valdés*. Jorge Anckermann's *sainete La Señorita Maupín* pokes fun at this fascination with a chorus of young women mad for the latest in French fashion.

31. The zarzuela's treatment of working women is discussed in Chapter 5.

32. Enrique Arredondo provides a particularly poignant account of these economic difficulties in his memoirs, *La vida de un comediante*.

33. It appears that the Regina's organizers took a while to come up with the best formula for the theater's success. The original version of the libretto for *La tierra de Venus*, for example, placed the work within the realm of the raunchier comedy associated with theaters like the Alhambra. The last scene originally called for an "aesthetic nude," which was struck down by the sensors. See Rio Prado, *La Venus de bronce*, 50.

34. "Ernesto Lecuona es el creador del Teatro Lírico en Cuba, y para crearlo realizó el milagro de convertir el repugnante "Molino Rojo" en un teatro al que asistían complacidas las familias. Justo es decir que una audáz empresa, de la que formó parte don Luis Estrada, sustituyó el teatrucho, donde habían imperado el descoco y el ludibrio, por una sala simpática y atrayente." From "La vida y la obra de Ernesto Lecuona," program notes from a 1936 performance of *El torrente* by Lecuona's Teatro Lírico Cubano. The author leaves out Grenet's participation in the opening of the theater. Personal archive of Pedrito Fernández.

35. "Ní un solo detalle de confort o de buen gusto falta al simpático coliseo." *Diario de la Marina,* Sept. 24, 1927, 6.

36. ". . . las más dilectas familias de nuestro mundo elegante." *Diario de la Marina,* Sept. 27, 1927, 8.

37. ". . . toda la *highlife,* toda la *elite,* el *bon ton* en pleno . . . se hallaba confortablemente acomodado en los sitiales novísimos del flamante coliseo." *Diario de la Marina,* Sept. 30, 1927, 9.

38. *Diario de la Marina,* Oct. 1, 1927.

39. Acceptance of the premiere of *La Niña Rita* as a historical benchmark is widespread. The view is shared by theater historians Leal, Robreño, and Tolón, by music scholars Ruiz Elcoro, Fajardo, Piñeiro, and Cañizares, and also by musicians themselves, including Rodrigo Prats.

40. The *género chico* began in Spain in the last decades of the nineteenth century as theater impresarios looked for a more lucrative way to present musical comedy. Works from the *género chico* tradition are shorter, usually an hour or less, and frequently treat comic themes.

41. I was not able to locate an original libretto for *La Niña Rita,* nor a musical score. I referenced an abridged version of the libretto used for a 1950s television adaptation. The libretto is found in the personal archive of Pedrito Fernández, now part of the Museo Nacional de la Música Cubana.

42. "*La Habana en 1830* es un sainete delicioso. La nota criolla retrospectiva está tratada en él con una finura y una gracia admirables." *Diario de la Marina,* Sept. 30, 1927.

43. The issue of historicism and nostalgia in the zarzuela is discussed in Chapter 1.

44. "*La tierra de Venus* interesó desde el primer cuadro. Es una revista llena de luz y de color; pintoresco desfile de animadísimos cuadros que mantienen al público un curiosidad constante. La obra fue montada esplendidamente. Acertadísimas las evoluciones, bajo la dirección experta de Esteban Palos que, además, se nos mostró justamente con la Strabeu, con Paquita López y con María Verdiales como un ballarín notabilísimo. En el role de La Gobernatora en *La tierra de Venus* obtuvo Soledad Pérez un éxito excelente. Lucía un turbante, creación de la elegante Maison de Ketty, que llamó poderosamente la atención de las damas. Merecen elogio E. Lecuona y E. Grenet el primero por su labor como director artístico y el segundo por su actuación de la orquesta." *Diario de la Marina,* Sept. 30, 1927.

45. Examples include the chorus of the *curros* from *María la O,* the Saint's Day festivities in *Cecilia Valdés,* and the *comparsa* scene in *Rosa la China.*

46. In *La tierra de Venus,* for example, the characters decide to "volunteer" for the trip to Venus because they have no money, they are hungry, and the debt collectors are after them. *Chaufer al Regina* deals with the transportation changes rocking Havana following the introduction of the automobile and their

accompanying social baggage, and *La liga de las señoras* pokes fun at the national Congress of Women organized in that same year.

47. Rodrigo Prats points out this distinction in a 1979 interview recorded with Ramón Fajardo. From the personal archive of Ramón Fajardo.

48. It has been suggested that the penchant for death and tragedy at the end of zarzuelas is related to early twentieth-century Cubans' taste for Italian opera. Enrique Rio Prado, personal communication.

49. A cursory look at the *Diario de la Marina* and *El Mundo* newspapers from the 1920s and 1930s shows that a surprising number of political and civic events were held in Havana's theaters, particularly the Teatro Nacional.

50. "Reseña biográfica" in "La música viva del cubano Ernesto Lecuona," 18–19.

51. Premiered in the Teatro Payret, March 1, 1930. Other works that premiered in the Payret include *El amor del guarachero* (July 12, 1929), *La mujer de nadie* (July 16, 1929), *El maizal* (March 7, 1930), and *El calesero* (March 15, 1930).

52. "En Cuba ya no podrá existir en forma estable una verdadera compañía de teatro cubano con el prestigio que se necesita mientras el gobierno no le brinde protección oficial." *Diario de la Marina,* June 15, 1937.

53. Lecuona's influence was not only as a producer of lyric theater. The composer was the president of the Federación de Compositores and exerted considerable influence over the publication of music in Cuba. He was soundly criticized for his control over Cuban composition in the Jan. 16, 1947, *Prensa libre* column "Babel: Nada humano me es ajeno," where the critic screams in boldfaced capital letters, "SE MUEREN DE HAMBRE LOS COMPOSITORES"—"Composers Die of Hunger." Lecuona also traveled extensively. Several of his lyric works premiered abroad, during his tenure in Spain from 1924 to 1927 and in Mexico in 1934. He was also well known in the United States, and his personal correspondence held in the archives of the Museo Nacional de la Música indicate that he had extensive business dealings with American publishing houses and, later, with Hollywood.

54. The Suárez–Rodríguez company opened on March 7, 1931. The company would perform continuously until the end of October 1936. Gisela de la Guardia notes that Roig's decision to form the company appears to have been based on his having been sacked as director of the Banda Municipal as a result of changes in city politics. Gisela de la Guardia González, "La zarzuela en Cuba en el período comprendido entre los años 1927 y 1940," 51.

55. The theater would close with a sarcastic parody by Agustín Rodríguez with music by Rodrigo Prats titled *El teatro se va* (*The Theater Goes Away*).

56. ". . . la importancia de esta temporada del Martí son sus cinco años consecutivos (1931–36), el número de obras estrenadas y el feliz desarrollo del género lírico. Fueron funciones, casi todas, a teatro lleno, con escenificaciones tarde y noche, con un elenco que no se enfermaba, ní padecía de ronquera. También es necesario destacar que esta temporada se mantuvo gracias al que hacer de los compositores y libretistas que coadyuvaron en esta ardua empresa, a pesar de sufrir la crisis política imperante." Pols, "Rodrigo Prats," 30.

57. "Al inaugurarse, el Regina Theater fué puesto en las manos de Lecuona, quien, para que todo fuera nuevo formó también las cuatro tiples que habían de mostrarse en el desempeño de las obras. Fueron Rita Montaner, que ya se sabe hasta donde ha llegado; Caridad Suárez, que tambien alcanzó rápidamente reputa-

204 Notes to Pages 37–42

ción y admiraciones; María Ruíz y Dora O'Siel." From "La vida y la obra de Ernesto Lecuona," anonymous program notes from a 1936 performance of *El torrente* by Lecuona's Teatro Lírico Cubano. Personal archive of Pedrito Fernández.

58. *Cuba Musical* (1927), 33–37.

59. Pedro Arias, personal communication, 1999.

60. Fajardo Estrada, *Rita Montaner.*

61. The Sunday concerts are generally recognized as a milestone in the history of Cuban music. Robin Moore examines the concerts' role in the Afrocubanism movement. *Nationalizing Blackness,* 174.

62. Listings for benefit concerts and recitals given by the daughters and wives of Havana's elite can be found in *Pro-Arte Musical* and occasionally appear in the "Habaneras" column of the *Diario de la Marina.*

63. The practice of holding concerts on Sunday mornings, and the smug self-selection that it produced, was still firmly in place in Havana until 1998. Until that date, audiences went to hear the Filarmónica perform in the Teatro García Lorca. With the opening of the Amadeo Roldán in 1999, orchestral performances were moved there and, with an eye to attracting tourists, the concerts were moved to the afternoon.

64. "Enchanting Maiden." Borja became so associated with the song from Lecuona's *Lola Cruz* that she was referred to by its title.

65. "María la O, Rosa la China, y Lola Cruz. Si fueran mujeres de nuestros días, lavarían con jabón 'La Llave.'"

Chapter 3: The Mulata Makes an Entrance

1. Writers who have made important contributions to the role of the *mulata* in Cuban arts and letters include Rine Leal, Vera Kutzinski, Reynaldo González, William Luis, Robin Moore, Jill Lane, and Norman S. Holland.

2. Homi Bhabha, "The Other Question," 66–84.

3. See, for example, Lope de Vega's *El nuevo mundo descubierto por Cristóbal Colón* (1598–1603), which contains music and dancing for both Moors and New World natives, and *El remedio en la desdicha* (1506–1603), in which a Moorish girl named Zara sings to a group of white men.

4. The relationship between racial caricature and, specifically, the formation of character types such as the *mulata* and the *negrito* with the social circumstances created by Cuba's full-fledged entry into the slave trade, has been discussed by many authors. Rine Leal makes this connection in his *Breve historia del teatro cubano,* 30–32, as does Robin Moore, *Nationalizing Blackness,* 43–45. Mary Cruz's monograph *Creto Gangá* examines one of the most influential models of the *negrito* character and ties his emergence to the rising social unrest, racial tension, and xenophobia that followed the increase in the slave trade.

5. My work has been greatly informed by Reynaldo González's influential essay found in *Contradanzas y latigazos* and by Vera Kutsinski's far-ranging, interdisciplinary critique *Sugar's Secrets.*

6. While there were rare examples of relationships between white women and black men and consensual partnerships and even marriages between white men and their slaves or free women of color, the nature of slave society and the anat-

omy of the power structure made the abuse of both slave and free black women tragically common. See Martínez-Alier, *Marriage, Class, and Color*, 11–19.

7. See Kutzinski, *Sugar's Secrets*, 17–42. Clearly, this mythology inverts logic, turning the masters into victims and the disenfranchised victims into masters.

8. It is worth speculating that the strength of the discourse against the *mulata* was not motivated by sexual mores, but by economic concerns. Mixed-race women became a disproportionate number of the free nonwhite population in Cuba's cities during the nineteenth century. They were heavily represented in the emerging wage economy for Afrocubans, and as independently earning seamstresses, cooks, domestic servants, and the like, these women symbolized a kind of economic and social mobility that was not possible for male Afrocubans or *mulatos*, or, for that matter, white women. See Helg, *Our Rightful Share*, and Martínez-Alier, *Marriage, Class, and Color*.

9. The discourse of *mestizaje*, Cuban identity, and the *mulata* becomes central to late nineteenth- and early twentieth-century Cuban letters. The *mulata*'s role as a central figure in nineteenth-century literature has been examined by writers such as Vera Kutzinski, Reynaldo González, Norman S. Holland, and William Luis.

10. Spanish for "Creole." Used to denote a person born in Cuba or sufficiently naturalized.

11. Kutzinski, *Sugar's Secrets*, 86–91.

12. Villaverde's novel has been the subject of numerous literary critiques. See González, *Contradanzas y latizgazos*; Luis, *Literary Bondage*; and Yanez, "Cecilia Valdés: La heroína corriente, la heroína solitaria." Lorna Valerie Williams offers a particularly interesting reading in regard to race and gender, and her careful unraveling of the novel's symbolism renders clear the extent to which the *mulata*'s image communicated through the realm of the semiotic. Williams, *The Representation of Slavery in Cuban Fiction*.

13. "*Mulata* of the street." This character was visually immortalized on tobacco boxes and sugar labels as a flashily dressed woman, bear-shouldered, wearing the typical ruffled train, or *bata de cola*.

14. Moore, *Nationalizing Blackness*, 53–55.

15. "La Mulata," by A. O. Halloran, published in *Guarachas cubanas: Curioso recopilación desde las más antiguas hasta las más modernas*, 5.

16. The 1882 edition actually reads, "en las varillas del malacó," which is most likely a typographical error. I have chosen to interpret the text as "malecó." Cuban musicologist Leonardo Acosta recounted to me that during the summer, lower-class *habaneros* would go to the "*varillas*," baths carved into the rocks along the Malecón, or sea wall, to bathe and relax. There were separate areas screened off for men and women. It is not clear from the text whether the man has somehow gained entrance to the women's baths, or if the *mulata* is merely in the area. If the original text were correct, the term "malacó" might refer to a type of mollusk and "las varillas del malacó" could be either a shell-inlaid fan or some type of corset. (Marial Iglesias Utset, personal communication.)

17. Examples of typical early twentieth-century *guarachas* can be found in the collection of Jorge Anckermann's musical scores, previously held in the archive of the Centro Odilio Urfé, which are now part of the holdings of the Museo Nacional de Música.

18. The first version of *Cecilia Valdés* was published by Villaverde in 1830, and he spent the next five decades further refining the tragedy. Pictoral depictions of the *mulata* as a tragic figure can be seen in Eduardo Laplante's popular engravings for tobacco *marquillas*, which are discussed by Kutzinski, *Sugar's Secrets*, 69–74.

19. There are a few cases where *salidas* are sung by men. The title character in Lecuona's *Julián el Gallo* (1934), for example, sings a full *salida*. Julián, a voracious *mujeriego*, or womanizer, is portrayed as possessing both a promiscuous sexuality and a deep connection to the earth and nature, both of which are "female" traits associated with the *mulata*. Lecuona and his librettist Sánchez Galarraga recast these traits in a macho mold, and Lecuona even goes so far as to have Julián sing the rhythms of the *guaracha*, allowing him to serve as a national icon in the *mulata*'s place. *Salidas* performed by white female characters, while rare, do occur. (See Chapters 5 and 6.) One might surmise that the *salida*, which usually takes place at parties or dances, is far too "public" a display for the white aristocratic women characters that appear on the zarzuela stage.

20. The *cinquillo* is a syncopated rhythmic pattern most commonly consisting of a five-note pattern (quarter, eighth, quarter, eighth, quarter) followed by four unsyncopated rhythms (quarter, quarter, quarter, quarter). The term itself refers only to the initial five notes.

21. Benítez-Rojo uses this term to describe the Caribbean people's unique way of ascribing their own identity within the repeating histories of postcolonial society.

22. Fajardo Estrada, *Rita Montaner*, 89.

23. The Manglar was located near where Havana's train station stands today. In the nineteenth and early twentieth centuries the neighborhood was famous for tales of violence, prostitution, and witchcraft.

24. ". . . si hubiera dudao de tus frases, tén por sierto, o que ya me hubiera muerto o que te hubiera matao! Matao! . . . Que como la Maja que hubo en la tierra española, bajo mi bata de cola también yo llevo navaja!"

25. Le Duc, "Los origenes de la zarzuela moderna," 14–15.

26. María la O's identification as lower-class, darker-skinned, sexually available, and potentially violent also begs comparison with the title character of Bizet's *Carmen*, and María la O's reference to the Spanish *maja* serves only to strengthen this connection. *Carmen* (whose protagonist shows a clear debt to popular representations of the *maja*) was quite popular in early twentieth-century Cuba. A 1925 edition of *Revista Pro-Arte Musical* contains a multipage photographic spread of the many Carmens that had been performed in Cuba's theaters. Benítez, "El quincuagésimo aniversario de Carmen."

27. The Virgen de la Caridad del Cobre is also an important figure in Afrocuban religion, where she is syncretized with the *orisha* Ochún, goddess of rivers, fertility, and sensuality.

28. Caridad's character is informed by the stock characterization of the *negrito catedrático* (see Chapter 4), and she is scarcely able to control her flowery verbosity.

29. "Gracías mil / yo no merezco lo que oí."

30. "In the Absence."

31. Social dances attended primarily by Havana's working- and middle-class

Afrocuban population. Such dances also drew a fair number of white men, who came seeking out nonwhite women.

32. "Bailada aquella anticuada pieza con bastante gracia por parte de la mujer y con aire grotesco por la del hombre, saludaron la primera los circunstantes con estrépitos aplausos . . ." Villaverde, *Cecilia Valdés*, 69–70.

33. The *cinquillo* is a pervasive rhythm throughout Cuban music and is especially typical in the *danzón* and *contradanza*. The rhythm can rightly be called a pan-Caribbean rhythm, as it is thought to have reached Cuba via Haiti and has a strong presence in the music of Puerto Rico and the Dominican Republic, most notably in the *merengue*. The rhythm is often used as a metaphor for *mestizaje*. See Austerlitz, *Merengue*, 16–17.

34. The late Cuban musicologist and composer Hilario González once noted that María la O's music almost appears to have been written originally for a man, because of the constant third-person distancing. (Ramón Fajardo Estrada, personal communication.)

35. *Tango-congos* are often used in pieces meant for coloristic or ethnic effect. These pieces are typically humorous or show deprecating views of black characters. The *tango-congo* of Dolores Santa Cruz, from Roig's *Cecilia Valdés*, is perhaps one of the most famous examples.

36. "Era su tipo el de las vírgenes de lo más célebres pintores. Porque a una frente alta, coronada de cabellos negros y copiosos, naturalmente ondeados, unía facciones muy regulares, naríz recta que arrancaba desde el entrecejo, y por quedarse algo corta alzaba un si es no es el labio superior, como para dejar ver dos sartas de dientes menudos y blancos. Sus cejas describían un arco y daban mayor sombra a los ojos negros y rasgados, los cuales eran todo movilidad y fuego. La boca tenía chica y los labios llenos, indicando más voluptuosidad que firmeza de carácter. Las mejillas llenas y redondas y un hoyuelo en medio de la barba, formaban un conjunto bello, que para ser perfecto sólo faltaba que la expresión fuese menos maliciosa, si no maligna. . . . A qué raza, pues, pertenecía esta muchacha? Difícil es decirlo. Sin embargo, a un ojo conocedor no podía esconderse que sus labios rojos tenían un borde o filete oscuro, y que la iluminación del rostro terminaba un un especia de penumbra hacia el nacimiento del cabello. Su sangre no era pura y bien podía asegurarse que allá en la tercera o cuarta generación estaba mezclada con la etíope." Villaverde, *Cecilia Valdés*, 69–70.

37. Cecilia's words "la danza a mí me fascina" can be understood in two ways. *Danza* is the name of a nineteenth-century dance genre that was one of the precursors to the *danzón*. However, the word is also an archaic Spanish word for "dance" (*baile* is the common term) and is used in Cuba to describe classical or "high culture" dance forms, particularly ballet.

38. *Mayombe* and *mayombera* refer to practices of herbology and herbal magic associated with Afrocuban religion practiced by descendants of the Congolese region of Africa. The Congolese practices are less well known than the Yoruba-derived ones and have generally been held in greater suspicion by whites as being agents of witchcraft.

39. *Palo monte*, also known as *palo congo*, or simply *palo*, is one of several African-derived religions practiced in Cuba. The religion's focus on the influence of the dead, and the use of ritualistic items such as bones and herbs, has frequently

led to fear and misunderstanding of its religious practices and has often resulted in charges of witchcraft.

Chapter 4: From the Negrito to the Negro Trágico

1. "Teniendo la cara negra / con el tinze que usarémos / no habrá quien se atreva/ á registrarnos el cuerpo/ para adquirir la certeza/ si somos negros pintados/ ó somos negros de versa." These words are spoken by the character of Dima, in Pedro N. Pequeño's 1882 blackface *bufo* play, *La africana.* Quoted in Lane, *Blackface Cuba,* 111–12.

2. The zarzuela's representation of black characters evidences an undeniable gender bias. While black women were only occasionally represented on the zarzuela stage, usually as anonymous participants in chorus production numbers, the black man was a continuous subject of interest. I make a distinction here (as did the zarzuela's creators) between *mulata* characters, who are well represented in the repertoire, and black female roles. I have found no examples of primary roles for black women characters. Even the slave woman Africa, who has a major role in *El cafetal* (discussed in Chapter 6) is described in most librettos as a *mulata.*

3. "[The stereotype] is a form of knowledge and identification that vacillates between what is always 'in place,' already known, and something that must be anxiously repeated . . ." See Homi Bhabha, "The Other Question," 66–84.

4. See Lott, *Love and Theft;* and Bhabha, "The Other Question," 66–84.

5. Bhabha, "The Other Question," 66.

6. Judith Butler, building on Jacques Derrida's discussion of mimesis in "The Double Session," reminds us that "the imitated is to some degree produced—or rather, *reproduced*—by imitation." Yet, "on the contrary, *imitation* does not copy that which is prior, but produces and inverts the very terms of priority and derivativeness." Butler, "Imitation and Gender Insubordination," 313. While Butler's work describes the politics of identity and meaning that take place in the subjective performance of gender, and particularly in drag performance, her work resonates intriguingly with Homi Bhabha's work on repetition and stereotype in "The Other Question," especially when one begins to examine how such imitations produce pleasure.

7. Enrique Arredondo, more popularly known by his stage name, "Bernabé," recounts his own process of familiarization in his memoirs. He offers a particularly amusing anecdote of his first appearance in blackface, in 1923, when, after performing for an unruly and hostile audience in the Esmeralda movie house, he did not know how to remove the black paint from his face and was unable to leave the theater, as ruffians awaited him outside. He was finally able to return home, at three in the morning, where his mother taught him to remove the paint with water and oil. Enrique Arrendondo, *La vida de un comediante,* 36–37.

8. The term *gallego* literally refers to somebody from the Spanish region of Galicia. In Cuba, however, the term was used to denote anybody who came from Spain.

9. Leal, *Teatro bufo siglo XIX,* 21, and Lott, *Love and Theft,* 5.

10. The Haitian revolution, 1791–1803, stands as the only successful slave revolt in the history of the Americas. Events in Haiti profoundly affected the Cuban

experience, not only because Haiti ceased to be a player in the international sugar trade, but also because the racial violence that accompanied the revolution caused great fears among white Cubans that similar events could happen in Cuba.

11. These fears erupted in 1844, with the so-called conspiracy of La Escalera. Fearful of an English-backed black insurrection, Spanish authorities tortured and executed a number of Afrocubans, concentrating especially on the growing class of educated mulattos and free blacks. See Robert Paquette's study of the La Escalera conflict in *Sugar Is Made with Blood: The Conspiracy of La Escalera and the Conflict between Empires over Slavery in Cuba.*

12. See Mary Cruz, *Creto Gangá.*

13. The collection was published in three parts by Oliva y Compañía in 1846. Cruz, *Creto Gangá,* 49–50.

14. ". . . por la puerta del caricaturismo y la crítica de costumbres." Ibid., 15.

15. Crespo y Borbón's writings were not the first appropriation of black speech; blacks speaking in *bozal* appear as early as the colonial *villancico*. See Stevenson, "The Afro-American Musical Legacy to 1800." However, Crespo y Borbón was unique in that he used the speech as the core of his work, in order to truly exploit and experiment with its possibilities.

16. The *poesía negra* movement of the 1920s and 1930s, led by poet Nicolás Guillén, valorized Afrocuban speech and customs. Unlike the *poesía negra* movement, however, Crespo y Borbón's plays and newspaper columns would not use an appropriated black speech to bolster Cuban nationalism, but rather to undercut it. Robin Moore has argued that the caricature of black culture within Cuban theater eventually led to the valorization and popularization of the culture that was being denigrated, and, in spite of Crespo y Borbón's overtly racist tone, the publication of Creto's *bozal* may be looked at as having had a similar effect. Moore, *Nationalizing Blackness,* Chapter 2. Laurie Aleen Frederik makes a similar claim in "The Contestation of Cuba's Public Sphere in National Theater and the Transformation from *Teatro Bufo* to *Teatro Nuevo,*" 11.

17. Moore, *Nationalizing Blackness,* 43–44.

18. See Chapter 1.

19. The creation of the *negro catedrático* is credited to Francisco Fernández.

20. The *negros curros* might be viewed as participants in one of Cuba's earliest black power movements. These groups formed in black *barrios* of Havana and tried to imitate the original blacks that were brought to Cuba as slaves from Spain. They were recognizable by their elaborate dress, earrings on the men, and, in some cases, dreadlocks. See Fernando Ortíz, *Los Negros Curros.*

21. *Ñáñigos*—Practioners of Abakuá, an Afrocuban religious secret society. The Abakuá were feared and distrusted by the white elite, although the early twentieth century saw increasing numbers of white Abakuá members.

22. "Black witches." This stereotype covers the *santero,* a practitioner of Yoruba-based Afrocuban religion not associated with the Abakuá. The practices of *santería* were often condemned as witchcraft by those, white and nonwhite, outside of Afrocuban religious culture.

23. Aline Helg, *Our Rightful Share,* 107–8.

24. This strategy is discussed by Helg, *Our Rightful Share,* and by de la Fuente, *A Nation for All: Race, Inequality, and Politics in Twentieth-Century Cuba.*

25. "Es que ahora el negro es 'libre,' potencialmente igual al blanco, y había

que hallar nuevos elementos de discriminación que demostraran su salvajismo o su incapacidad para emparejarse con el resto de la población." Leal, *La selva oscura*, v. 2, 234.

26. See Moore's discussion of *negrito* performance, *Nationalizing Blackness*, 46–48.

27. In the 1920s, the coachman character played by Montaner in *La Niña Rita* was a recognizable figure in Cuban folklore. The character, known as a *negro calesero*, was drawn from colonial-era stereotypes surrounding the slaves who were selected to drive their master's coach. In the second volume of *La selva oscura*, Rine Leal documents that during the nineteenth century, such slaves were educated from an early age in the arts of etiquette and were identifiable by their manners and speech as well as by their luxurious dress. Havana's wealthy would compete in seeing whose coach and coachman were the most lavishly decorated. The special status of the *caleseros* made them the subject of caricature as *costumbrista* artists and playwrights sought to show them as vain, pretentious womanizers, as in Victor Patricio Landaluze's famous lithograph *Calesero cortejando una cocinera*.

28. The piece is credited to Grenet, although García Garófolo has shown that the song's origins are much older. Moore, *Nationalizing Blackness*, 108.

29. See Moore, *Nationalizing Blackness*, 166–90, and "The Commercial Rumba: Afrocuban Arts as International Popular Culture," 165–98.

30. Moore, *Nationalizing Blackness*, 180.

31. "Será la primera que haré en mi vida, pues si bien he cantado mucho en público, tanto en La Habana como en los Estados Unidos, nunca había salido al escenario viviendo un tipo, moviéndolo y hablándolo sobre las tablas." *Diario de la Marina*, Sept. 22, 1927, 8.

32. "Pensamos siempre que el calesero lo interpretara un hombre, pero al llevar la obra al teatro Regina . . . nos encontramos con que el empresario . . . no tenía, ni quería tener, 'negrito' en la compañía." *El Mundo*, Sept. 21, 1932, 8.

33. Ibid.

34. "Casí todos los números musicales fueron repetidos. Gustaron muy especialmente el de La Clavelera y Los Caleseros, en los cuales la notable tiple cantante María Ruiz hizo alarde de sus facultades." *Diario de la Marina*, Sept. 30, 1927, 8.

35. This maintains the *teatro vernáculo*'s use of the *negrito* as primarily a speaking character. Examples of nonsinging *negritos* from zarzuelas include Papa Yeyo in *Lola Cruz*, Monguito in *Amalia Batista*, and Tirso in *Cecilia Valdés*. I distinguish the musical performance of the *negrito* in zarzuelas from incidental music performed by anonymous blackface characters. Production numbers featuring *rumbas*, *comparsas*, and *congas* abound, such as "El Cabildo de Reyes" and "Los curros del Manglar" in *María la O*, "La conga se va" in *Rosa la China*, and "Etanilá" in *Cecilia Valdés*. These numbers are invariably performed by unnamed soloists and anonymous choruses who have no dramatic function in the larger work.

36. "Eto é un corral. Aquí er que no é gallo, é toro. Yo, por se acaso, voy a empesal a cantál, pá que no me confundan."

37. The realities of slavery would have given black house servants, male or female, access to family secrets. Thus, the construct that knowledge of domestic gossip is a feminine trait is itself based on a racialized model of (white) male mo-

bility and (white) female domesticity. This model was subverted by the structure of slavery.

38. "Toma mulatica bebe der coquito que para tu boca tu negrito abrió." The consistent use of diminutive endings (in *mulatica, coquito, negrito*) serves not only to show the intimate nature of the relationship between Chea and Felo but also to assist the choppy, singsong nature of the melody.

39. In Cuba, the phrase *romper el coco*, literally, "to break the coconut," means to realize a long-held sexual desire, making the allusions between the characters' dialogue and sexual activity even more explicit.

40. During slavery it was common for the children of slave owners to be called "Niño" or "Niña" by their slaves; although the term means "child," it could be used well into adulthood.

41. The colonial term *criollo* denotes a person of Spanish or European descent who is born on the island.

42. Moore, *Nationalizing Blackness*, 139.

43. Anselmo Suárez y Romero, *Francisco*.

44. Gertrudis Gómez de Avellaneda, *Sab*.

45. In Cuba, as in the United States, alliances were quickly drawn between the abolitionist movement and emerging feminist and women's groups. See Sánchez-Eppler, *Touching Liberty: Abolition, Feminism, and the Politics of the Body*.

46. Hensen, "Victor Capoul, Marguerite Olagnier's *Le Säis*, and the Arousing of Female Desire," 421.

47. Ibid., 455.

48. "Lamento esclavo" is from Grenet's zarzuela *La virgen morena*, which was popularized in Spain. The song was published separately as sheet music and is found in Grenet's 1939 anthology of Cuban music, *Música popular cubana*. The Cuban slaves lament also bears a strong similarity to North American musical theater numbers such as "Old Man River" from the 1929 Kern/Hammerstein musical *Showboat*.

49. Such terms refer to the linguistic and geographic origin of the different groups of Africans who were forcibly brought to the island. *Carabalí* referred to those who were descended from the Efik people, who came from the region of Calabar, in what is now southern Nigeria, while *Arará* refers to members of the Fon-Ewe ethnic groups from the Dahomey region of West Africa.

50. An example of this trend is found in *Cecilia Valdés*, where the slave woman María de Regla becomes Villaverde's advocate for abolition, telling her story with an eloquence and rhetorical skill that seems out of place next to the author's representation of other slaves.

51. Rhythmic terms such as *tango-congo* can be used to denote a particular rhythmic pattern as well as musical genres based upon that pattern.

52. An example of this appears in the *salida* of *María la O*.

53. When Lecuona wrote *María la O*, he originally intended to write a zarzuela on *Cecilia Valdés* but could not get rights to use the novel. Fajardo Estrada, *Rita Montaner*, 89.

54. The years following abolition saw the *negrito* figure treated with increasingly harsh caricature. Along with the *negro catedrático*, who made fun of educated blacks by affecting a fancy vocabulary he could not control, appeared more violent representations of blackness. These new black characters were thieves, thugs, and practitioners of witchcraft. Leal, *La selva oscura*, v. 2, 251.

55. The Manglar was located near where Havana's train station stands today. In the nineteenth and early twentieth centuries, the neighborhood was famous for tales of violence, prostitution, and witchcraft.

56. The correct Spanish would be, "Y le digo que, si cuida su pellejo, siga a la letra el consejo de respetar a esa, amigo! Porque no hay por que aclarar lo que usted sabe y yo sé; que usted con esa mujer tiene una deuda sagrada."

57. "Vete, María la O . . . Los curros vienen toos lo dias a cantá y a bailá a eita hora . . . Vete que no quiero que te vean aquí."

58. Subsequent performances of José Inocente's lament often changed the text of the last line to "la pena inmensa de la esclavitud" ("the immense pain of slavery"), further strengthening the song's connection to the slave lament. This change occurs in the 1979 EGREM recording of *María la O* and was published as sheet music in the 1930s.

59. See Chapter 5.

60. José Ruiz Elcoro, "Las bodas de oro de *Cecilia Valdés*."

61. Clara Díaz, José Ruiz Elcoro, and Victoria Eli Rodríguez all claim (without evidence) that the number was written for the work's premiere in 1932 but did not get performed until 1954.

62. The title means "Runaway Slave." Premiered in the Teatro Martí on October 14, 1936. Music by Gonzalo Roig, libretto by Marcelo Salinas. I discovered the autograph of this score in July 2000, misfiled with the orchestra parts of *La hija del sol.*

63. *Diario de la Marina*, Oct. 15, 1936, 8.

64. The theater closing was the subject of a new comedy that opened only two weeks after *El cimarrón*, titled *El teatro se va* (*The Theater Goes Away.*) Rio Prado discusses the economic and political circumstances that surrounded the theater's closing in *La Venus de Bronce*, 130–36.

65. As an older man, de Grandy performed the tragic black baritone repertoire.

66. Another example of this trend is Eliseo Grenet's song "El cimarrón," where the female narrator laments her abandonment.

67. The musical examples of "Dulce quimera" duplicated here belong to a copy that was part of the collection of Blanca Varela, now held in the Museo Nacional de Música. The key is transposed a step up from the key in which the piece is performed in *Cecilia Valdés*, but a step lower than the original, written as part of *El cimarrón.*

68. The text change at the beginning of Example 4.6 (from "Cecilia" to "traidora") appears in the original version and is a frequent substitution of the text for performances outside the context of the zarzuela. Some arrangements of the melody feature a *beguine* rhythm in the accompaniment, others a *son.*

69. See, for example, Heller, *Emblems of Eloquence: Opera and Women's Voices in Seventeenth-Century Venice.*

70. Tompkins, "Sentimental Power: *Uncle Tom's Cabin* and the Politics of Literary History," 122–46.

Chapter 5: Ingenues and Fallen Women

1. It is telling that author and politician Morúa Delgado would choose to write a novel that establishes "Otherness" in terms of class rather than race, as the au-

thor, of mixed race himself, argued that inequality would be erased only through a denial of racial difference. For a discussion of Morúa Delgado's views of racial politics, see Helg, *Our Rightful Share*, 153–54.

2. Isabel Ilincheta, Leonardo's sanctioned love interest in *Cecilia Valdés*, is the only exception. When the independent, headstrong girl with a mind for business who appears in the pages of Villaverde's novel is adapted to the zarzuela stage, Agustín Rodríguez and Gonzalo Roig undermine Isabel's independent spirit by writing out aspects of her character not considered crucial to the love plot.

3. It is not until Agustín Rodríguez's 1952 libretto of *La bella cubana* (the zarzuela was intended to have a musical score by both Roig and Prats, but only the libretto survives) that a white female character appears who possesses all of the attributes of early twentieth-century bourgeois female sensibility.

4. A representative scene occurs in *María la O*, when the ingénue Niña Tula excitedly meets at home with Santiago, the shoemaker.

5. Rules for courtship were quite rigid. In the colonial period, in which many of these zarzuelas are depicted, courting couples were closely chaperoned, being left alone only in highly public venues, at a dance, for example, or in an open carriage with others close by. The advent of the automobile caused quite a furor, as the closed sides granted couples a dangerous privacy. Cuban historian Julio César González is one of the first scholars to look closely at the connection between transportation and gender roles in Cuba. I am indebted to him for sharing with me his work in progress.

6. The issue comes up again in the surviving libretto for *La bella cubana*, in which the young Estrella finds herself alone in the garden with her beloved, dressed only in her nightdress. She virtuously flees. Her malevolent cousin then appears and, not having the morals to take her leave, ends up pregnant.

7. Term coined by George W. Bush during the 2000 presidential election campaign.

8. The most discussed of these relationships occurs in Villaverde's novel *Cecilia Valdés*, where Cecilia and her white half-sister Adela were raised by a black wet nurse, María de Regla. The two girls are said to be almost identical, and they bear an uncanny resemblance to María de Regla's own black daughter, Dolores. Thus, the wet nurse may be looked at allegorically as the mother of white, mulatto, and black: the Cuban nation. Conversely, the physical resemblance of the three girls that she nursed might also be read as conferring upon her a kind of illegitimate motherhood in the same sense that Don Cándido is the illegitimate father of Cecilia. The mistreatment of María de Regla by Don Cándido's wife follows the strategy of showing women as complicit in the evils of slavery, common in abolitionist literature in the United States as well as Cuba. See Sánchez-Eppler, "Bodily Bonds: The Intersecting Rhetorics of Feminism and Abolition."

9. "Que gueno etá eto! L'ama en er suelo, y la negra ecrava en el sillón"

10. *Tula:* "Tú no eres mi esclava, Ña Salú. Eres mi madre, desde que mi verdadera madre murió." *Salú:* "Madre negla como er carbón, con hija blanquito como la nieve."

11. Of the zarzuelas that emphasize cross-racial romance, I have located only one, Prats's *Amalia Batista*, that takes place in the twentieth century. The lack of contemporary plots dealing with race suggests that such topics were deemed more palatable when set in the past. Throughout the Republican period, focusing on the racism of the past was a recurrent strategy in downplaying contemporary

racial tensions, and Aline Helg has documented that criticisms of racism in contemporary culture were routinely criticized as divisive and incendiary. Helg, *Our Rightful Share*, 16–17 and 105–6. The head-in-sand practice of critiquing racism of the past but ignoring or denying its existence in the present continues to this day in Cuba. Since the 1959 Revolution, it has been common to discuss the discrimination in place under Batista but to ignore the pervading influence of racism still in place in Cuban society. Only recently has the Cuban government begun to take the discussion of race seriously, signaled by the Fifth Congress of the Cuban Communist Party, held in 1997, in which the government admitted that problems of racial discrimination had not been eradicated by the Revolution as had once been thought. Academic and artistic dialogue on race has become more frequent and open on the island, and the publication, in English, of a small portion of this dialogue has been an important step. See Pérez Sarduy and Stubbs, eds., *Afrocuban Voices: On Race and Identity in Contemporary Cuba*.

12. Niña Flor in Lecuona's *El cafetal* is the most prominent of these women.

13. Prats himself added music for the role of Carmita as he moved toward the goal of converting *Amalia Batista* into an opera. Lecuona's works have been less prone to heavy revisionism than either Prats's or Roig's, although new numbers were frequently added in the weeks following a show's opening. Thus, the *romanzas* given to Tula in later performances have been the result of artistic license, rather than compositorial intent, with performances such as the 1995 EGREM recording showcasing Maribel Ferrales's talents. (The recording also features extra music for Fernando, sung by Rodolfo Chacón, and Fernando's mother, sung by María de los Angeles Santana.)

14. Miguel de Grandy's 1961 revision of the libretto portrays Isabel in a light slightly more true to the novel.

15. The *romanza* is the zarzuela equivalent of the operatic aria. Given this literal definition, all of the zarzuela's major character types sing what are, technically, *romanzas*. However, composers most often refer to these pieces by their subgenres, be they rhythmic (*tango-congo*, march) or expressive (lament, serenade). Only the ingenue—and the *mulata*—perform musical numbers that are consistently referred to as *romanzas*. While *romanzas* written for the *mulata* are invariably tragic, sung near the zarzuela's end as the protagonist laments her inability to change fate, *romanzas* sung by the white ingenue are quite different, focusing instead on romantic love.

16. "Prayer" *romanzas*, or *plegarías* (discussed later), are somewhat an exception to this, for they begin with quite a limited range, although the range may expand as the piece develops.

17. It was typical for new musical numbers to be added in the days and weeks following a work's premiere, possibly because the work wasn't entirely finished by opening day, or as a marketing tool to further ticket sales, or to furnish showcase numbers for famous additions to the cast who were contracted once the work was deemed a success.

18. "Si tú supieras cuanto me interesa de verdad ese tal Alberto, no sé cuanto . . . y lo ansiosa que estoy porque llegue . . ."

19. "Yo quisiera un día sentir tu amor en sueño."

20. "Amor eterno, eterno amor, sublime loco arrobador que siempre en mí vivirá."

21. Another stratospheric *romanza* is that sung by Azucena in Gonzalo Roig's *El Clarín*, which similarly features an extended coloratura vocalise. Also written for the voice of Maruja González, Azucena is perhaps the most difficult soprano role in the zarzuela repertoire.

22. A descendant of the Italian operatic *preghiera*, the genre has a long history in Cuban lyric theater. Fidelia, the heroine in Hubert de Blanck's 1899 opera *Patria* sings a *plegaría* very similar to those found in the zarzuela.

23. "Bajo un palmar en noche de luna incierta / con un amor soñaba yo despierta / y eran tus ojos y eran tus labios / los que miraba yo en mi ilusión."

24. "Pero fue mi sueño fugaz cual la brisa del palmar y murió la bella illusion fugaz que no volverá."

25. "Pues yo sé que aunque el corazón arde en fé, jamás volverá la que se fue."

26. The art of sizing up the ingenue against an exotic Other is not unique to the zarzuela. The most familiar model is Bizet's *Carmen*, where Micaela's near-tuneless aria contrasts sharply with the folk-melodic character of Carmen's music. The effect of the contrast is not to emphasize Carmen's difference; indeed, her music is much more approachable than Micaela's. Rather, it is Micaela who seems out of place—"Other"—throughout the opera. The difference, however, between what occurs in Bizet's opera and what occurs in zarzuelas like Lecuona's *Lola Cruz* is that Micaela does not try to express herself using Carmen's musical rhetoric.

27. Several well-known Cuban intellectuals feared the mixture of Afrocuban culture with an officially sanctioned Cuban identity. Eduardo Sánchez de Fuentes was perhaps the most virulent of these critics. See Zoila Lapique Becali, "Figura musical de Eduardo Sánchez de Fuentes."

28. It must be remembered that the "blackness" originally suggested by musical genres such as *salidas*, *guarachas*, stage *rumbas*, and *tango-congos* was itself the product of an identity described and manipulated through a white lens, resulting in a musical version of blackness that was drawn up against the norms of whiteness. Robin Moore has shown that during the first decades of the twentieth century, the white Cuban establishment came to embrace Afrocuban-derived popular music, and sounds that had once been denigrated and censored were exploited as "national" music. Moore suggests that this "inclusive" appropriation served to further white hegemony in two ways. First, at a time when the *négritude* movement was sweeping the Caribbean, the white appropriation of black music disempowered that music's potential to participate in the black movement. Second, white appropriation "refined" black musical forms by giving them sophisticated arrangements and new dance steps, by downplaying the role of hand percussion—or even by reinterpreting them as light opera. While there is nothing unusual—or explicitly racist—about this kind of musical mixing, the popular new forms problematically came to be viewed as authentically "Cuban," while the original Afrocuban genres were criticized as lewd, primitive, or unmusical. See Moore, *Nationalizing Blackness*.

29. The *danzón*, a salon dance genre that blended European-style instrumentation with Afrocuban rhythmic elements, was considered lewd, dangerous, and overly black at its inception. Later, the genre became an icon for national culture, and cultural critics began a campaign to divest the *danzón* of its blackness. Sán-

chez de Fuentes actually went as far as stating that the *danzón* had absolutely no Afrocuban elements at all. Sánchez de Fuentes, "Influencia de los ritmos africanos en nuestro cancionero," 167. See also Moore's discussion in *Nationalizing Blackness*, 23–26, and Lane, *Blackface Cuba*, 149–79.

30. Quoted in Lane, *Blackface Cuba*, 154.

31. The Ten Years War (1868–78) was the first, and most prolonged, of a series of armed conflicts that pitted Cuban *mambises*, or independence fighters, against Spanish colonialists.

32. Aside from *Lola Cruz, Rosa la China* is the only exception I can think of, and even in *Rosa la China*, while the protagonist is ostensibly white, her nickname, "la China," suggests the possibility of racial mixture. Roig's zarzuela *Carmiña* (1934) does not quite fit into this convention, because its title lacks the protagonist's complete name.

33. A botched courtship had the power to ruin a reputation, since once a woman's family allowed a man to take the liberty of seeing their daughter, there was no saying what else might have occurred. See Suárez Findlay, *Imposing Decency*, 25.

34. "María la O, it's all finished"; "Amalia Batista, you played at love"; "María Belén Chacón, you can't sing any longer"; "Rosa la China, why did you dream, bird without nest, branch without flower."

35. "*Lola Cruz, qué ilusión te alumbraba, pero ya que tiembla ahora ves . . . Negra noche ya tu vida será pues tu sueño no volverá.*"

36. Felo and Chea's duet is discussed in Chapter 4.

37. Suárez Findlay, *Imposing Decency*, 25.

38. ". . . prez y gala deslumbrante del salón."

39. "People of bad living."

40. Stoner, *From the House to the Streets*, 63–73.

41. "no . . . como un pecado sino como un fenómeno social o patológico que debía ser curado en vez de condenado." Pogolotti, *La Republica de Cuba al través de sus escritores*, 54.

42. Stoner, *From the House to the Streets*, 130, 144.

43. "Se Hará Un Raid En Matanzas Contra La Gente De Mal Vivir

Una enérgica campaña moralizadora, un *raid* extensivo para todos los barrios extremos de la ciudad, contra la gente de mal vivir que vienen ofendiendo la moral pública, con detrimento de las buenas costumbres. La acción moralizadora será llevada a cabo por el Supernumerario del Ordén Público, Octavio Cánovas Martínez, quien con personal a sus órdenes viene realizando una amplia labor de investigación contando ya con una enorme lista de mujeres que hacen vida non sancta . . . En Matanzas se han efectuado ya otros *raids* de esta naturaleza . . . resultando siempre en tales casos, que han sido solamente víctimas las más infelices e indefensas de la clase, mientras las que activan y fomentan el vicio en alta escala, las dueñas de lonocinios y conocidos souttenuers, han seguido gozando de la mayor impunidad en la población." *Diario de la Marina* (March 2, 1929): 5.

44. The title can be translated as "*The Troublemaker*." The libretto does not carry the full name of the librettist, who is named only as "H. J. T." A musical score for the work has not surfaced in my research.

45. All of the named prostitutes (excluding Rosa) in this work are described in

the cast list to the libretto as *mulatas*. The list does not provide a racial description of Rosa.

46. "[Dulzura] es el marido de Rosa la China, el cuál vive de ella, pués la obliga
a hacer una vida que Rosa detesta, en una palabra: ha metido a Rosa en la vida
alegre, para explotarla."

47. I have noticed a certain reticence on the part of contemporary supporters of
lyric theater in Cuba to recognize Rosa's occupational status. When questioning
whether Rosa was a prostitute, I was told by various informants that no, she was
"low class," married to a "delinquent," or "maybe she helped her husband steal of
something, but she wasn't a prostitute." The reason behind this defense of Rosa's
moral standing sheds a curious light on contemporary cultural politics in Cuba.
In my interviews it seemed as if the defense of Rosa's honor was somehow tied
to a defense of Lecuona and his work (*Rosa la China* is one of his better-known
zarzuelas and one of the few to be recorded) and of the zarzuela genre in general.
These sentiments were relayed to me by Reynaldo Fustier, Anton Fustier, and
Nelson Moore of the Centro Pro Arte Lírico (personal communication, 1999); by
Jorge Bosque, stepson of Rodrigo Prats (personal communication, 1998); and by
the late Pedrito Fernández (personal communication, 1998). Their views were
echoed by several young singers I interviewed in between rehearsals at the Centro
Pro Arte Lírico, although interestingly, women seemed more willing than men
to admit that Rosa was probably engaging in prostitution.

48. Like María la O, Rosa sings her *guaracha* with a heavy street accent, an
accent that will vanish completely in her later musical numbers, as well as in
most of her spoken dialogue.

49. Although Rosa is explicitly not called a *mulata* in the libretto, her nickname
suggests a kind of racial ambiguity. *China*, or *chino*, can be a term of endearment
among Cubans of all races, and it is also used for those with slightly slanted eyes,
a trait popularly associated with central African or Chinese ancestry. This racial
ambiguity would have been heightened by the fact that at the work's premiere
the role of Rosa was played by Candita Quintana, one of Cuba's most celebrated
performers of *mulatas*.

50. Both *Carmen* and *La Traviata* were popular operas in Cuba during the Republic. Verdi's *La Traviata*, first performed in Havana in 1856, has been considered
the most popular opera in Latin America. See Rio Prado, *La música italiana a
Cuba*; and Versenyi, *Theater in Latin America*, 129.

51. From the stage directions in the libretto.

52. Woolf, *A Room of One's Own.*

53. The work premiered Oct. 3, 1941, in Havana's Teatro Principal de la Comedia. Agustín Rodríguez's libretto was the only source available in my research.
The catalogue of Lecuona's works put out by the Spanish Sociedad General de
Autores y Editores claims that there was a complete score in the holdings of the
Centro Odilio Urfé. That archive has since merged with that of the Museo Nacional de Música Cubana (which previously held a few isolated orchestral parts
for the work), and the score in question is one of the many items that has not yet
been catalogued because of lack of space, or because it did not remain with the
collection during the move.

54. *La de Jesús María* is the only work I have encountered that openly references the revolutionary struggles of the 1930s.

55. Charo's actions hearken back to *La Traviata*, where Violetta's self-sacrifice aims to preserve another's purity and innocence.

56. María Teresa de la Cruz Muñoz's libretto *Dos vidas*, performed in the Teatro Martí in 1934 with music by Rodrigo Prats, provides one of the few women's voices in the music theater industry. Cruz Muñoz's libretto fights the stereotype against working women when the young heroine María is thrown out of her convent school upon the death of her father. Destitute, she obtains a job as a clerk. Abandoned by her former friends, one of whom even pretends not to recognize her in the street, María maintains her virtue although she eventually loses her job after shunning the advances of her employer. The former friend who avoided her, meanwhile, leaves her husband for another man and sows social chaos wherever she goes. The moral lessons offered in Muñoz's libretto were not, however, a model for the zarzuela at large. A copy of the libretto can be found in the Biblioteca Nacional José Martí, but no copies of the musical score appear to have survived. Cruz Muñoz was the wife of José Sánchez Arcilla, one of the librettists of *Cecilia Valdés* and *María Belén Chacón*.

Chapter 6: Ambivalent Heroes and Sensual Peasants

1. ". . . Uds. son seres inferiores, que se dedican de una manera morbosa a una sola mujer. Yo digo como el Poeta: las novias pasadas con copas vacías, en ellas pusimos un poco de amor. Pasaron las horas, volaron los días . . . traed nuevas copas, con nuevo licor." The zarzuela's libretto was written by Agustín Rodríguez as an homage to Gonzalo Roig. The undated libretto is held in the Museo Nacional de la Música Cubana.

2. Librettists occasionally used the *galán*'s student status to address the growing nationalist movement among Cuba's university students in the 1920s and early1930s. The Federación de Estudiantes Universitarios, or F.E.U., was founded in 1922. The group became a primary voice for dissent, criticizing governmental corruption and the increasing foreign ownership of Cuban resources. The male protagonist Andrés, in Agustín Rodríguez's libreto for *La de Jesús María*, embodies the role of the left-leaning student activist and is an excellent example of this trend.

3. A present-day singer in Havana's Centro Pro-Arte Lírico expressed her disdain for the *galán*'s lack of appeal one day in rehearsal when she exclaimed in frustration to her duet partner, who was in bad voice, "Oye, ya me cuesta mucho trabajo enamorarme con Leonardo, pero cuando gritas es imposible!" ("Look, it's already a lot of work to make myself fall in love with Leonardo, but when you yell, it's impossible!") Name withheld upon request. Rehearsal, Centro Pro-Arte Lírico, Havana, July 14, 2000.

4. See Regidor Arribas, *La voz en la zarzuela*.

5. A notable exception is the character of Ricardo in Lecuona's *Lola Cruz*, who introduces himself while singing of his past transgressions. At the end of the zarzuela, Ricardo again stretches the stereotypical mold of the *galán* as he sings with two *mambises* (revolutionary fighters) of his decision to go off to war in "La guerra chiquita."

6. The tradition still exists among Spain's university students, as well as student groups in Mexico.

7. This song was not in the original production of *Amalia Batista* but was added in later revisions.

8. A similar "seduction" duet occurs between Eugenio and Dulce María in *Julián el Gallo.* Like Flor, Dulce María's resistance to Eugenio is defeated by the music's arrival to 3/4 meter.

9. "Mi amor y mi ayuda por siempre. Podrá el mundo odiarnos pero separarnos, no podrá jamás."

10. "Dime que ya no la quieres. Júrame que no la ves. Júrame que sólo eres de tu Cecilia Valdés."

11. The duet between Alberto and Africa, as well as the *concierto final* that ends the zarzuela, premiered on March 11, 1929, ten days after the show's opening. *Diario de la Marina,* March 11–12, 1929.

12. Literally, "Creole." The term *criollo* was used to differentiate those Cubans born in Cuba from immigrants who were born in Spain. In popular theater, the resulting contrast between the *criollo* and the *gallego* (Spaniard) led to the direct association of the *criollo* type with Cuban nationalism.

13. It is a curious irony that Julián, the most nationalistic of all of the zarzuela's male leads in his lyrics and behavior, is perhaps the character whose vocal delivery most resembles the Spanish zarzuela tradition.

14. The *décima* is a ten-line poetic form with a tradition that dates back to medieval Spain. In western Cuba, the poems are freely improvised over a fixed melody with instrumental *ritornelli* and are known as the *punto guajiro* (country *punto*), *punto libre* (free *punto*), or *punto pinareño* (*punto* from the region of Pinar del Rio).

15. "En el remoto confín de la manigua cubana, en el monte y la sabana su canción canta el Clarín."

16. "Canta el ave, canta el río, y también canta la palma [repeat] y si me quieres bien mío, alegre canta mi alma."

17. The work was premiered by tenor Miguel de Grandy and soprano Maruja González, both noted for their vocal virtuosity.

Epilogue

1. See the discography for more information about individual recordings. For more information about Fernando Montilla and the rise of Montilla Records, see Cristobal Díaz Ayala, *Música cubana,* 241–45, 250.

2. Archive of the Museo Nacional de Música. It appears from Roig's correspondence that none of the requests ever received a positive response to their query—Roig jealously guarded the rights to his music. Roig did register the rights to *Cecilia Valdés* with the E. B. Marks Music Company in 1948, but it was never published.

3. Molina, *150 años de zarzuela en Puerto Rico y Cuba,* 307.

4. Martínez, "Esther Borja."

5. Ibid., 307.

6. A particularly valuable archive is the library of the Sociedad General de Autores y Editores, located in Madrid. Information on the locations of Lecuona's works can be found in Bestard, ed., *Catálogo de obras de Ernesto Lecuona.*

7. See Robin Moore, *Music and Revolution,* Chapter 2.

8. Pro-Arte Grateli maintains an important and vibrant presence in Miami to this day. It continues to be directed by the indefatigable Pili de la Rosa. Zarzuelas have also been produced by Spanish-language companies in New York, in New Jersey, and throughout South Florida, and Cuban tenor Pedro Gómez moved to Puerto Rico and became active in zarzuela production there. See Molina, *150 años de zarzuela*, 331–39, and Sturman, *Zarzuela*.

9. Pedrito Fernández had been Lecuona's personal secretary. Ramón Fajardo Estrada, from an interview with María de los Angeles Santana. Personal communication.

10. Ramón Fajardo Estrada, personal communication.

11. Pedro Arias, one of the Teatro Lírico founders, personal communication.

12. Particularly the government's dismantling of the Sociedad Nacional de Autores Cubanos. See Moore, *Music and Revolution*, 120.

13. See Rivera García, "Una Amalia sin mayombe"; Anonymous, "Amalia Batista en el García Lorca"; and Royero, "Amalia Batista: Hacia dónde va el teatro lírico?," 23–24.

14. Reynaldo Fustier, personal communication.

15. "Un intento de analizar pasiones y situaciones con cierto enfoque ético, aportando así al género una relative validez social, lo que ayuda a destruir la falsa imagen de la zarzuela cubana como género socialmente intrascendente, ya que en todas subyace una denuncia y un cuestionamiento del orden social y moral imperante." De la Hoz, "Cafetal en penumbras."

16. See Moore, *Nationalizing Blackness*, 62–86.

BIBLIOGRAPHY

Abbreviations

BN	Biblioteca Nacional José Martí
COU	Archive of the Centro Odilio Urfé
CPF	Private collection of Pedrito Fernández
JRE	Private collection of José Ruiz Elcoro
MNM	Museo Nacional de la Música Cubana
OBP	Private collection of Olga Bosque de Prats
PA	Private collection of Pedro Arias
RG	Private collection of Radamés Giro
ST	Private collection of Susan Thomas
TLN	Archive of the Teatro Lírico Nacional de Cuba

Contemporary Sources: Books and Articles

Anonymous. "La Alianza Feminista: El esfuerzo mínimo." *Diario de la Marina* (March 8, 1929).

Anonymous. "Babel: Nada humano me es ajeno." *Prensa libre* 16 (January 1947). (MNM).

Anonymous. "'El cafetal' y 'Las mulatas de Bombay' mañana en el Regina." *Diario de la Marina* (March 10, 1929): 8.

Anonymous. "Entrevista con Ernesta Lecuona." *Alerta* (January 23, 1952): 7. (MNM).

Anonymous. "Hoy, dos funciones en el Teatro Regina." *Diario de la Marina* (October 7, 1927): 8.

Anonymous. "'No existe la música afrocubana' dice el maestro Jorge Anckermann." *Melodías* (February 1, 1939): 5, 42.

Anonymous. "Regina, Lunes Popular: *Las mulatas de Bombay* y *El cafetal.*" *Diario de la Marina* (March 10, 1929): 8.

Anonymous. "Se hará un raid en Matanzas contra la gente de mal vivir." *Diario de la Marina* (March 2, 1929): 5.

Anonymous. "El teatro musical cubano y español a través de la estampa (1850–1940)." Pamphlet. Havana: Ministerio de Cultura, Centro de Documentación Musical, s.f.

Anonymous. "La vida y la obra de Ernesto Lecuona." Playbill for Teatro Lírico Cubano de Ernesto Lecuona, 1936. (CPF).

Arrom, José Juan. *Historia de la literatura dramática cubana.* New Haven, Conn.: Yale University Press, 1944.

Benítez, Nena. "Jorge Anckermann ha muerto." *Diario de la Marina* (February 5, 1941): 8.

———. "Jorge Anckermann Bafart." In "Música y Músicos." *El País* (February 3, 1942).

Bolet, Alberto. "Ha muerto Jorge Anckermann." *El País* (February 3, 1941): 15.

Callejas, José María. *Historia de Cuba,* ed. Ortíz. Havana: Editorial Ortíz, 1841.

Carrión, Miguel de. *Las honradas y las impuras.* (First published 1917, 1919). Havana: Letras Cubanas, 1978.

Diario de la Marina. Número centenario, 1832–1932. Havana, 1932.

Gómez de Avellaneda, Gertrudis. *Errores del corazón.* Havana: Editorial Arte y Literatura, 1977.

———. *Sab.* Havana: Editorial Arte y Literatura, 1976.

Guarachas cubanas: Curiousa recopilación desde las más antiguas hasta las más modernas. Havana: Librería Principal, 1882.

Herrera, José María. "Entrevista con Rita Montaner." *Diario de la Marina* (September 22, 1927): 8.

Hills, Elijah Clarence. *Bardos cubanos: Antología de las mejores poesías líricas de Heredia, "Plácido," Avellaneda, Milanés, Mendive, Luaces, y Zenea.* Boston: D.C. Heath, 1901.

Lamar, Hortensia. "La mujer cubana: Su preparación y concepto social de la vida." *Diario de la Marina. Número centenario, 1832–1932* (1932): 127.

Lizaso, Félix. *Panorama de la cultura cubana.* México: Fonda de Cultura Económica, 1949.

Machado, Gerardo. "Cuba Musical." *Diario de la Marina* (March 29, 1929): 10.

Martí, Agenor. "Cara a cara con Rodrigo Prats." *Cuba.* s.f. 48–50. (RG).

Orbón, Julián, and Hilario González, eds. "Presencia cubana en la música universal." Pamphlet. Havana: Grupo de Renovación Musical, 1945. (RG).

Ortíz, Fernando. *Bailes y el teatro de los negros en el folklore de Cuba.* Havana: Letras Cubanas, 1981.

———. "El estudio de la música afrocubana." *Musicalia* 5 (January 1929).

———. *Los negros curros.* Havana: Editorial de Ciencias Sociales, 1989.

Peraza, Carlos. *Machado: Crímenes y horrores.* Havana: Cultural S.A., 1933.

Roig, Gonzalo. "Música." In *Historia de la nación cubana.* Vol. 7. Havana: Editorial Historia de la Nación Cubana, 1952.

Sainz de la Peña, J. "La interprete sonriente de la voz de la calle" *El País.* Sección Dominical. S.f. 4. Anckermann archive (MNM).

Salazar, Adolfo. "El siglo XX, hijo del siglo XIX." *Musicalia* 8 (September 1929): 41–47.

Sánchez de Fuentes, Eduardo. "Los compositores del primer concierto local." *Pro-Arte Musical* 4 (November 15, 1926): 6–7.

———. "Influencia de los ritmos africanos en nuestro cancionero." *Anales de la academia nacional de artes y letras* 11 (1927): 115–66.

Suárez y Romero, Anselmo. *Francisco.* Havana: Editorial Arte y Literatura, 1984.

Villaverde, Cirilo. *Cecilia Valdés.* Havana: Editorial Letras Cubanas, 1982.

Scores, Librettos, and Musical Recordings

Anckermann, Jorge. *Afrodita.* 1923. Piano vocal score. Archive of the Odilio Urfé. (MNM).

———. *America en la guerra.* 1918. Piano vocal score. Archive of the Centro Odilio Urfé. (MNM).

———. "Los Amores del Zangano" and "El Sereno." Sound recording sung by Caridad Castillo and Ramón Espigul. Victor Records, 1910's. (JRE).

———. *La carretera central.* 1928. Piano vocal score. Archive of the Centro Odilio Urfé. (MNM).

———. "El chauffer" and "Arriba la canela." Sung by Ramon Espigul. Victor Records, s.f. (JRE).

———. *Napoleon.* 1908. Piano vocal score. Archive of the Centro Odilio Urfé. (MNM).

———. *La niña bonita.* 1915. Piano vocal score. Archive of the Centro Odilio Urfé. (MNM).

———. *La Señorita Maupin.* 1918. Piano vocal score. Archive of the Centro Odilio Urfé. (MNM).

———. "El quitrín." Sheet music. Havana: Casa del Anselmo López, s.f. (ST).

———. "El quitrín." Sung by Rita Montaner. Columbia Records, s.f. (JRE).

——— and Federico Villoch. "Los patos de Florida" and "La bisabuela de teatro cubano." Comic sketches recorded by Blanca Becerra. Columbia Records, 1915. (JRE).

Arrieta, Emilio. *Marina.* Opera española en tres actos. Madrid: Unión Musical Española, 1946.

Centeno, Modesto, and Gilberto Enríquez. *Cecilia Valdés.* Adaptation of libretto by A. Rodríguez and J. Sánchez Arcilla. S.f. (PA).

Chapí, Rupert. *La tempestad.* Madrid: Sociedad Anónima Casa Dotesio, s.f. (MNM).

De Blanck, Hubert. *Patria.* Opera en un acto y dos cuadros (1899). Unpublished piano vocal score. Havana: Museo Nacional de la Míúísica Cubana. (MNM).

"Galleguíbiri Macuntíbiri." Comic sketch recorded by Sergio Acebal and Adolfo Atero. Columbia Records, s.f., ca. 1923. (JRE).

Grandy, Miguel de. *Cecilia Valdés.* Libretto based on the original by Agustín Rodríguez. Havana: Consejo Provincial de Cultura, Impresa Modelo, 1961.

Grenet, Eliseo. "Cimarrón." *Canción afro-cubana.* Sheet music. Havana: s.f. (ST).

———. "Lamento cubano" (*son*). New York: Southern Music Publishing, 1932.

———. "La mora" (*danzon*). Copy by Choe Belén Puig. Havana. (RG).

———. "Las perlas de tu boca" (*bolero*). Havana: Editores Culturales, s.f.

Guerrero, J. *Los gavilanes.* Zarzuela en tres actos. Madrid: Unión Musical Española, 1925.

Guridi, J. *El caserio.* Comedia lírica en tres actos. Madrid: Unión Musical Española, 1927.

Lecuona, Ernesto. *í_ílbum de obras.* No. 3. Havana: Lecuona Music Co., 1929.

———. "Ali Baba" and "Pirulero" from *La guaracha musulmana.* Sung by Margarita Cueto. Victor, s.f. (JRE).

———. *El cafetal.* 1929. Copy of original piano-vocal score. (MNM).

———. *El cafetal.* Sound recording. Serdisco 7432133582. 1995.

———. "Canción de la Flor" from *El cafetal.* Sheet music. Havana: Ediciones Ernesto Lecuona, 1929.

———. *María la O.* Sainete, 1930. Piano-vocal score. (MNM).

———. *María la O.* Sound recording. EGREM CD 0122, 1995.

———. "Romanza" from *María la O.* Sheet music. Havana: S. Iglesias é Hijo, 1929. (MNM).

———. "Romanza" from *Rosa la China.* Sheet music. Havana: Copyright Ernesto Lecuona, 1932. (MNM).

———. *Rosa la China.* Sainete lírico. 1932. Piano-vocal score. s.f. (MNM).

———. *Rosa la China.* Sainete lírico. 1932. Piano-vocal score copied by Edilia Piñon González, 1980. MNMC Undated copy of piano vocal score. (CPF).

———. *Rosa la China.* Sound recording. Serdisco 74321334572, 1995.

———. "Triste es ser esclavo" from *El cafetal.* Sheet music. Havana: Ediciones Ernesto Lecuona, 1929.

Lehar, Franz. "Eva." Recorded by the orchestra of the Teatro Alhambra. Columbia Records, 1909. (JRE).

Luna, Pablo. *Molinos de viento.* Opereta en un acto. Madrid: Unión Musical Española, 1929.

Meluza, Francisco. *La plaza del catedral.* 1944. Libretto for television version, 1952. (PA).

Moreno Torroba, F. *Luisa Fernanda.* Comedia lírica en tres actos el segundo dividido en tres cuadros. Madrid: Unión Musical Española, 1932.

Prats, Rodrigo. *Amalia Batista.* Autograph piano-vocal score, 1936. (OBP).

———. "Espero de tí." Unpublished manuscript. (ST).

———. "El Heladero" (1928) Unpublished manuscript. (ST).

———. "Madre . . .!" from *El gran desfile* (1933). Unpublished manuscript. (TLN).

———. "Miedo al desengaño." Unpublished manuscript. (ST).

Primelles, Carlos. *La tierra de Venus.* Revista fantástica. Original libretto. Havana: 1927. (CPF).

Rodríguez, Agustín. *Amalia Batista.* Original libretto, 1936. (OBP).

———. *La bella cubana.* Zarzuela en tres actos. 1952. Original libretto. (PA).

——— and José Sánchez Arcilla. *Cecilia Valdés.* Original libretto, 1932. (MNM).

Roig, Gonzalo. "Canción de cuna" from *Cecilia Valdés.* Sheet music. Published in *Carteles*, s.f. (MNM).

———. *Cecilia Valdés.* Autograph orchestral score, 1932. (MNM).

———. *Cecilia Valdés.* Autograph piano vocal score, 1932. (MNM).

———. *Cecilia Valdés.* Copy of piano-vocal score authorized by composer. (MNM).

———. *Cecilia Valdés.* Sound recording. EGREM LD4675–6, 1990.

———. *Cecilia Valdés.* Sound recording. EMI CDZ 5734172, 1999.

———. "Duo de Isabel y Leonardo" from *Cecilia Valdés.* Sheet music. Havana: Ediciones Roig, 1932. (ST).

"Los timbales" and "El pajarito." Sound recording. Comic sketches performed by "Los negritos de Palatino." Victor, 1909. (JRE).

———. "Po po po" from *Cecilia Valdés*. Sheet music. Havana: Ediciones Roig, 1932. (ST).

Roldán, Amadeo, and Alejandro García Caturla, Eliseo Grenet, and Emilio Grenet. *Motivos de son*. Havana: Editorial Letras Cubanas, 1980.

Sánchez Galarraga, Gustavo. *El cafetal*. Original libretto. Havana: 1929. (CPF).

———. *María la O*. Sainete. Original libretto. Havana: 1930. (CPF).

———. *Rosa la China*. Sainete lírico. Original libretto. Havana: 1932. (CPF).

Secondary Sources: Books and Articles

Acosta, Leonardo. *Dal tamburo al sintetizzatore: La míúísica cubana e afrocubana*. Vol. 2. Bolsena, Italy: Massari Editore, 1998.

———. "Ernesto Lecuona: El centenario y otras consideraciones. *Revista 91.9 10* (April–May, 1996): 34–38.

———. *Música y descolonialización*. Havana: Editorial Arte y Literatura, 1982.

———. "Universo de Hilario González." *Revista Clave* 1 (July–September, 1999): 14–17.

——— and Olivier Cossard, René Espí, and Helio Orovio. *Fiesta Havana: 1940–1960: L'age d'or de la musique cubaine*. Paris: Editions Vade Retro, 1999.

André, Naomi Adele. "Azucena, Eboli, and Amneris." PhD dissertation, Cambridge, Mass.: Harvard University, 1996.

Anonymous. "Amalia Batista en el García Lorca." *Trabajadores*, 1979.

Anonymous. "Eliseo Grenet, el prolífico autor de 'Mama Inés.'" *Granma* (April 7, 1985): 5.

Anonymous. "Homenaje a Eliseo Grenet." Program notes. Havana: Delegación Provincial de La Habana, Consejo Nacional de Cultura, 1966.

Anonymous. "El mar en la música: Grenet." *Mar y Pesca* (January 1985): 56–57.

Anonymous. Program notes to *El cafetal*. Presented in the Gran Teatro de la Habana: Festival Iberamerican de la Zarzuela, 1990.

Arblaster, Anthony. *Viva la Libertá! Politics in Opera*. London: Verso, 1992.

Ardévol, José. *Introducción a Cuba: La música*. Havana: Instituto del Libro, 1969.

———. "Nuestra música en los años treinta: Vivencias." *Unión* 1 (1980): 120–33.

Barcía Zequeira, María del Carmen. "Entre el poder y la crisis: Las prostitutas se defienden." In Luisa Campuzano, ed. *Mujeres latinamericanas: Historia y cultura, siglos XVI al XIX*. Vol. 1. Havana: Casa de las Américas, 1997.

Bean, Annemarie, James V. Hatch, and Brooks McNamara, eds. *Inside the Minstrel Mask: Readings in Nineteenth-Century Blackface Minstrelsy*. Hanover, N.H.: Wesleyan University Press, 1996.

Béhague, Gerard. *Music in Latin America: An Introduction*. Englewood Cliffs, N.J.: Prentice-Hall, 1979.

Behar, Ruth, and Deborah A. Gordon, eds. *Women Writing Culture*. Berkeley: University of California Press, 1995.

Belliard-Acosta, Marianella. "Del lecho al hecho hay un gran trecho: Mestizaje, sexo y concubinato; construcción social de la mujer de color en *Cecilia Valdés*."

In Luisa Campuzano, ed. *Mujeres latinamericanas: Historia y cultura, siglos XVI al XIX.* Vol. 2. Havana: Casa de las Américas, 1997.

Benítez-Rojo, Antonio. *La isla que se repite: El caribe y la perspectiva posmoderna.* Hanover, N.H.: Ediciones del Norte, 1989.

———. *The Repeating Island: The Caribbean and the Postmodern Perspective.* Trans. James Maraniss. Durham, N.C.: Duke University Press, 1992.

Benjamin, Jules R. *The United States and the Origins of the Cuban Revolution.* Princeton, N.J.: Princeton University Press, 1990.

Bestard, Hamilé Rozada, ed. *Catálogo de obras de Ernesto Lecuona.* Madrid: Sociedad General de Autores y Escritores, 1995.

Bhabha, Homi K. *The Location of Culture.* London: Routledge, 1994.

———, ed. *Nation and Narration.* London: Routledge, 1990.

Bowers, Jane, and Judith Tick. *Women Making Music: The Western Art Traditions, 1150–1950.* Chicago: University of Chicago Press, 1987.

Bowlby, Rachel. "Breakfast in America—*Uncle Tom's* Cultural Histories." In Homi K. Bhabha, ed. *Nation and Narration.* London: Routledge, 1990.

Brand, Peggy Zeglin, and Carolyn Korsmeyer. *Feminism and Tradition in Aesthetics.* University Park: Pennsylvania State University Press, 1995.

Brennan, Timothy. "The National Longing for Form." In Homi K. Bhabha, ed. *Nation and Narration.* London: Routledge, 1990.

Burton, Antoinette. *Burdens of History: British Feminists, Indian Women, and Imperial Culture, 1865–1915.* Chapel Hill: University of North Carolina Press, 1994.

Butler, Judith. "Imitation and Gender Insubordination." In *The Lesbian and Gay Studies Reader.* New York: Routledge, 1993.

Cairo, Ana. *El grupo minorista y su tiempo.* Havana: Editorial Ciencias Sociales, 1978.

———. *La revolución del 30 en la narrativa y el testimonio cubanos.* Havana: Editorial Letras Cubanas, 1993.

Calderón González, Jorge. *Nosotros, la música y el cine.* Xalapa: Universidad Veracruzana, 1997.

Campuzano, Luisa. "Blancas y <<blancos>> en la conquista de Cuba." In Luisa Campuzano, ed. *Mujeres latinamericanas: Historia y cultura, siglos XVI al XIX.* Vol. 1. Havana: Casa de las Américas, 1997.

———, ed. *Mujeres latinamericanas: Historia y cultura, siglos XVI al XIX.* 2 vols. Havana: Casa de las Américas, 1997.

Cañizares, Dulcila. "La creatividad en Gonzalo Roig" Pamphlet. Havana: Ministerio de Cultura, Instituto de la Míúísica Cubana, Museo Nacional de la Míúísica, 1990.

———. *Gonzalo Roig.* Havana: Editorial Letras Cubanas, 1978.

———. *Gonzalo Roig: Hombre y creador.* Havana: Editorial Letras Cubanas, 1999.

Cantón Navarro, José. *Historia de Cuba: El desafío del yugo y la estrella.* Havana: SI-MAR S.A., 2000.

Carbonell y Rivera, José Manuel. *Las bellas artes in Cuba.* Havana: Imprenta "El Siglo XX," 1928.

Carpentier, Alejo. *Crónicas.* Vol. 1. Havana: Editorial Arte y Literatura, 1975.

———. *Crónicas.* Vol. 2. Havana: Editorial Arte y Literatura, 1976.

———. *La música en Cuba.* Havana: Editorial Pueblo y Educación, 1989.

———. *Temas de la lira y del bongo.* Havana: Editorial Letras Cubanas, 1994.

Carreras, Julio A. *Contradicciones de clases en el siglo XIX.* Havana: Editorial de Ciencias Sociales, 1985.

Cid Pérez, José. "Introduction." In *El teatro en Cuba republicana.* Havana, 1958.

Clément, Catharine. *Opera, or the Undoing of Women.* London: Virago Press, 1989.

Cordero, Tania. "Teatro musical: La luna impaciente." *Tablas* 3 (1998): 14–19.

Cortázar, Octavio. "Bola y Rita: La memoria, la música y el amor." *Gaceta de Cuba* 30 (July–August 1992): 22–27.

Cruz, Anne J. *Discourses of poverty: Social Reform and the Picaresque Novel in Early Modern Spain.* Toronto: University of Toronto Press, 1999.

Cruz, Mary. *Creto Gangá.* Havana: Unión de Escritores y Artistas Cubanos, 1974.

Davis, Martha Ellen. "'Bi-musicality' in the cultural configurations of the Caribbean." *Black Music Research Journal* 14, no. 2 (Fall 1994) 145–60.

Depestre, Leonardo. *Cuatro músicos de una villa.* Havana: Editorial Letras Cubanas, 1990.

Deschamps Chapeaux, Pedro. *El negro en la economía habanera del siglo XIX.* Havana: Unión de Escritores y Artistas de Cuba, 1971.

Díaz Ayala, Cristóbal. "Discografía activa de Lecuona." In *Ernesto Lecuona: Homenaje a la música viva del compositor cubano.* Program for concerts November 23 and 24, 1995. Madrid: Casa de America, 1995.

———. *Míúísica cubana del areyto a la nueva trova.* Miami: Ediciones Universal, 1993.

Díaz Pérez, Clara. *De Cuba soy hijo: Correspondencia cruzada de Gonzalo Roig.* Madrid: Editorial Música Mundana, 1995.

———. "Gonzalo Roig Lobo (1890–1990): Centenario de su nacimiento." Pamphlet. Havana: Ministerio de Cultura, Instituto de Música Cubana, Museo Nacional de Música, 1990.

———. "Luisa María Morales." Pamphlet. Havana: Ministerio de Cultura, Dirección Nacional de Música, Museo Nacional de la Música, 1987.

Días-Ruiz Soto, Antonio, Mercedes Humpierre Alvarez, and René Marquéz Castro. *La sociedad neocolonial cubana.* Havana: Editorial de Ciencias Sociales, 1984.

Dorr, Nelson. "*María la O* en España." *Clave* 14 (1989): 45–46.

Duharte Jiménez, Rafael. *El negro en la sociedad colonial.* Santiago de Cuba: Editorial Oriente, 1988.

Dunn, Leslie C., and Nancy A. Jones, eds. *Embodied Voices: Representing Female Vocality in Western Culture.* Cambridge, UK: Cambridge University Press, 1994.

Encima Cortizo, María. "La zarzuela romántica. Zarzuelas estrenadas en Madrid entre 1832 y 1847." In *Actas del congreso internacional "La zarzuela en España y Hispanoamérica: centro y periféria, 1800–1950." Cuadernos de música iberoamericana,* vol. 2–3, 1996–1997.

Evora, Tony. *Ernesto Lecuona: Homenaje a la música viva del compositor cubano.* Program for concerts November 23 and 24, 1995. Madrid: Casa de America, 1995.

Fajardo Estrada, Ramón. *Rita Montaner: Testimonio de una época.* Havana: Casa de las Américas, 1997.

Fanon, Franz. *Black Skin, White Masks.* New York: Grove Press, 1976.

Feijoo, Samuel. *El negro en la literatura folklórica cubana.* Havana: Editorial Letras Cubanas, 1980.

Fernández de Castro, José Antonio. *Tema negro en las letras de Cuba (1608–1935).* Havana: Ediciones Mirador, s.f.

Fernández Robaina, Tomás. *Historias de mujers públicas.* Havana: Editorial Letras Cubanas, 1998.

———. *El negro en Cuba: 1902–1958.* Havana: Editorial de Ciencias Sociales, 1994.

Ferrán, Yamilé, and Maithée Rodríguez. *Luz y sombra de mujer.* Havana: Editorial Letras Cubanas, 1998.

Figueras, Francisco. *Cuba y su evolución colonial.* Havana: Editorial Isla, s.f.

Flinn, Caryl. *Strains of Utopia: Gender, Nostalgia, and Hollywood Film Music.* Princeton, N.J.: Princeton University Press, 1992.

Frederik, Laurie Aleen. "The Contestation of Cuba's Public Sphere in National Theater and the Transformation from *Teatro Bufo* to *Teatro Nuevo,* or What Happens When *El Negrito, El Gallego,* and *La Mulata* meet *El Hombre Nuevo." Hewlett Foundation Working Papers Series.* Chicago: Center for Latin American Studies, 1998.

Fuente, Alejandro de la. *A Nation for All: Race, Inequality, and Politics in Twentieth-Century Cuba.* Chapel Hill: University of North Carolina Press, 2001.

Fulcher, Jane F. *The Nation's Image: French Grand Opera as Politics and Politicized Art.* New York: Cambridge University Press, 1987.

Fusco, Coco. "Adventures in the Skin Trade." *The Utne Reader* 82 (July 1, 1997): 67–69, 107–9.

Gadles Mikowsky, Solomon. *Ignacio Cervantes y la danza en Cuba.* Havana: Editorial Letras Cubanas, 1988.

Galán, Natalio. *Cuba y sus sones.* Valencia: Ediciones Pre-Textos, 1997.

García, Andra. "La zarzuela en Cuba." *Clave* (June 1987): 24.

García Franco, Manuel, and Ramón Regidor Arribas. *La zarzuela.* Madrid: Acento Editorial, 1997.

Garciaporra, Jorge. "Rosita Fornés, su mundo lírico." *Clave* (November 1988): 13–16.

Gillman, Susan. "The Mulatto, Tragic or Triumphant? The Nineteenth-Century American Race Melodrama." In Shirley Samuels, ed. *The Culture of Sentiment: Race, Gender, and Sentimentality in Nineteenth-Century America.* New York: Oxford University Press, 1992.

Giro, Radamés, "Bibiliografía: Historia, literatura, música, filosofía, etnografía, sociología." Havana: Radamés Giro, 1998. (RG).

———, ed. *Panorama de la música popular cubana.* Havana: Editorial Letras Cubanas, 1998.

Gómez Cairo, Jesús, ed. *El arte míúísical de Ernesto Lecuona.* Madrid: Sociedad de Autores y Editores, 1995.

Gómez Cairo, Jesús. "Ernesto Lecuona en la orbita de su creación." In Jesús Gómez Cairo, ed. *El arte musical de Ernesto Lecuona.* Madrid: Sociedad de Autores y Editores, 1995.

Gómez García, Zoila. *Música latinoamericana y caribeña*. Havana: Editorial Pueblo y Educación, 1995.

González, Hilario. "*Écue Yamba-O!* por dentro" *Iman* 2 (1984–85): 5–24.

———. "El Lied en Ernesto Lecuona." In Jesús Gómez Cairo, ed. *El arte musical de Ernesto Lecuona*. Madrid: Sociedad de Autores y Editores, 1995.

——— and María Antonieta Enríquez. "Ernesto Lecuona: Fisonomía de lo cubano." *Gaceta de Cuba* (September–October, 1995), 12–18.

González, Jorge Antonio. *La composición operística en Cuba*. Havana: Editorial Letras Cubanas, 1986.

———. "Entre nota y nota: En el 70 aniversario del estreno de *Domingo de piñata* y otras obras de Ernesto Lecuona durante el verano de 1919." *Revista Clave* 14 (1989): 39–51.

———. "Establecimiento y desarrollo de la zarzuela en La Habana durante el siglo XIX." *Boletín Musical* 25 (1972): 5–11.

González, Reynaldo. *Contradanzas y latigazos*. La Habana: Letras Cubanas, 1992.

———. *La ventana discreta*. Ciego de Avila, Cuba: Ediciones Avila, 1998.

———. "A White Problem: Reinterpreting Cecilia Valdés." In Pedro Perez Sarduy and Jean Stubbs, eds., *Afrocuba: An Anthology of Cuban Writing on Race, Politics, and Culture*. Melbourne, Australia: Ocean Press, 1993.

González Freire, Natividad, ed. *Teatro cubano del siglo XIX*. 2 vols. Havana: Editorial Arte y Literatura, 1975.

Gramatges, Harold. "Editorial." *Nuestro tiempo* 1, no. 2 (April 1954): 1–14.

———. "Notas sobre Ernesto Lecuona." Read at concert program, "Recordar . . . a Ernesto Lecuona," at the Biblioteca Nacional "José Martí," December 19, 1983. (RG).

Guadarrama González, Pablo, and Miguel Rojas Gómez. *El pensamiento filosófico en Cuba en el siglo XX: 1900–1960*. Havana: Editorial Félix Varela, 1998.

Guardia González de la, Gisela. "La zarzuela en Cuba en el período comprendido entre los años 1927 y 1940." Thesis. Havana: Instituto Superior de Arte, 1989.

Guerra y Sánchez, Ramiro, ed. *Historia de la nación cubana*. Havana: Editorial Historia de la Nación Cubana, 1952.

Guillén, Nicolás. "Eliseo Grenet." *Seminario habanero* (November 13, 1950).

Hadlock, Heather. *Mad Loves: Women and Music in Offenbach's* Les Contes D'Hoffman. Princeton, N.J.: Princeton University Press, 2000.

Hamm, Charles. *Irving Berlin: Songs from the Melting Pot; The Formative Years, 1907–1914*. New York: Oxford University Press, 1997.

———. "Towards a New Reading of Gershwin." In *The Gershwin Style: New Looks at the Music of George Gershwin*. New York: Oxford University Press, 1999.

Helg, Aline. *Our Rightful Share: The Afro-Cuban struggle for Equality, 1886–1912*. Chapel Hill: University of North Carolina Press, 1995.

Heller, Wendy Beth. "Chastity, Heroism, and Allure: Women in Opera of Seventeenth-Century Venice." PhD dissertation, Waltham, Mass.: Brandeis University, 1995.

———. *Emblems of Eloquence: Opera and Women's Voices in Seventeenth-Century Venice*. Berkeley: University of California Press, 2003.

Henríquez, María Antonieta. *Alejandro García Caturla*. Havana: Ediciones Unión, 1998.

———. "Lo permanente en nuestra música." *Nuestro tiempo* 22 (March–April 1958). Reprinted by Editorial Letras Cubanas, s.f. 287–301.

——— and Hilario González. "Lecuona en primer plano." *Revolución y cultura* 10 (October 1985): 46–54.

Henríquez Ureña, Max. *Panorama histórico de la literatura cubana*. Havana: Reedición Revolucionaria, 1967.

Holland, Norman S. "Fashioning Cuba." In Andrew Parker, Mary Russo, Doris Sommer, and Patricia Yaeger, eds., *Nationalisms and Sexualities*. New York: Routledge, 1992.

Howard, Philip A. *Changing History: Afro-Cuban Cabildos and Societies of Color in the Nineteenth Century*. Baton Rouge: Louisiana State University Press, 1998.

Ibarra, Jorge. *Un análisis psicosocial del cubano: 1898–1925*. Havana: Editorial de Ciencias Sociales, 1994.

———. *Cuba, 1898–1921: Partidos políticos y clases sociales*. Havana: Editorial de Ciencias Sociales, 1992.

———. *Nación y cultura nacional*. Havana: Editorial Letras Cubanas, 1981.

Jones, Willis Knapp. *Behind Spanish American Footlights*. Austin: University of Texas Press, 1966.

Kallberg, Jeffrey. *Chopin at the Boundaries: Sex, History, and Musical Genre*. Cambridge: Harvard University Press, 1996.

Kerman, Joseph. *Opera as Drama*. Berkeley: University of California, 1988.

Knight, Franklin. *Slave Society in Cuba during the Nineteenth Century*. Madison: University of Wisconsin Press, 1970.

——— and Colin A. Palmer, eds. *The Modern Caribbean*. Chapel Hill: University of North Carolina Press, 1989.

Kondo, Dorinne. "Bad Girls: Theater, Women of Color, and the Politics of Representation." In Ruth Behar and Deborah A. Gordon, eds. *Women Writing Culture*. Berkeley: University of California Press, 1995.

Koskoff, Ellen. *Women and Music in Cross-Cultural Perspective*. Chicago: University of Illinois Press, 1989.

Kuhlman, Erika A. *Petticoats and White Feathers: Gender Conformity, Race, the Progressive Peace Movement, and the Debate over War, 1895–1919*. Westport, Conn.: Greenwood Press, 1997.

Kutzinski, Vera. *Sugar's Secrets: Race and the Erotics of Cuban Nationalism*. Charlottesville: University of Virginia Press, 1993.

Lane, Jill. *Blackface Cuba, 1840–1995*. Philadelphia: University of Pennsylvania Press, 2005.

Lapeña-Bonifacio, Amelia. *The "Seditious" Tagalog Playwrights: Early American Occupation*. Manila: Zarzuela Foundation of the Philippines, 1972.

Lapique Becali, Zoila. "Figura musical de Eduardo Sánchez de Fuentes." Biblioteca Nacional José Martí. *Revista* 16, no. 2 (May–August 1974): 217–30.

———. *Música colonial cubana en las publicaciones periódicas (1812–1902)*. Havana: Editorial Letras Cubanas, 1979.

Leal, Rine. *Breve historia del teatro cubano*. Havana: Editorial Letras Cubanas, 1980.

———. *En primera persona*. Havana: Instituto del Libro, 1967.

———. *La selva oscura, vol. 1: Historia del Teatro Cubano desde sus orígenes hasta 1868*. Havana: Editorial Arte y Literatura, 1975.

———. *La selva oscura, vol. 2: De los bufos a la neocolonia*. Havana: Editorial Arte y Literatura, 1982.

———, ed. *Teatro bufo: Siglo XI*. Havana: Editorial Arte y Literatura, 1975.

León, Argeliers. "Actitudes del compositor cubano en el siglo XIX." *Revista de la Universidad de La Habana* 32, no. 192, "edición extraordinaria" (October–December, 1968).

———. "La canción y el bolero." Pamphlet. Departamento de Música, Biblioteca Nacional "José Martí," s.f.

———. *Del canto y el tiempo*. Havana: Editorial Pueblo y Educación, 1974.

———. "El ciclo del danzón." *Nuestro Tiempo* 2, no. 4 (March 1955): 1–3.

———. "Del eje y la bisagra." Pamphlet. Havana: Biblioteca Nacional "José Martí", 1987.

———. "Ensayo sobre la influencia española en la música cubana." *Boletín metodológico* 3 (December 1976).

León, Carmela de. *Ernesto Lecuona: El maestro*. Havana: Editorial Musical de Cuba, 1995.

Levine, Lawrence. *Highbrow Lowbrow: The Emergence of Cultural Hierarchy in America*. Cambridge, Mass.: Harvard University Press, 1988.

Linares, María Teresa, and Faustino Nuñez. *La música entre Cuba y España*. Madrid: Sociedad de Autores y Editores, 1998.

Lope de Vega. *El nuevo mundo descubierto por Cristóbal Colón*. In Menéndez y Pelayo, ed., *Obras*. Madrid: Biblioteca de Autores Españoles, 1966.

———. *El remedio en la desdicha*. Cambridge: The University Press, 1931.

López, Oscar Luis. *La radio en Cuba*. Havana: Editorial Letras Cubanas, 1981.

Lott, Eric. *Love and Theft: Blackface Minstrelsy and the American Working Class*. New York: Oxford University Press, 1992.

Luis, William. *Literary Bondage: Slavery in Cuban Narrative*. Austin: University of Texas Press, 1990.

Mañach, Jorge. *Ensayos*. Havana: Editorial Letras Cubanas, 1999.

Martín, Edgardo. "Recuerdo a Rita Montaner." *Nuestro tiempo* 5, no. 23 (May–June, 1958): 9.

Martínez, Orlando. *Ernesto Lecuona*. Havana: UNEAC, 1989.

Martínez-Fernández, Luis. *Fighting Slavery in the Caribbean: The Life and Times of a British Family in Nineteenth-Century Havana*. New York: M. E. Sharpe, 1998.

Martínez-Malo, Antonio. *Rita: La í_ínica*. Havana: Editorial Abril, 1988.

Martínez Rodríguez, Raul. "Esther Borja." Program notes for recital performed for the "Día Internacional de la Mujer." Havana: Ministerio de Cultura, Instituto Cubano de la Música, Museo Nacional de la Música, 1990.

———. "Felo Bergaza (1917–1969). Recordación por el 20 aniversario de su muerte (1969–1989)." Havana: Ministerio de Cultura, Museo Nacional de Música, 1989.

———. "Ignacio Villa y Fernández, Bola de Nieve. En su 75 aniversario de natalicio y 15 de fallecido." Pamphlet. Havana: Ministerio de Cultura, Museo Nacional de Música, 1986.

Martínez Tabares, Vivian. "*Parece blanca:* Una relectura de *Cecilia Valdés* desde el teatro cubano." In Luisa Campuzano, ed. *Mujeres latinamericanas: Historia y cultura, siglos XVI al XIX.* Vol. 2. Havana: Casa de las Américas, 1997.

Martínez Villena, Rubén. "Las contradicciones internas del imperialismo yanqui y el alza de movimiento revolucionario." *Pensamiento crítico* 39 (April 1970): 72–84.

Martínez, Mayra. "Eliseo Grenet: Del danzón al sucu-sucu." *Revolución y cultura* 130 (1992): 78–79.

McClary, Susan. *Feminine Endings: Music, Gender, and Sexuality.* Minneapolis: University of Minnesota Press, 1991.

———. *Georges Bizet:* Carmen. Cambridge, UK: Cambridge University Press, 1992.

McClintock, Anne. *Imperial Leather: Race, Gender, and Sexuality in the Colonial Contest.* New York: Routledge, 1995.

Medina Martín, Alicia. "Fernando Anckermann (1890–1933). Catálogo de partituras." Pamphlet. Havana: Ministerio de Cultura, Museo Nacional de Música, 1987.

Méndez Bravet, Alina. "Testimonios." In Jesús Gómez Cairo, ed. *El arte musical de Ernesto Lecuona.* Madrid: Sociedad de Autores y Editores, 1995.

Méndez Capote, Renée. *Memorias de una cubanita que nació con el siglo.* Havana: Editorial Gente Nueva, 1998.

Merchán, Rafael M. *Patria y cultura.* Havana: Ministerio de Educación, 1948.

Milanés, José Jacinto. *Antología lírica.* Havana: Editorial Arte y Literatura, 1975.

Miller, Jonathan. *Don Giovanni: Myths of Seduction and Betrayal.* New York: Faber and Faber, 1990.

Moore, Robin D. "The Commercial Rumba: Afrocuban Arts as International Popular Culture." *Latin American Music Review* 16, no. 2 (Fall/Winter 1995): 165–98.

———. *Music and Revolution.* Berkeley: University of California Press, 2006.

———. *Nationalizing Blackness: Afrocubanismo and Artistic Revolution in Havana, 1920–1940.* Pittsburgh: University of Pittsburgh Press, 1997.

———. "Representations of Afrocuban Expressive Culture in the Writings of Fernando Ortíz." *Latin American Music Review* 15/1 (Spring/Summer, 1994).

Mordden, Ethan. *Coming Up Roses: The Broadway Musical in the 1950s.* New York: Oxford University Press, 1998.

Moreno Fraginals, Manuel R. "Hacia una historia de la cultura cubana." *Revista de la Universidad de la Habana* 227 (May–June 1986): 41–63.

Moríúía Delgado, Martín. *Sofía.* Havana: Editorial Arte y Literatura, 1977.

Muguercia, Alberto, and Ezequiel Rodríguez. *Rita Montaner.* Havana: Editorial Letras Cubanas, 1985.

Muñoz Alburquerque, Carmelina. "Moisíéís Simons Rodríguez, Centenario de su nacimiento (1889–1989)." Pamphlet. Havana: Ministerio de Cultura, Instituto de la Música, Museo Nacional de la Música, 1989.

Muñoz de Quevedo, María. "Una Mujer." *Musicalia* 13–14 (September–December, 1930): 123–24, 128.

———. "Profesión de fé." *Musicalia* 10 (January 1930): 19–20.

Neuls-Bates, Carol, ed. *Women in Music: An Anthology of Source Readings from the Middle Ages to the Present.* Boston: Northeastern University Press, 1996.

Newman, Karen. *Fashioning Femininity and English Renaissance Drama*. Chicago: University of Chicago Press, 1991.

Ojeda Fernández, Norka. "Eliseo Grenet: Mamá Inés tiene 60 años." *Granma* (July 24, 1987): 5.

Oramas, Joaquín. "*Rosa la China* y el rescate de nuestro género lírico." *Granma* (August 10, 1975).

Orovio, Helio. *Diccionario de la música cubana*. Havana: Editorial Letras Cubanas, 1981.

Ortner, Sherrie. *Making Gender: The Politics and Erotics of Culture*. Boston: Beacon Press, 1996.

———. "Theory in Anthropology in the 1960s." In Nicholas B. Dirks, Geoff Eley, and Sherry B. Ortner, eds. *Culture/Power/History: A Reader in Contemporary Social Theory*. Princeton, N.J.: Princeton University Press, 1994.

Osa, Enrique de la. *Crónica del año 33*. Havana: Editorial de Ciencias Sociales, 1989.

———. *Sangre y pillaje*. Havana: Editorial Pablo de la Torriente, 1990.

Paquette, Robert L. *Sugar Is Made with Blood: The Conspiracy of La Escalera and the Conflict between Empires over Slavery in Cuba*. Middletown, Conn.: Wesleyan University Press, 1988.

Parker, Andrew, and Mary Russo, Doris Sommer, and Patricia Yaeger, eds. *Nationalisms and Sexualities*. New York: Routledge, 1992.

Pérez, Louis A. *Cuba: Between Reform and Revolution*. New York: Oxford University Press, 2005.

Pérez de la Riva, Juan. "Los recursos humanos de Cuba al comenzar el siglo: Inmigración, economía, y nacionalidad (1899–1906)." In *Anuario de estudios cubanos* 1. Havana: Editorial de Ciencias Sociales, 1975.

Pérez Sarduy, Pedro, and Jean Stubbs, eds. *Afro-Cuba: An Anthology of Cuban Writing on Race, Politics, and Culture*. New York: Ocean Press, 1993.

———. *Afro-Cuban Voices: On Race and Identity in Contemporary Cuba*. Gainesville: University Press of Florida, 2000.

Pichardo, Esteban. *Diccionario provincial casí razonado de vozes y frases cubanos*. Havana: Editorial de Ciencias Sociales, 1979.

Piñeiro Días, José. "Cronología artística de Alice Dana Plasencia (soprano y pedagoga)." Pamphlet. Havana: Ministerio de Cultura, Dirección Nacional de Música Cubana, Museo Nacional de la Música, 1988.

———. "Ernesto Lecuona." *Dos Musicalia* 1, no. 1 (January–March 1997): 12–19.

———. "Francisco Fernández Dominicis: Centenario de su natalicio (1883–1983)." Pamphlet. Havana: Ministerio de Cultura, dirección de patrimonio cultural, Museo Nacional de la Música, 1983.

———. "Homenaje a Carmelina Santana Reyes (1907–1981)," Pamphlet. Havana: Ministerio de Cultura, Dirección Nacional de Música, Museo Nacional de la Música Cubana, 1989.

———. "Recordando al maestro Rodrigo Prats." *Revista de la Biblioteca Nacional José Martí* 27, no. 3 (September–December, 1985): 76.

———. "Rita Montaner, 80 Aniversario 1900–1980." Pamphlet. Havana: Ministerio de Cultura, Museo Nacional de la Música Cubana, 1980.

———. "Rodrigo Prats Llorens, director de orquesta y compositor. Quinto aniversario de su fallecimiento (1980–1985)." Pamphlet. Havana: Ministerio de Cultura, Museo Nacional de la Música Cubana, 1985.

———. "Teatros de Cuba." Pamphlet published as part of the Festival International de Arte Lírico de La Habana. Havana: Ministerio de Cultura, Museo Nacional de la Musica Cubana, 1987.

Pogolotti, Marcelo. *Los apuntes de Juan Pinto*. Havana: 1951.

———. *Del barro y las voces*. Havana: Union de Escritores y Artistas Cubanos, 1968.

———. *La historia de Cuba al través de sus escritores*. Havana: Editorial Lex, 1958.

Pols, José A. "Entrevista con Rodrigo Prats." *Revolución y Cultura* 67 (1975): 20–38.

Poumier, María. *Apuntes sobre la vida cotidiana en Cuba en 1898*. Havana: Editorial de Ciencias Sociales, 1975.

Powers, David M. "The French Musical Theatre: Maintaining Control in Caribbean Colonies in the Eighteenth Century." *Black Music Research Journal* 18, no. 1–2 (Spring–Fall 1998): 229–40.

Ramirez, Arturo. *El canto de la Alondra*. La Habana: Editorial Lex, 1957.

Regidor Arribas, Ramón. *Aquellas zarzuelas . . .* Madrid: Alianza Editorial, 1996.

———. *La voz en la zarzuela*. Madrid: Real Musical, 1991.

Rey Alfonso, Francisco. "Gran Teatro de La Habana: Cronología mínima, 1834–1987." Pamphlet. Havana: Banco Nacional de Cuba, 1988.

Rio Prado, Enrique. *La miúísica italiana a Cuba: Prime rappresentazioni delle opere di Verdi e Morlacchi a L'Avana*. Lecce, Italy: BESA Editrice, 1996.

———. *La Venus de bronce: Hacia una historia de la zarzuela cubana*. Boulder, Colo.: Society of Spanish and Spanish-American Studies, 2002.

Rivera García, José. "Una Amalia sin mayombe." *El Caimíáín barbudo* (August 1979). (RG).

Le Riverand, Julio. *La república: Dependencia y revolución*. Havana: Editorial de Ciencias Sociales, 1971.

Roa, Raul. *Retorno a la alborada*. 2 vols. Las Villas, Cuba: Universidad Central de Las Villas, 1961.

Robinson Caivet, Nancy. "El homenaje a Rodrigo Prats." *Granma* (January 22, 1980). (MNM).

———. "Rodrigo Prats y el estreno de *Amalia Batista*." *Granma* (June 21, 1979). (MNM).

Robreño, Eduardo. *Como lo pienso, lo digo*. Havana: Unión de Escritores y Artistas Cubanas, 1985.

———. *Como me lo contaron, te lo cuento*. Havana: Editorial Letras Cubanas, 1981.

———. *Cualquier tiempo pasado fue*. Havana: Editorial Letras Cubanas, 1981.

———. *Historia del teatro popular cubano*. Havana: Oficina del Historiador de la Ciudad, 1961.

———. Program notes to recording of *Amalia Batista*. Havana: EGREM, 1980.

———, ed. *Teatro Alhambra: Antología*. Havana: Editorial Letras Cubanas, 1979.

———. *. . . y escrito en este papel*. Santiago de Cuba: Editorial Oriente, 1989.

Rodríguez, Olavo Alén. "The Afro-French Settlement and the Legacy of Its Music to the Cuban People." In Gerard H. Bíéíhague, ed., *Music and Black Ethnicity: The Caribbean and South America*. New Brunswick, N.J.: Transaction Publishers, 1994.

Royero, Maida. "Amalia Batista: Hacia dónde va el teatro lírico?" *Revolución y cultura* 85 (1979): 23–24.

Ruiz Elcoro, José. "En las bodas de oro de Cecilia Valdés." *Tablas* 2 (1992): 29–35.

———. "Pensamiento musicológico de Cuba: Antecedentes e iniciadores." *Clave* 1, no. 1 (July–September, 1999): 42–45.

———. "Surgimiento y desarrollo de la zarzuela cubana: Estructura, morfológica y análisis." In *Actas del Congreso Internacional La Zarzuela en Espana e Hispanoamerica. Centro y periferia, 1800–1950.* Madrid: SGAE,1995.

———. "El teatro musical de Ernesto Lecuona." In Jesús Gómez Cairo, ed. *El arte musical de Ernesto Lecuona.* Madrid: Sociedad de Autores y Editores, 1995.

Samuels, Shirley, ed. *The Culture of Sentiment: Race, Gender, and Sentimentality in Nineteenth-Century America.* New York: Oxford University Press, 1992.

Sánchez, Juan. *Fidelio Ponce.* Havana: Editorial Letras Cubanas, 1985.

Sánchez Cabrera, Maruja. "Orquesta Filarmónica de La Habana (1924–1989). 65 aniversario de us fundación." Pamphlet. Havana: Ministerio de Cultura, Museo Nacional de la Música Cubana, 1989.

Sánchez-Eppler, Karen. "Bodily Bonds: The Intersecting Rhetorics of Feminism and Abolition." In Shirley Samuels, ed. *The Culture of Sentiment: Race, Gender, and Sentimentality in Nineteenth-Century America.* New York: Oxford University Press, 1992.

Sarmiento Sánchez, Lázaro. "El tenor más grande del mundo: El doble musical de Miguel Barnet." *Salsa* 1, no. 3 (1997): 16–19.

Schechter, John M., ed. *Music in Latin American Culture: Regional Traditions.* New York: Schirmer Books, 1999.

Schwartz, Rosalie. "Ideales de una Raza; Caste, Class, and Consciousness in 1920s Cuba." Unpublished paper presented at the Latin American Studies Association conference, s.f.

Seoane Gallo, José. *Eduardo Abela: Cerca del cerco.* Havana: Editorial Letras Cubanas, 1986.

Simon, Pedro. "La danza en Ernesto Lecuona." In Jesús Gómez Cairo, ed. *El arte musical de Ernesto Lecuona.* Madrid: Sociedad de Autores y Editores, 1995.

———. "Ernesto Lecuona." *Bohemia* 77, no.44 (November 1985): 14–19.

———. "Ernesto Lecuona en su nonagésimo aniversario." *Cuba en el ballet* 4, no. 4 (July–December 1985).

Smart, Mary Ann, ed. *Siren Songs: Representations of Gender and Sexuality in Opera.* Princeton, N.J.: Princeton University Press, 2000.

Solie, Ruth A. *Musicology and Difference: Gender and Sexuality in Music Scholarship.* Berkeley: University of California Press, 1993.

Sommer, Doris. "Irresistible Romance: The Foundational Fictions of Latin America." In Homi K. Bhabha, ed. *Nation and Narration.* London: Routledge, 1990.

Starr, Larry. "Musings on 'Nice Gershwin Tunes.'" In Wayne Schneider, ed. *The Gershwin Style: Form and Harmony in the Concert Music of Gershwin.* New York: Oxford University Press, 1999.

Stein, Louise K. *Songs of the Mortals, Dialogues of the Gods: Music and Theatre in Seventeenth-Century Spain.* Oxford, UK: Clarendon Press, 1993.

Stevenson, Robert. "The Afro-American Musical Legacy to 1800." *Musical Quarterly* 54, no. 4 (October 1968): 475–502.

Stoner, K. Lynn. *From the House to the Streets: The Cuban Woman's Movement for Legal Reform, 1898–1940.* Durham, N.C.: Duke University Press, 1991.

Sturman, Janet L. *Zarzuela: Spanish Operetta, American Stage.* Chicago: University of Illinois Press, 2000.

Suárez Durán, Esther. "Otra mirada al bufo sin prejucios, con amor." *Gaceta de Cuba* (September–October, 1995): 28–31.

Suárez Findlay, Eileen. *Imposing Decency: The Politics of Sexuality and Race in Puerto Rico, 1870–1920.* Durham, N.C.: Duke University Press, 1999.

Subirá, José. *Historia de la música teatral en España.* Barcelona: Labor, 1945.

Teurbe Tolón, Edwin. *Historia del teatro en la Habana.* Sta. Clara, Cuba: Universidad Central de las Villas, 1961.

———. *Teatro lírico popular de Cuba.* Miami: Ediciones Universal, 1973.

Urfé, Odilio. "Aporte negro en la música cubana. (Breves acotaciones a tan complejo como interesante tema)." *Nuestro tiempo* 5, no. 29 (May–June, 1959): 3–4.

Vallejo, Catharina. "*Las feministas,* la zarzuela inédita de Virginia Elena Ortea." In Luisa Campuzano, ed. *Mujeres latinamericanas: Historia y cultura, siglos XVI al XIX.* Vol. 2. Havana: Casa de las Américas, 1997.

Vasquéz, Roland. "The Quest for National Opera in Spain and the Re-Invention of the Zarzuela (1808–1849)." Dissertation, Cornell University, 1992.

Versényi, Adam. *Theatre in Latin America: Religion, Politics, and Culture from Cortés to the 1980s.* Cambridge, UK: Cambridge University Press, 1993.

Vidaurreta, José Luis. "La música cubana en el periódo republicano." In *Panorama de la música cubana.* Unpublished manuscript. (RG).

Vitier, Cintio. *Lo cubano en la poesía.* Havana: Editorial Letras Cubanas, 1998.

Weiss, Judith A., ed. *Latin American Popular Theatre: The First Five Centuries.* Albuquerque: University of New Mexico Press, 1993.

Williams, Lorna Valerie. *The Representation of Slavery in Cuban Fiction.* Columbia: University of Missouri Press, 1994.

Woolf, Virginia. *A Room of One's Own.* New York: Harcourt Brace Jovanovich, 1957.

Yanez, Mirta. "Cecilia Valdés: La heroína corriente, la heroína solitaria." In Luisa Campuzano, ed. *Mujeres latinamericanas: Historia y cultura, siglos XVI al XIX.* Vol. 2 Havana: Casa de las Américas, 1997.

Yglesia Martínez, Teresita. *El segundo ensayo de república.* Havana: Editorial de Ciencias Sociales, 1980.

INDEX

Abbate, Carolyn, 4
Abela, Eduardo, 20
abolitionist literature, 94, 98, 111
Acebal, Sergio, 86, 196n50
Afrocuban culture and music: *afrocubanismo*, 19–21; feeling associated with, 107–8; folkloric ensembles, 181; as hegemonic musical discourse of zarzuela, 120–21; ingenue's musical behavior contrasted with, 120; intellectual opposition to, 18–19, 197n60, 215n27; in Lecuona's *María la O*, 101–2; *mulata* character in popularization of, 21, 43; *negrito* character in popularization of, 93; *poesía negra* movement, 209n16; in Prats's *Amalia Batista*, 72, 78; in Roig's *Cecilia Valdés*, 62, 103; whites appropriate, 120–21, 217n28; zarzuela in popularization of, 2, 3, 20–21
afrocubanismo, 19–21
Alianza Feminista Cubana, 31
Allenbrook, Wye J., 4
Alma de raza (Lecuona), 36, 184
alma guajira, La (Salinas), 103
Amalia Batista (Prats): central conflict of, 144; chronology of lyric works by Prats, 189; cross-racial romantic intrigue in, 112, 213n11; enshrined as classic, 179; female protagonist of, 27; *galán* in, 155; *guaracha* in, 71–74; ingenue in, 112; "Juventud," 157; Lecuona's *Lola Cruz*'s tragic *romanza* compared with, 130; *mulata* in, 40–41, 70–80; *negrito* in, 91, 212n35; as

pedagogical text, 80; premiere of, 37, 40; revisions to, 22, 183, 198n75, 214n13; *salida* of, 71–80; twentieth-century setting of, 70, 78
América en la guerra, 17, 195n41
Anckermann, Jorge, 16, 17, 38, 196n48, 196n51, 201n30
antislavery literature, 94, 98, 111
Arcilla, José Sánchez, 218n56
Arderius, Francisco, 14
Arias, Pedro, 38
Arredondo, Enrique ("Bernabé"), 86, 196n45, 196n50, 208n7
Arrieta, Emilio, 198n75
Auditorium Theater, 17, 31, 36, 38, 201n27
"Ay Mamá Inés" (Grenet), 86–87, 88, 91, 95

Ballagas, Emilio, 20
Batista, Fulgencio, 27, 177, 181, 200n5
bella cubana, La, 91, 213n3, 213n6
bella del Alhambra, La (film), 17, 196n46
Bellman, Jonathan, 4
benefit concerts, 38
Benítez-Rojo, Antonio, 48
Bernabé (Enrique Arredondo), 86, 196n45, 196n50, 208n7
Bhabha, Homi, 41, 82, 208n6
Bizet, George, 144, 197n55, 206n26, 215n26, 217n50
blackface: history in Cuban theater, 82–86; Lecuona's *Lola Cruz*'s Concha Cuesta compared with, 135; nationalism associated with, 84;

SUSAN THOMAS is associate professor
of music and women's studies
at the University of Georgia.

The University of Illinois Press
is a founding member of the
Association of American University Presses.

Composed in 9.5/12.5 Trump Mediaeval LT Std
at the University of Illinois Press
Manufactured by Sheridan Books, Inc.

University of Illinois Press
1325 South Oak Street
Champaign, IL 61820-6903
www.press.uillinois.edu